APPROXIMATE MAN

& OTHER WRITINGS

TRISTAN TZARA

APPROXIMATE
MAN

& OTHER WRITINGS

▼

translated with an introduction,
essay & notes by

MARY ANN CAWS

BLACK
WIDOW
PRESS

Boston, Mass.

APPROXIMATE MAN & OTHER WRITINGS
TRISTAN TZARA

Black Widow Press edition, December 2005

These translations of Tristan Tzara's work were originally made with the permission of Christophe Tzara. Translations of L'Homme approximatif (© Editions Gallimard, Paris, 1968) are permitted by arrangement with Gallimard Publishing, France. Extract from First Poems (Les Premiers Poèmes) © Edition Seghers, 1965. Tristan Tzara: Oeuvres Complètes, © Flammarion, Paris (1975–1982). Cover photo: "Tristan Tzara, Paris, 1927." André Kertesz, © Ministère de la Culture—France. Interior art: Nude Descending a Staircase (No. 2), Marcel Duchamp, 1912, used by permission, The Philadelphia Museum of Art/Art Resource, NY. Three Standard Stoppages (3 Stoppages Étalon), Marcel Duchamp, 1913–14, used by permission, Digital Image © The Museum of Modern Art/Licensed by SCALA/Art Resource, NY. Etant donnes: 1 la chute d'eau, 2 le gaz d'eclairage (Given: 1. The Waterfall, 2. The Illuminating Gas, 1946–6, used by permission, The Philadelphia Museum of Art/Art Resource, NY. The Bride Stripped Bare by Her Bachelors, Even (The Large Glass), 1915–23, used by permission, The Philadelphia Museum of Art/Art Resource, NY.

Black Widow Press is an imprint of Commonwealth Books, Inc., Boston.
Joseph S. Phillips, Publisher.

Black Widow Press
www.blackwidowpress.com

ISBN-13: 978-0-9768449-1-4
ISBN-10: 0-9768449-1-5

Library of Congress Cataloging-in-Publication Data

Tzara, Tristan, 1896-1963.
    [Poems. English. Selections]
    Approximate man & other writings / Tristan Tzara ; translated with an introduction, essay, & notes by Mary Ann Caws.
        p. cm.
    Includes bibliographical references.
    ISBN-13: 978-0-9768449-1-4 (trade : alk. paper)
    ISBN-10: 0-9768449-1-5 (trade : alk. paper)
    1. Tzara, Tristan, 1896-1963—Translations into English. I. Title: Approximate man and
        other writings. II. Caws, Mary Ann. III. Title.

PQ2639.Z3A23 2005
841'.912--dc22   2005027819

Printed in the United States

10 9 8 7 6 5 4 3 2

. . . this path is earth and could not disappear. A path gifted with a life of its own, a way of living, a vertiginous story, a mirror, nothing more. Nothing more, not even a tear.

—SEEDS AND BRAN

CONTENTS

Preface

Tristan Tzara seems a perfect fit with our present time. As T. S. Eliot's *Waste Land* marked its moment in the early twentieth century and continues to mark ours, so does Tzara's *Approximate Man*—in its mental landscape, climate, and style, a true epic. Tzara developed the all important concept of approximation throughout the years 1920–1930. Preferring, however, a kind of exactness to an approximate translation, this rendering of *Approximate Man* remains as close as possible to the original; this will be noticeable particularly in the cases where a freer and more lyric line could be obtained only at the expense of a slight switch in meaning.

The extensive notes comprise a series of selected variants, as well as thematic and general annotations. The technique followed in the selection of both writings and the notes is deliberately subjective; there is little effort, for instance, to balance in quantity the choices between the various epochs. Each period and each variety of attitude and style is exemplified in this volume, from Tzara's earliest Rumanian lyrics to his last prose poems, but the more interesting works are represented at greater length. The same technique prevails in the choice of variants. Only the more valuable ones appear after the others have been sorted out, in an attempt to show Tzara's method of composition without inflicting a mass of details on the reader. In short, this work is a combination of abbreviated edition, informal commentary, and critical choice, in the spirit of Tzara's own formula: "this freedom of mind which I call poetry."

My warmest thanks to Christophe Tzara, for his generous permission to consult and to quote from the extensive collection of his father's manuscripts and notebooks in the Fonds Tzara at the Bibliothèque littéraire Jacques Doucet, to François Chapon for his counsel and to Jacqueline Zacchi, to Professor Serge Gavronsky for his helpful suggestions on some difficult lines, and to Peter Caws for his collaboration in the translation of *Appro-*

ximate Man. The material for the annotations was collected with the aid of grants from the George N. Shuster Faculty Fellowship fund of Hunter College and the Faculty Research Fellowship fund of the Graduate Center of The City University of New York.

introduction

tion on language, form the basis of Tzara's surrealist theories and expression. When closely examined, however, these works exhibit the best aspects of Dada and of the surrealist inspiration.[1]

The Development of a Dada-Surrealist Style

> *I am not waiting for someone*
> *to pronounce the word which*
> *will open the door for me. The*
> *key is in me and I am lost.*
>
> —"AWAKENING," MINE

The collection of writings assembled here reveals the various facets of Tzara's style: from the deliberately disconnected to the sustained and lyric; from the fragmentary to the visionary and the epic; from the tormented or the nostalgic to the serene; from the simple to the complex. The accent falls constantly on two recurring elements, however, on action or the spectacle of action and on the attempt to find a language which will translate it.

Tzara's Rumanian poems, written from 1911 to 1915, are postsymbolist in imagery and sentimental in tone. Of particular interest are the alternations from light to dark imagery and the ironic asides, both of which continue and are intensified in the later poetry, which also occasionally exhibits the accompanying accent of romantic melancholy especially in the period from 1925 to 1935.

The great works of the Dada years, that we can date from 1916 to 1924 approximately, the works for which Tzara is best known, are structurally simple but brilliantly colored cinematic panoramas of motion and antirational violence. The elements of action are juxtaposed without any apparent grammatical or semantic links. This lack of cohesion is partly due to the awkwardness of Tzara's French at this time (although there is some controversy even about that), but, more importantly, it represents a stylistic choice. This technique produces the instantaneous effect of vivid discontinuity. Even on the surface, however, there are indications of an interior order which Tzara describes as the genuine orientation of the poetic vision and of an underlying rhythm that he views as characteristic of the apparently frenetic transcription. Traces of the sentimental crisis Tzara mentions at this time are also visible, together with his ironic reaction against them: "I only react by contrast," he writes in a letter to Jacques Doucet.[2]

By the time of *Travelers' Tree* (*L'Arbre des voyageurs*), published in 1930, Tzara's concern for language is of an equal interest with that of the examination of the poet's own feeling and the display of the violence done to logic by his poetry. The leitmotif of voyage prefigured in the sea journey of *Cloud Handkerchief* (*Mouchoir de nuages*) and in the allusions to roads and paths in *Heartway Guide* (*Indicateurs des chemins de coeur*) and *Circuit by the Moon and Color* (*Circuit par la lune et par la couleur*) is transformed into the epic interior pilgrimage of *Approximate Man*. Here the theme is interwoven with a reflection on the progress, the power, and the severe limits of language. During this period, Tzara's most intensive linguistic experimentation and poetic development can be described as a lyric journey in itself, as the early unevenness and catalog of spectacle give way to a poetry of range and continuity. Gradually, the bizarre and the bright join with the deeply pathetic and the majestic in a total impression of cosmic inspiration.

In the period from 1931 to 1938, a more sustained lyricism emerges from the linguistic and visionary force of the preceding years, as the image of *Noontimes Gained* (*Midis gagnés*) leads finally to an emphasis on clarity, combined with the profound impulses of night and the dream world. The bizarre is given less weight. The manuscript changes, for example, are frequently a simple substitution of one term, perhaps more euphonious, for another of the same tone, in contrast to the preceding period, where the changes were overwhelmingly toward the more startling or the more grandiose. Tzara now demonstrates a personal involvement in the concerns of the surrealists with whom he is once more, although temporarily, associated. The concept of ennui, dear to Breton, dominates a good part of "The Despairing' ("Le Désespéranto") in *The Antihead*. The experimental use of the dream as a transforming and scientific process, an idea advocated by the group of *Inquisitions* which attracted Gaston Bachelard and others of equal eminence, is responsible for the title "Radiant Mutations" ("Les Mutations radieuses") and for much of *Seeds and Bran*.

After 1938, Tzara enters a period of increasing political commitment. In his work, he places an even stronger emphasis on fullness, illumination, and height, as in *At Full Flame* (*A haute flamme*), on the possible generosity of the earth, *Permitted Fruit* (*Le Fruit permis*), *Earth upon Earth* (*Terre sur terre*), together with man's necessary acceptance of the ways of nature, "Acceptance of Spring" ("Acceptation du printemps"), and on the possible efficacity of human action in the world. Tzara's late poems, centered rather weakly on repeated unspecified images of clarity, fullness, immobility, and vague movement and on simple verbs of vision and motion do not have the poetic strength of his earlier work. The critical works on Rabelais and Villon which Tzara left unfinished at the time of his death as well as his published essays on Rimbaud and Corbière indicate his continued fascination with the poetic presence of certain larger-than-life literary figures, as do the essays on art and artists of which he left so many. His taste and his own tendencies inclined toward the powerful rather than the subtle, direct primitive force rather than the indirect sensitivity, the massive and the epic rather than the understated and the brief. His conception in the earlier *Approximate Man* of the dubious and slow-moving approximation of a hero who follows on the overtly negative steps of the earlier *Antiphilosopher* is presented not as an incoherent and modest lament but as a great and deliberately prolonged poetic journey. This is the focal point for a great pilgrimage of language, of which all the other writings are only stages along the way.

Self and Language

to clear the way in yourself for
crisis and for fortune

—SEEDS AND BRAN

Probably the clearest insight into Tzara's poetic personality is afforded by his incomplete autobiographical novel *Place Your Bets* (*Faites vos jeux*), the successive parts of which were published in *Les Feuilles libres* starting in 1923. As the title indicates, the novel is concerned with a game played, in this case, by the poet against himself. The more tragic elements of his nature win out over the others as he balances the concepts of risk, error, and failure against pride in individual assertion: "I play my life on the tornado of every present moment." The romantic "snobbism of melancholy" and the consciousness of a heart constantly bankrupt prevent the poet from acquiring the "taint of mediocrity," as he says. At times, Tzara describes himself ideally as an adventurer with sweeping gestures; but here he calls his actions nearsighted and terms the experiments he makes with language as much of a failure as the sentimental ones he makes in life. He views himself as only a "word merchant, changing ideas and elements of life into images and crystallized sentences and vice versa."[3] This emphasis on despair and uselessness is perhaps most strongly revealed in the following statement found on the back of an envelope among Tzara's manuscripts: "I detest artifice and lies. I detest language which is only an artifice of thought. I detest thought which is a lie of living matter; life moves outside of all hypocrisy, hypothesis; it's a lie that we have accepted as a starting point for the others."[4]

Tzara's spirit of negativity is also reflected in a wide range of poems, beginning with the first melancholy neo-symbolist effusions. Tzara speaks of undergoing a severe psychological crisis around 1916 and then of trying to efface the sentimental from his poems.[5] For this purpose, he incorporates into the poems sounds, scraps of pseudo-language, and phrases resembling African dialects (see his "Note on Negro Art" of 1917 and the longer essay on primitive art). However, the negative intensity continues with images of burning, breaking, imprisoning, cutting, and other modes of suffering in the

distinguished: images associated with the sky or the seasons, with death and dream, and with water. As in other surrealist writings, they create an atmosphere of the fluid state, the liberated consciousness called poetry. Even the deliberately rough surface of the poetry, the often irritating imagery and overloaded texture, and the seemingly non-sequential nature of the lines serve as signals. They point to the inadequacy of language, to Tzara's doubts concerning the role of poetry. Moreover, they place the reader in a position exterior to the epic from which he can judge its brilliant but uneven character, the extraordinary power and the tragic failure of the poetic word. This strength and this weakness can only be seen approximately, as if there were another more absolute text behind the visible one, which the Dadaist would call "the groupings of an interior order."

In the puzzling and diverse nature of *Approximate Man* can be seen the poet's struggle between his desire to recapture the bizarre imagery of his former poetry, on one hand, and, on the other, his spontaneously lyric effusions, emphasized by repetition. Thus a whole series of remarkable extensions of verbally induced images is interrupted by a sort of tragic chorus, repeated from time to time at key points. Appearing at the conclusion of a part, the reiterated phrase casts an emotional aura over all the disjointed brilliance before it. These lyric patterns serve as guides to the rest; in contrast to the other passages in the notebooks, manuscripts, typed pages, and printer's proofs, where Tzara patiently complicates the imagery, these passages are almost never touched. Only their position is changed, as Tzara makes of them the changing centers of his mobile poem on motion:

> consolation . . . consolation . . . consolation

> morning/ morning/ morning sealed in crystal
> above nocturnal peace nocturnal peace/ and
> so many others and so many others
> peace on the outside of this world reversed
> in the mold of unanimous approximations/
> and on so many others and on so many others

> I have pledged my waiting . . . I have pledged my waiting

These refrains express a certain universality, patience, and peace. They are the obvious threads leading to the final hope, as incomplete man in all the humility and uncertainty of his vocabulary is led by a shepherd of absolute language toward a final ordeal of fire and waiting, the agents of his possible transformation. They are not only the visible centers of lyric continuity and the sustained focus of the mutal involvement of poet and reader, but also the stages of an invisible progression toward unity and completeness in language and in vision.

Even as early as *The Second Celestial Adventure of Mr. Antipyrine*, the concept of centers forms the focus of an eight-line incantation. Tzara himself refers to the roundness of his "semi-language"; and a passage from *The Antihead* reads as a description of the rapid, wheel-like motion of the ideal giratory language as it revolves about the specific center of its desire: "Each wheel boasts of its facial construction; its giratory expansion, lucid regularity, or coquetry sing of the way in which they stupefy quickness, etc. The desires of the wheels, the specialities of the centers tear apart the brain and break the mirrors systematically, break through the corridors. . . ." Corresponding to this roundness is the fundamental notion of centers, or kernels; see, for instance, one of the leading refrains of *Approximate Man*: "Je pense à la chaleur que tisse la parole/ autour de ce noyau ce rêve qu'on appelle nous" ("I think of the warmth spun by the word/ about this center the dream we call ourselves," p. 28). Tzara refers constantly to images of centers, as if language continued to be the *circus* it had been during the Dada epoch: "des hommes chantent en rond," "le geste rond des mains," "comme pour la jeter une boule," and so on. The refrains themselves in *Approximate Man* are the centers of the whole: in many cases, they appear before the rest of the work and are never altered.

Like *Approximate Man*, the prose poems of the latter part of *The Antihead* (the first parts of which date from the same period as the *Twenty-Five Poems* and *Seeds and Bran*) are based on continuous thematic structures and repetitions of corresponding verbal rearrangements. Through their lengthy accumulations of details and their eloquent invocations of night, boredom, and dream, there is built up a linguistic and dramatic momentum of unmistakable force. They are structurally as impressive as *Approximate Man*.[7]

The Verbal Origin of Tzara's Imagery

all words are forgotten limitless
—WHERE THE WOLVES DRINK

For the comprehension of Tzara's process of creation, a close study of the various stages of the manuscripts is illuminating. Six steps can be distinguished, though not all are always of interest. Tzara frequently jotted down his first inspiration in notebooks or on little slips of paper. He reworked these passages in longhand and on typed sheets, later edited the printer's galley proofs (sometimes extensively), and occasionally published a preliminary version in a small magazine before the appearance of the final printed form. An examination of these stages reveals that Tzara's poetic verve and bizarre imagery are based not on visual perception but on an interior play of sounds and echoes. This stylistic habit, characteristic also of many surrealist writers, is consistent with his theoretical writings.

The first Dada poems, concentrating on the circus and performance, emphasize the impression of noise as much as sight:

NTouC mouimbimba nfnfnftatai

Through a solely auditory progression, the word *buts* occurs next to *buveurs*, *maille* and *dalle* give *malle*, *pomme nom de crayon* leads to *nom de plomb*, and *premier venu* leads to *grenier venu*.

In Tzara's notebooks and manuscripts, one can trace some steps in his favorite method of "knotting" words together, as he describes it. This non-Frenchman was apparently fascinated by particular sections of French vocabulary. He developed the habit of starting with a list of words (from five or less to eighty or more), which became the kernel for a series of sentences.

These in turn served as the centers of some passage of prose or poetry. As an example of this method and of the *aural* origin of many of the most striking passages, we may take a typical list, in which we find the words:

ne fera pas long feu
s'endormir à coeur joie
liasse
liesse
laisse
pythie dans les sources
tirer à la courte paille
où boivent les chamelles
et pissent les serpents
pépin
fientes
égarement
surexcitation
terrifiant
incognito
certificat
agité
incurable
brebis
immoler
piédestal
le dernier mot idylle
mythique
déboires
affranchir
les vagissements de l'avachissement
le protecteur (de la République)
s'esseuler
aboli
extase
bouleversement

The list then yields a lengthy passage from which the following excerpts are taken (key words are italicized):

L'ombre courte. *A la courte paille.*

. . .

Rire *mythique*. *Brebis*. Au croisement du contrepoint.

. . .

Le dernier mot incurable . . . Les têtes de *piédestal*. Les *incognitos!*
Laissez-nous rire. Du rire en *liasses*. En *liesse*. Des *liasses* d'*idylles*.
L'*assis* en rire. Où prient *les chamelles pissent les serpents*.
Il ne fera pas long feu. Disent les *coeurs joie*. S'en *donner au
long feu*. Et fera *coeur joie*. Non, non et non. . . .
D'abord il y eut le non. Ne vous ai-je déjà rencontré
quelque part? Ce fut un non plein d'arbres. D'*égarements*. De
certificats. Un non touffu et *agité*. D'abord ce fut un *pépin* de
non. Un prophète *pépiant*. . . . Un *pépin* de tête. Presque une
pépine. Un vrai *pépin*. Un *pépin* de plus. Soyons bons pour les
pépins.. . . [The play on these words continues here.] Les clients
sont *terrifiants*. Même sous la peau de locomotive. Les *pépins*
sont grands. Ils sont jolis. . . . Immolons les *déboires* . . . ne
crois pas à une vaine *surexcitation*, tout peut servir, rien ne se
perd, que personne ne sorte de ce couloir ou la pensée est
abolie et l'*extase* en *bouleversement* . . . regarde, dis-je, avant de
croire, car alors ta tête aussi sera *certificat*. . . . comme tant
d'autres, regarde, ce sont les *pépins* de papa . . . qui en veut
pour les *pépins*? Mourons pour les petits oiseaux.

And, in the next section:

ce jour infatigable de revers de médaille, une *pythie dans la source*
de mandoline . . . ce jour . . . sitôt qu'il vit *l'attroupement* de
toutes les bonnes consciences, mit sa pelouse dans sa poche et
le *vagissement de l'avachissement* . . . ce jour de lapins couchants,
de soleil frais, de *brebis* frileuses . . . *Protecteur* des lettres et
des arts. . . . Les *brebis* frileuses de gale *s'esseulaient* sur des
lopins de mer.[8]

The sounds, not the meanings, of the words suggest other sounds, exten-
sions, and elaborations. *Liasses* and *liesse* lead to *l'assis*; *pépin* suggests *pépine*
and *pépiant*; *pépiant* suggests the omitted *pépiement* and thus the small birds at

the end of the passage; *lapins* leads to *lopins*. Numerous other examples could be given.

A look at the striking images and the transitions between them in the manuscripts of *Approximate Man* verifies the fact that it was their aural impression which determined their order. In the line:

> avec un coeur comme valise et une valse en guise de tête
> (with a heart like a suitcase and a waltz as a head)

the word *valise* leads to a *valse* by sound and certainly not by sense, while the image of the candle in the following line comes from the sound *bout* which is then discarded, having served its purpose as the generator of the image:

> j'attends j'attends la patience de mon destin atteint la fin de
>   la bougie
> (I wait I wait the patience of my waiting reaches the
>   candle's end)

Tzara's aural sensitivity not only determines the construction of certain verbally "rich" passages and the alteration of others, but, in some cases, also determines the complications sensed by the reader. In *Approximate Man* a long section is built around the image of whiteness—glacier, clouds, swans, white of water (a pun on egg white)—where the phrase

> surgie de quel mordant glacier dont le dehors blanc se
>   gargarise de nuages
> (arisen from what biting glacier whose white outside gargles
>   with clouds)

leads to the perfectly natural description of the outside landscape:

> dehors et blanc
> (outside and white)

and then, by what appears on the manscript as a probable error in writing based again on the priority of the aural in all Tzara's transcriptions, to

    dehors est blanc,
    (outside is white)

a phrase which he finds so convincing that it repeatedly occurs as a kind of litany and thematic center for the poem. Of course, this procedure illustrates the scheme of *chance* on which both Dada and surrealism rely. In certain key passages, expressions are changed to their exact opposite to satisfy the exigencies of rhythm or phraseology. Once Tzara has placed the new images on the page, they become the starting points for a new text, of which they seem to have been the temporary approximations. In general, nine out of ten changes made by Tzara in his poetry and poetic prose before 1935 are aesthetically defensible, even if such a criterion as the aesthetic is found unacceptable in itself. Banalities are transformed into unique expressions, the ordinary is transformed into the extraordinary, and the oversentimental into the majestically simple. The remarkable acuity of Tzara's aural perception bears primary responsibility for the remarkable nature of his poetry.

    The distance between the initial text and the second one can only be felt within the context of the whole, but perhaps three examples of differing importance and kind will suffice to give an idea of the peculiarities found in the manuscripts. In *The Antihead*, for example, an entire passage which had given the impression of brightness is suddenly clouded over by one word change, from *des hauteurs festives* (festive heights) to *des hauteurs menacées* (threatened heights). The second expression is undeniably stronger, both in sound and in shock potential. In *Approximate Man*, a recurring melancholy passage on the eternal nonmeeting of things, the nonmeshing of sentiments in a Proustian sense, ends with the negative phrase:

    le coeur tournevis ne les rencontre pas.
    (the screwdriver heart does not meet them.)

Finding the assertion too definite, or, more probably, finding the "pas" not satisfying to the ear as an ending, Tzara changes the line to read:

    le coeur tournevis va à leur rencontre
    (the screwdriver heart goes to meet them)

The positive version has the advantages of indefiniteness, possibility, and an accented last word, the sound of which is aesthetically pleasing. The third and most subtle change which typifies Tzara's attitude toward his text occurs in *Mine*, his late and masterful collection of prose poems. In a brief passage Tzara describes the vision of a lone horse standing on a hill in the early morning, parallel to but pathetically removed from his own sudden hopes for the day and the life he has still to live. The poet ends with the semioptimistic question to himself:

> Mais puis-je dire aujourd'hui que les promesses n'ont jamais été tenues?
> (But can I say now that the promises were never kept?)

The implied answer is negative, or perhaps: "No, for some of them have been kept." But Tzara makes many successive changes in these words, first to the openly pessimistic:

> Mais je ne saurais pas affirmer que les promesses ont été tenues
> (But I could not say certainly that the promises were kept)

where the slightly awkward rhythm is appropriate to the hesitant answer. Finally, after several alterations, he arrives at the brief, highly ambiguous, and intense phrasing characteristic of his best work:

> Mais qui saurait dire que les promesses ont été tenues.
> (But who could say that the promises were kept.)

A passage from the conclusion of a long meditation in *Seeds and Bran* on the phrase "pain de minuit aux lèvres de soufre" ("midnight bread with sulphur lips") provides the most fitting example of the minute attention Tzara always paid to sound. After a brilliant consideration of the points of falling and of triumph expressed by the preceding syllables, Tzara finally comments on the final syllable "fre": "[it] will be the final stopping place of an elevator, deadened by pads of cotton in bags of wool imitating the elephant feet of the toys of children (preferably blond)—a sound held neither too long nor too briefly, like a book one chooses, but a velvet book where the length of the lines will lead one to think that regular poems are printed in it, but needless to say, nothing will be readable in this pseudobook of velvet poems, where the patient reader may see only hints of the beauty whose momentary author he will be" (pp. 31–32).

Notes to Introduction

1   One could apply the adjective Dada (only on condition that the adjectival form should lose none of the nominal brilliance) in conjunction with the adjective surrealist under the same proviso to *Approximate Man*, and to the collections, *The Antihead* and *Seeds and Bran*, all of which represent the best aspects of both movements.

2   In an unpublished letter to Jacques Doucet of October 30, 1922 (quoted by the generous permission of M. Christophe Tzara and the Fonds Doucet), Tzara describes a first book of poems, *Mpala Garoo* which he wrote before *The First Celestial Adventure of Mr. Antipyrine*. Here he was reacting against his early sentimental poems, two of which appear here in translation. The letter is of primary importance for understanding the poet's attitudes and techniques during the period of the *Twenty-Five Poems*.

   "It was during the winter of 1916 that I decided to destroy the whole edition [of *Mpala Garoo*]. After a nervous sickness from which I suffered greatly, I had completely changed my pattern. I fell, after a savage and completely lawless life, into a sort of convalescent mystic crisis. This mysticism, which had no connection with any existing religious or political idea, was purely abstract and purely cerebral. . . . I was playing with dubious sentimentality and an irony resulting from surprise at the banality of my phrases. As I only reacted by contrast, all my poems of 1916 were only a reaction against the preceding ones, too gentle and careful; they were of an excessive brutality, containing cries and strongly accentuated and rapidly moving rhythms. I think they have one great defect: often they are declamatory, made only to be recited and contain exterior effects. Since then, everything that is pathetic is quite disagreeable to me. In 1916 I tried to destroy literary genres. I introduced into my poems elements [which would have been] judged unworthy of being there, like newspaper phrases, noises and sounds. These sounds (which had nothing in common with imitative sounds) were supposed to be the equivalent of the research of Picasso, Matisse, Derain, who used in their paintings different subject matters. Already in 1914 I had tried to take away from words their meaning, and to use them in order to give a new global sense to the verse by the tonality and the auditory contrast. These experiments ended with an abstract poem, "Toto-Vaca," composed of pure sounds invented by me and containing no allusion to reality." This letter is the best possible introduction to the early poems of Tzara, to his revolutionary attitude toward poetry, to his particular sense of Dada.

See also, in *Place Your Bets* (*Faites vos jeux*), the passage on writing as an attempt to destroy personality (quoted above).

3 *Faites vos jeux; Les Feuilles libres* no. 32, 1923, p. 145. The title of the preceding section of the "novel," *Le Coeur sans rides* (*Unwrinkled Heart*) reminds us of Breton's *Les Mots sans rides* (*Unwrinkled Words*).

4 This envelope is among the overwhelming, frequently illegible, mass of material for *Approximate Man*. On the other side of the envelope the poet works out a passage beginning "Il n'y a qu'une seule maladie la mort nous la portons tous en nous" ("There is only one sickness death we all carry it in us") and continues on the subject of approximation, falsehood, and language in the same vein.

5 Letter to Jacques Doucet; see note 2 above.

6 Of even greater interest is his attitude toward the tragic. As he openly states in an essay on collage, every work of expression is accompanied by a double which is its tragic sense ("Le papier cone ou le proverbe en peinture"): the notion of this double is associated with all the references to the man and his echo, to the approximate man walking alongside the other. We have, says Tzara in reference to Picasso, a sharply divided nature; Tzara's own work stresses that division continually. "The end of life is to die . . . ." (*Place Your Bets*). Every expression itself is a murder: "You have to kill the moving reality of the world as it appears in order to have its fruit come forth" ("A Philippe Bonnet"). Even more precise is his essay on the painter Miró: "For the identification of the loving object with the loved object is not free of a certain tragic sense. In identifying himself with the object, the artist must empty himself of all foreign substance so completely that his receptivity is total, open to the flaming wings of the death that occasionally visits him."

7 In the poems and prose after 1936, the same effort is not visible; the modifications, as numerous as before, are not modifications of tone. Almost none of them changes in any way the feeling, the imagery, or the problems raised in the initial text. Tzara's poetry becomes expansive and purposeful, in accordance with his increased political involvement, and the texts become linear in nature. These poems prove, or they lament, or they exalt or exult; they rarely show the changing and perplexing char-

acter of *Approximate Man.* The notion of approximation has gone, and the tension of verbal experiment played against a deliberately repetitious lyricism is now replaced by one of sustained feeling. These last writings make little effort to balance one tone against another, to have a spectacle moving in more than one ring at a time, and they are therefore structurally limited in spite of their universal scope. However, even taking into account the lessened interest of the manuscripts and variants for all the later works, there is not the same divergence of quality or effect between the earlier and later prose poems (such as *Mine*) as there is between the verse poems of earlier and later periods.

8   *The Antihead, Cahiers libres,* 1933, p. 17.

APPROXIMATE MAN

Part I*

sunday heavy lid on the seething of blood
weekly weight crouched on its haunches
fallen inside oneself found again
the bells ring for no reason and we too
we will rejoice at the clank of chains
that we will sound within us with the bells

what is this language lashing us we start in the light
our nerves are whips in the hands of time
and doubt comes with one drab wing
tightening compressing crumpling up in us
like the wrinkled paper of the unpacked box
gift of another age gliding like fish of bitterness

the bells ring for no reason and we too
the eyes of fruit watch us closely
and all our actions are ruled nothing hidden
the water of the river has washed its bed so long
it carries off the gentle threads of looks which have lingered
at the foot of walls licked up lives in bars
enticed the weak compounded temptations desiccated ecstasies
dug to the depths of old possibilities
and loosened the springs of imprisoned tears
the springs enslaved by daily stiflings
the gazes taking in shriveled hands
the day's bright creation or the dark apparition
extending the anxious profusion of the smile
fixed like a flower in the buttonhole of morning

---

*For variants and annotations to the text, see "Notes to Approximate Man,"
  beginning on 249.

those who ask for rest or stimulation
electrical shocks sudden jolts
adventures fire certitude or slavery
looks that have slithered the length of discreet storms
worn thin the city streets expiating many indignities by charity follow
close on one another around ribbons of water
and flow seaward taking in their passing
human wastes and their mirages

the water of the river has washed its bed so long
that even the light glides on the smooth wave
then falls to the bottom with the heavy clatter of stones

the bells ring for no reason and we too
the cares we carry with us
which are our inner clothing
that we put on each morning
that night undoes with the hands of dream
decorated with useless metallic puzzles
cleansed in the bath of circular landscapes
in the cities prepared for carnage for sacrifice
near the seas of sweeping horizons
on the mountains of uneasy harshness
in the villages of painful nonchalance
the hand weighing on the head
the bells ring for no reason and we too
we leave with the departures arrive with the arrivals
leave with the arrivals arrive when others leave
for no reason a little dry a little hard severe
bread sustenance no more bread to accompany
the bawdy song on the scale of the tongue
the colors lay down their burden to think
and think or cry out and stay to feed
on delicate fruits hovering like the smoke
that thinks of the warmth spun by the word
around its center the dream called ourselves

✕　　✕　　✕

the bells ring for no reason and we too
we walk to escape the multiplying ways
with a flask of scenery one illness only one
one single illness that we nurture death
I know I carry the tune in me and am not afraid
I carry death and if I die it is death
who will carry me in its imperceptible arms
subtle and light as the smell of thin grass
subtle and light as the parting for no reason
without bitterness without commitments without regret without
the bells ring for no reason and we too
why seek the end of the chain that links us to the chain
ring bells for no reason and we too
we will ring in ourselves the broken glasses
the sterling coins mixed with the counterfeit
the debris of festivals burst in laughter and in tempest
at whose doors chasms might open
the tombs of air the mills crushing the arctic bones
these festivals that whirl us skyward
and spit on our muscles the night of molten lead

I speak of the one who speaks who speaks I am alone
I am only a little sound I have several sounds in me
a frozen sound bruised at the crossroads dropped on the damp
        sidewalk
at the feet of hurried men running with their deaths
around death that stretches out its arms
on the clockface of the hour alone living in the sun

the obscure breath of the night thickens
and along the veins sing the sea flutes
transposed on the octaves of layers of diverse lives
lives repeating themselves to infinity to atomic sparseness
and above so high we cannot see
and with these lives on the sidelines that we do not see

the ultra violet of so many parallel paths
those we could have taken
and not have come into the world
or have already left it long ago so long ago
that the epoch and the earth which would have sucked our flesh
would be forgotten
liquid salts and metals limpid in the depth of wells

I think of the warmth spun by the word
around its center the dream called ourselves

Part II

the earth holds me clenched in its fist of stormy anguish
Let no one move! we hear the hour preparing its insect flight
and rejoining the day in search of an end
let us clench in our jaws the minutes that part us

hands up! welcome the angel about to fall
shedding his leaves in a snow of fireflies on your heads
sky weakened by the wind that has blown so long
we will pay the innumerable debts of suffering

whistles thicken the air of the railway station
so many intentions swim in the bitter gloom
that the shrill sound guides the gnawing flood
with black and fetid indignations frothing guts of the earth
to the velvety surfaces toward what goals drinkers of hopes
that are bought at the price of slow seeds
marked by the traces of the bodies of trades
that are drunk in the troughs with quivering nostrils of horses

that are chased in circles in the village carrousels
let the old pipe of eagles be smoked
shepherds let the roofs be kept smoking at evening
glimpsed in the mirrors sensed in the heart of stones
in the depth of oil wells on crossbars of heavy shafts
in the barns where life is measured with the grain
clear cushions of the water foams seated in the sun

approximate man like me like you reader and like the others
heap of noisy flesh and echoes of conscience
complete in the only element of choice your name
transportable absorbable polished by the docile inflections
          of women's voices
diverse misunderstood according to the pleasure of inquiring currents
approximate man moving in the almosts of destiny
with a heart like a suitcase and a waltz for a head
vapor on the cold glass you block your own image from your sight
tall and insignificant among the glazed frost jewels of the landscape
nevertheless men sing in a circle under bridges
with mouths blue and drawn from the cold on the other side
          of nothingness
approximate man magnificent or miserable
in the fog of chaste ages
cheap lodging eyes ambassadors of fire
that each questions and cares for in the fur caresses of his ideas
eyes that rekindle the furies of the supple gods
rushing forth at set free the toothed springs of laughter
approximate man like me like you reader
you hold in your hands as if to throw a ball
luminous number your head full of poetry

door of the night closed forever the fruit of lovely limbs
long cross so solemn on the breath of dew
in the confines of evening day's shirt undone
while the tunnel lengthens the accordion of its sides
slides on the string of the rail long arching caravan of trains

and on the other side for lack of sun there is death perhaps
waiting for you in the uproar of a dazzling whirlwind with
      a thousand explosive arms
stretched toward you man flower passing from the seller's
      hands to those of the lover and the loved
passing from the hand of one event to the other passive
      sad parakeet
the teeth of doors are chattering and everything is
      impatient to make you leave quickly
man amiable merchandise eyes open but tightly sealed
cough of waterfall rhythm projected in meridians and slices
globe spotted with mud with leprosy and blood
winter mounted on its pedestal of night poor night weak and sterile
draws the drapery of cloud over the cold menagerie
and holds in its hands as if to throw a ball
luminous number your head full of poetry

round gesture of the hands offering the image to the air
vigilant nightingale closing the circuit of your content
in the glare of laments you deceive yourself
more secret than any other you are the most distant
you lift yourself to perfect chords on astronomic spars
you feed on incestuous delights at the steps of calvaries
your jealousy bursts forth from the narrow semblance
that stows time away in the purse of your life
you only conceive of a life where you can play it safe
while you age without knowing why the hinges of your head are
      rusting
your joints swelling up pride is dampened like the leaf in the rain
greedy you grip the door so hard your nails sink in the flesh
the dark throat where the clouds pile up
where unappeased pride can no longer be renewed
already stretches its delirium toward the lawns of death by
      holocaust as far as the eye can reach
and the water is always cool at the meeting of your loves

the lines of your calloused hands traced by an angel at your birth
your route gifted with all earthly success
the rubber of your false life effaced them and you soil what you touch
you wallow in the death-rattle and the gold the incandescent lies
all you have left from life is the despair of escape thwarted
and still night undoes in its bosom the knots of the bells the stars
the cadenced frame of musical scaffoldings tossed helter-skelter
nevertheless men huddle in a circle under bridges
and leaf through tepid evenings in photo albums
among so many bitter buds that memory brought to flower
      around the heavy tablecloth
defend with your teeth your patch of world so you can sleep from
      one weekend to the next
anonymous and ridiculed in the age-old nourishment of your breed
nevertheless men sing in a circle under bridges
and pull apart the nest of the meninges scratch
to find hidden at the bottom the cool orange of their brain

in the furies of snow let the hour erupt in remorse and torture let
the blood gush forth in you from the newest mouth astronomy
and spread through each cell of anatomic prisons
let the minutes swarming in the lung sac sow the meadows
of nursing homes the terraces with several rows of billiards
let crime at last flower young and fresh in heavy garlands
      along the houses
fertilize with blood the new adventures the harvests of future
      generations
the eagles dissolving like sugar in the mouth of years
dissolving the sugar of days spent in the bowl of ocean
flying from one flower to the next skin petals on their wings
insects or microbes loading with suffering the beds the seasons
the acid sleeps dragging our carcasses like beasts of burden
and pulling us toward them suspended in a dream hoisted on
      the crane of the celestial port
putrefaction sweet with sun with neither crows nor worms in the
whiteness invincible immaculate

Part III

what links us with our mothers' wombs
with those to whom for the moment we will give bitter life walking
near the flowered delights
unable to crack the kernel

and while the hollow ringing fills our horizons with alarm
you lick the flesh of fruit and there is mystery within
you cradle the moments' rhythm to let the time of mystery go by
the time go by and may death surprise you without too much
        bother with eyes too open
fill with fright each moment without break or haste
I drink the acid terror of what I shall never understand
happiness in seeds of lilies I have buried you serenely

I empty myself before you pocket turned inside out
I have given up to my sadness the wish to unravel mysteries
I live with them I adapt myself to their lock
rusted instrument honeyed voice of the phenomena of continual
        surprise
alluring mysteries signs of death death among us
in the stores with time-scorched smiles
in the concert halls the cypress grows watches
shrewd adolescence what none could tell or show you
where concealers of domestic cares
run fat fingers through the flora of labels
around loves with painful inconsistencies feigned by rebellions
at the hairdresser's you let your head fall lifeless and the snow
emerging from the daily winding-sheet take care that the brain's hands
don't graze the sticky mass of nightmare
in the arenas where brusque thoughts lead the flood
        with its apostolic din

at the gardeners' where in the dung and the debris
an illegible sun is shaped of flowers
risen from tomblike plexus with the seasons and their ample audacities

you come in you look around you feel your pockets
sobered tempests with discolored coins
that the gold-bearing streams have won by the torture of wrinkled
          time
you go out just as poor dandling your bones in the clothing of the
          flesh
wrinkled to the soul tired of the bustle of the world
wrinkled to the soul tired
but the day begins again color of fertile logarithms
upright in the elegance of your eyes you pace the sidewalks
your pride concealed in emphatic indolence
you know you will fall apart at your life's end but you
          conceal yourself and cntcr
flower knot of ribbons of human skin
and so few things have moved me brothers and make me weep
in stations—but I could never say enough of stations—there are born
          fragmented pleasures greetings too brief in shabby hotels
where even love is only a part of dusty legend
I have worn out my youth which cannot wake again
while the course of life outside falls in with trees of train-sleep
gardens of women with lovely shoulder blades resting in their
          waterlily languor
thus begging light each consumes all that's wanted
and in the mines you choose to forget that day exists and sirens
the word alone suffices for seeing
in hospitals there are numbers that suffice
to stretch out on a bed the white hope of a near death
in the church of Saint Eustache I saw two strolling prostitutes
while old women at seven in the morning
carrying baskets on their arms and children in their heads
dipped their guileless experience and faith in the wine of holy law

×   ×   ×

despite the wrongs done us by disdainful time
bad weather spat out copiously by the desert from the summit
        of its hills of night
despite the thick cry of the death-doomed beast
the breach opened in the heart of the army of words our enemies
the glacial laziness of fate that lets us run as we please
our dogs ourselves running after us
alone in the barking echo of our own mental waves
despite the ineffable fullness surrounding us with the impossible
I empty myself before you pocket turned inside out

facing others you are another than yourself
judging on the staircase of waves the texture of each look
dissimilar voiceless hallucinations that resemble you
the boutiques of bric-a-brac that resemble you
that you crystallize around your rainy calling—where you
        find portions of yourself
at each turn of the road you change into another self
in the houses—clenched jaws—where the surly shutters
        of the heart are closed
the light wipes itself on anemic sheets
in the pampas virile scent of heroism
a heart-rending tune precedes you in asylums
and without satellites the usury of our sins evolves in a narrow
        universe
man of dizzy somersaults in space
I've seen animals with human feelings grossly forming in them
the lotuses in sunday best blanket us in theaters
in convents murmuring impulses mechanize their game
among the peasants careless pleasures in the shadow aged
        with scornful gestures
in post offices where manners and countries touch
at the jewelers' we try on miniature landscapes
and in seaports the earth ends with slender arms
in alcohol I've found my one oblivion freedom
in music halls with shrill exhibitions

of enthusiasm and of patient gestures of proffered risks and of excess
in waiting rooms crickets my sisters
in the inns of impenetrable lives the cages lovely in the groves
but let us leave roads and breakwaters on the surface paneling of maps
so many sanguine appeals have attached us to the carnal masonry
that the bouquets of smoky hands have built in prisons
the heads tossed about from one hand to the next from day to night
incalculable flowering of hatred on the faded ships
among the disillusioned lonely ones harsh wheat
the creepers and the buildings fold their arms
above nocturnal peace strong fragrance nocturnal peace
and so many others and so many others

Part IV

filters the flower colander of clearing
the strawberry rolls its fat eye on the padded inside of lips
and the pistil's forefinger touches the incredulous wound of the sky
pillaged by the nightly attacks of otters
spread out near us where suspicious tight-rope walkers fall in the net
on the willow is hung the armor of sadness
that the long fall days have slicked with hammocks' caresses

the linen in white flames laughs in its alcoholic tongue
and the insect pram prepares its bags and springs
it goes off down the beardless road where the word embroiders the
        cork
and the tree sucks the resin from bowls of torrid hearts

cannonfire stiffens red globules under the tent
where the sleepy rockets live in electric colonies
and it gathers in its apron of rays the peelings of the evening horizon

the shapeless modeler sees in each tree a living welcome
on the beardless road where the word embroiders the altitude
the breathless forest has reached the summit of mathematical
        conception
and its breast flutters cloudless about cuckoos changed to minutes
but the twilight coolness of the spirit will soon appease our
        appetite for worlds
and tarnish the portions of life we discard from step to step
in the empty spinning escaped from the orbit of death
from the sack so miserably laden with the resounding
        dross of unspeakable punishments
of shocks and incalculable weariness for no result
tormented as we are by microscopic mental predictions
poor souls unable to avert our gaze from the heel of death
when the shapeless modeler sees in each tree a living alibi
autumn draws along on crutches the stammering wind
and the fins of bushes no longer weep secretly
sleep sleep
the alfalfa closes on your eyelid
the seed of mountains
the water stares at you
caravan of water
grain of stare
wrinkles the leaves eyebrows of mountains
coddled under the fingers of water the bells incline
the fan of the tunnel opens on the evening's bosom
the dreams have rung throughout the vacation

bearded tree-stump fist raised for the battle of droughts
thunder valve of doleful valleys
chanting monotony of kiosks lined up like cups of coffee
and supernatural threads linking the medical paths
attached to the ramparts of stalwart necks
fluttering circles around the death of phosphorus
the harrow of rotten grimaces has skirted the unreality of warlike teeth
but you heedless of what has neither weight nor omen

substantial lightning
hardly smiling at the chance play of muscles the eyes and the wind
like the tongues of snow licking the deep salts of the cliffs
      teeming with spheres
sleep sleep
the poplar will take flight
the hawthorn will ride the wreck of cloud
the scale is bitten on its side
where the landscape weighs on its donkey's back the penalty assessed
      against the mountain dwellers
flowers smaller than grains of dust
will carry you on an alphabet of accordions
and on the rolling roofs of butterflies
sleep fixed transparency of frost
in the night's abundance
and the lake's clear basket
new violins are growing on the violin trees
new children are appearing the flying violins
sleep sleep
the rain has fled paddler of white

scattered on the bunches of keys to springs beneath the limestone
      carpets
the black bands of marauding maxims still lounge in the vicinity of
      sleep
and the ridges of crystal sing on the organ the dorsal framework
      of the cargo pondering its strength
at the reaches of the tar smell move the heavy tribes of fleshy
      furniture
but when the pride of the petal blooms they once more become
      forests of stags to die
and the geysers of the flute and of the conscience tousled on
      the millstones' foreheads
mold under the thatch umbrellas where the equator hangs its nests
by the fireplace where silence blends with the henna of the stars
and the bark deceitful colors loosened

the tanned fruits shed the mourning hedges of old maids
that the trade-wind stories have beaten on the parapet of bridges
in the grotto the gypsum music lights up
the fir tree will keep the sheep of shadow unwinding acetylene lamps
the fair with muted shellfish
rings clear in the horn of mica
the procession of voyages is set in motion
the poppy of folded hands is injured
swallow's chrysalis
sleep with the whiteness forbidden to wolves

and the diffuse mythology of our wild fragments of knowledge
turns the crested millstone of the planet
a long unbroken departure of birdsong
and the faultless amber of your majestic torment
thus are joined to metallic truths the holidays that we are
that we wish to be
united in the same tress of fluid hummocks
hearts slip the length of the knots when the diver descends
      to the depth of tears
always near us the smell of catastrophe shed by the moon
sleep under the armpit of water
wander alone
grip tight the late-blooming flower
to the chest where the sailors' loneliness pitches its tent
night has put the jennets in prison
man has rid himself of his tackle
the nightjars tame the narrow sound
and the crowns of scrap-iron whitened to the bones
are hung above the anger issuing from fjords
about to fall in the boiling excess their breasts scalloped with slate
mesh with newborn infants' care in the toothed rack of the rising sun
the threat of cruel abductions breaks the junctures of nerves
bars the road of terror to the sleepbearing hampers filling
      all the breaches of feeling

clamorous nothingness folds its arms on the enchanted chasm
        where peace smokes its sorrow
in the layers at the heart of writhing vegetation
the eyelids grow tipsy in the allegory of sheets
I cast the anchor of disordered sleep in the bay whose wailing
        with incantations is so familiar
and the laments lit at night in the alembic of lies
beg from the demented crew the truce of wandering regret

reason is captive to a fable of discord
like the beetle containing in itself its fugitive confusion
cloistered in the praise of its occult remedy
subjected to the giant rites of useless passions
and the cave where insult slays the deer of the lofty oath
where lodge the pits of hell where saunter the slanders of bats
the pilots of the quarrel dismiss the captivating expression
        of the just man's rule
collapses from the weight of flaming logs and sorrows slaves to furies
and across the delirious distance of brandy and remnants of pride
the example of revenge assesses the skillful ransom

guardian of the immaterial shanties of repose
bottle on the wave pregnant with monstrous immortalities
you carry locked in the secret of your entrails the key
        to great coincidence
you let no envy penetrate the restless fissures of the tribe of fruits
but eternal agitation is common light for us
and chains us to its stalk-studded dreams from age to age
peace on the outside of this world inverted in the mold
        of unanimous approximations
and on so many others and on so many others

Part V

from your eyes to mine the sun sheds its leaves
on the threshold of dream beneath each leaf is a hanged man
from your dreams to mine the word is brief
along your folds spring the tree weeps its resin
and in the palm of the leaf I read the lines of your life

the label of the plant which is a bottle of sky
and on your heart also the labels keep their secrets
with the silent announcement I am pasted flat against the pharmacy
of the fat earth flattened the triumphant sickness of the clouds shatters
the horizon and the castle of weather maps crumbles
but to what avail trumpet of seasons
newspaper unfolded on the terrace of the firmament
through which an equivocal breeze of astral dispatches is filtered
         with scorn

sleep heavy with tired trees
the mute tortures the struggles of flesh in its bruised husk
furtive twilights avalanches of angelic nudities
hammer the days with the plodding step of your loves
you leave in the nest of dream the winged seed your giant bird
sleep heavy with tired trees
braided crowns of summits intertwined with clouds
lake cut cleanly in the damp forehead of earth
far far very close to death and unquenchable
in the womb of the sleep that closes on you its fingers of
         humble obsessions
the rivers of geographic life cut into the map of the past
sleep heavy with tired trees
with a single eye turned inwards
valve of the danaides will never fill the sack the gleam
and on your lunar enamel god of dream I will scratch the
         march of caravans

whose long whistles attest the foggy departure
a fountain in the breast and the inexhaustible savor within
toward the magic insolence of words that conceal no sense
straddling the tortures taken in their girdle of valleys by leaps and
      hiccups
when I open the drawer of your cool voice without a name
ribbons lace of the ages bracelet of teeth
I put it around my wrist when I break down the door of dream
to go out on day's threshold lacerated with the beating of heart
      and of drum

scarcely awakened my frank flesh placed on the flagstone
flowers the open tomb of easter and of solar cloths
in the sky I have gathered all the extra sky
at the outskirts of the village assembled with the beasts
boiled sky where parchments and skeletons float
guiding the tree trunks back to the sawmill
I have left behind real life overflowing with the manners
      of gentlemen travestied in dream
the fish of clouds swimming against the current of veins filled
with liqueurs snatched from flames that iron hands have twisted
in the steelworks of volcanoes where planets are prepared
      for cannons
impalpable linen caressing the skin of the uncertain country

through the open window the houses enter my room
with disordered rooms of awakenings and of open windows
the carafes of belltowers bellow in the freshness of gums
under the magnifying lens of the heart the grass braids
      its stained-glass window
the grass offers the network and detail of fabrics
but depart fresh memories and forecasts of springs past and coming
leave me to my winter of leather my underground work
nerves nourished on leisurely faithfulness the dampness of living stars
sees the evil from the root to the stone
the wind reaps the tresses of our hopes

×   ×   ×

waking at the boundary of the ends of suspicious sentences
waking boundary I enter into day sleep inside out
swimming I emerge in the spacious feast of air heavy with synonyms
I have walked on the sky head down
among the bushes of smoke of algae the milky paths
the marine reefs of thermometers and of planets
where hats lighthouses and pavilions of gramophones grow
the chain of golden mountains on the stomach
the sun a watch and the frontage of the world
the scissors of needles cut the shadow as far as night
man grows infinitely shorter with the year

the rivers unroll their film across the landscape
the cowboy decorates his farm with lasso trees
the horizon bareheaded serves him as umbrella and his heart
his love springs forth from the geyser's heat its mane in the wind
and life shrivels up when he sells his skin to the devil
I have walked on the sky infinitely with the year
you follow the anatomical forest where messages are planted
man grows shorter with the shadow until nighttime
and the rain falls upward splashing the tribe of nomadic gods
I have walked on the sky in the shop window of the world
where the stars flit from one flower to the next and suck
         the honey of their feather springtime

at bottom at the very bottom he has concealed he sees
he sees another eye hidden within
at the meeting of the currents of carnal tendencies
the kernel is forgotten in its eyelids and petals
while the posters tear the lining of the wall
but there are signs saying something's not outside
and he picks up the leaves that his fall laid on the ground
and the snow falls already and the churches spread out
         carefully in the streets
and the cats in your arms turn into tiny trains

surrounded as we are by birds and fortifications
northern silence silence with one eye open like a mouth
and teeth of snow in the place of lashes
motionless packet of houses tied up ready to sink
in the luminous chasm of the sea splendid cataract and crisis
though the branches have insinuated their crystalline bareness
      frozen everywhere
how many strange mathematics play in your smile near the
      ornamented fire
and how many ships furrow the memory of your arteries
the latitudes of your body bitten in the dazzled flesh
under the thaw of your delicate words falling from the corner
      of your navigable eyes

but let the door open at last like the first page of a book
your room full of triumphant loving coincidences sad or gay
I shall slice the long net of the fixed gaze
and each word will be a spell for the eye and from page to page
my fingers will know the flora of your body and from page to page
the secret study of your night will be illumined and from page to
      page
the wings of your word will be fans to me and from page to page
fans to chase the night from your face and from page to page
your cargo of words at sea will be my cure and from page to page
the years will diminish toward the impalpable breath
      that the tomb already draws in

Part VI

even under the bark of birches life is lost in bloody hypotheses
where the peaks peck at stars and the foxes sneeze insular echoes
but from what depths arise these flakes of condemned souls

that intoxicate the ponds with their searing idleness
is it the swan who sprays his white of water
white is the reflection whose vapor plays on the shudder of the sea
      lion
outside is white
a singing rift of wings absorbs the south wind in its peacock corolla
that the rainbow unfastens from the cross of memory
rubbing the teeth of the sky beating the linen at the river
the white windmills whirl
among the flakes of soul smoked by addicts in the shade
      of sparrow-hawks

between contradictory dispatches the mouth clamps tighter
like the world unforeseen between its jaws
and the dry sound breaks against the window
for never has word crossed the threshold of bodies
dead is the force that brought the bad weather to a boil
in the jars of poor ugly heads our neighbors
and despite the city mud of our feelings
outside is white
what does disgust matter since our strength is more fireproof than
      death
and its ardor will destroy neither our colors nor our loves
shells and small stones stratified in tiers of proverbs
meaning is the only unseen fire consuming us
since the origin of the first number
the breeders of birds speak a simple tongue
formed from an alphabet of birds with white exteriors
white is the finger that the thinkers rubbed so long against their
      temples
we are not thinkers
we are made of mirrors and air
and yet unsatisfied obscure morose impervious
the saw teeth that decorate our forehead border on death
and catch the eye from one thing to the next through the whole
      dictionary

rubbing the teeth of the sky beating the linen at the river
vomited from the white crests the fog solidifies among us
and soon we will be taken into the dense and muddy matter
soon will be absorbed by the spongy lethargy of iron
that by the length of a sad litany reaches beyond the coffin and
      the lie
risen from what biting glacier whose white exterior gargle of cloud
sucks at the roots of our irises the honey of ages to come

withered the unruly tonic of synthesis
flowered with curls and free of skin
high as a wall
haunts daily death my day is frail insomnia
laughs with one face and weeps with the other

shells and small stones stratified in tiers of proverbs
are read from top to bottom careful fragile glass
the climbing laughter seeds with storm the constellations of bees
and the snails sniff the accursed riot of downpours
laughs with one face and weeps with the other
for outside is always white
and like the trout struggling against the current leaping over the weirs
in the opposite direction from waterfalls
you go back in your graying youth to the place where the sun
      laid its eggs
and if from each calm shimmer rises a quivering halo of greetings
no one knows what high tide of magic rushes forth to conquer
      new points of return
thus you gather in nets of shadow the rough desires that spend
      their lives dying through them
and the constant deaths which do not succeed in dying
man milks the eternal subtraction from each slice in himself
that remains for him to ripen in his black debt toward the harsh suns
laughs with one face and weeps with the other

      ×   ×   ×

straddler of spasms deep is the drawer of antiquity
that the twilight peach and the glacial gift have watched until
        the words reposed there
edifice stuff of cities
rubbing the teeth of the sky beating the linen at the river
not much milk not much sugar not much
in the shadow of smoking brambles under the arcades of your heart
sings as a night light a rosary of waxen eyes
and joyless the free escape in the volcano's eye lights up
from the plane the frothing hollow of free air
straddler of spasms wind is your thought lightning the sought after
storm the botanical obsession your bed
the bouquet of paths rises and walks at the front
and the long slopes slide easily the processions down there
the exodus of leaves toward other meadows more unctuous dawns
thus melts in the candle your bewildered memory
the rain has gnawed at the sickness of pious stones
food of mice the hooks quarrel over the prey of the shelters
and the ashes of corpses carry to the creaking abysses cupped
        in each other
in the shadow of smoking bramble nightlights their
        treacherous uselessness
who will tell us the bitter hour when the thyme dies of trickery
its color melting in the tender water of mocking kisses
on the tree the fruits range in tiers their visual stammering
outside is white
white is your smile also sign of your body whiter than all experience
rubbing the teeth of the sky beating the linen at the river
if I steel myself at the precise sources of iron dragonflies it is that I
and if I wander it is that I
straddler of waterfalls time has run its risks and the premiums
I was stronger and the long ago was my marble companion
the fists of dead trees rise up again
and rage against the autumn of the firmament
it is my hope

×   ×   ×

now I plunge your eyes in the black depth of the song of straw
the wine will be livelier filtered through vespers of your pupils
        butterfly
now I melt in the candle bewildered memory
wandering with labyrinths hanging on the shadow of my steps
with heavy bundles of labyrinths on my back
lost inside myself lost
where no one ventures carried on the stretcher of oblivion's wings
and in spite of rockets fired inside the globe
earth's coat of arms drowses in the throat of the mountain
whose indecipherable silence is troubled by crows
turning their hard wide spirals of steel around the unique flight
lost inside itself where no one but oblivion ventures

Part VII

when the sparse grass freezes to the brim
and the night wears thin at the first sight of land
when the beacon grows dim on whitened hair
when it is dark in the crying of the child forgetting to cry
whom the ravaged black of spells turns blue
when charmer of black the poet or his laugh
slows down on the shadow awakening the mirror
when the beliefs in harsh colors come down the mountains
burned by panic angers stride pell-mell over writhings and caryatids
and lose themselves in the outrage of carnal multitudes—their habits—
when—sickly lantern on the tyrannical face of the island—
the fleeing mermaid—slum without a cove substance without scruple—
draws from the knell the pearly fire of pleasure
and from pleasure the insolent distress—tamer of pardons—
when desire—smoky nonchalance—licks the hoop-nets of the sun
shakes the tide-gates—rips the axles from their spine—
huntress pride—somber gag—

sniffs the waverings of misfortune and the ardent odor of their
      bushes—
when rough and fearful—born of a steady night—
alarming the myths choking all the cries—
sumptuous lassitude on the path of drunkenness—
you come spurting in the hand—star of rafts moving
      among the nightlights
when you yourself—harassed by confused visions
you return to the aid of your heart like a stranger
when vision on vision and shadow cut against shadow
effacing from the view the vow enforced by your retreat
can follow no longer the shore under your steps—
the heavy shutters of your youth swing open
a wind as far as the days can reach moves in you
the windows opened on the pediment of things
send old reminders coursing through you
the anxious avidities submit without restraint
to the carnal bitterness of the lichen ambush
the doors gaping the windows bled and your body
sold to squalls to beatings—on a platter of sun
offered to the highest to the cruelest
the vibrant modesty of uncertain days

artful invitation to southern pallors
under the tent that holds out muted
the mortal word which formed of so many successive rebirths
consumes itself in flying buttresses the seductive spring
      slips away chanting under your feet
you wonder where you're going the weighty heritage of trees survivals
and why you move about under this sign
garden invaded by evil loves
the seductive pallors found outside yourself
what you are what you do not know
sibilant insect searching between the lines
then you wonder then you ask yourself
the lisping flower seeking to know

thus there plays with me and plots a tall unseen child
and hurls me from one corner to the other in the enclosure
          of my used-up days
trailing tatters of temporary meaning
rigid pallors of knowledge and of wells

oblivion the buried the indiscoverable belief
buried in the swells the heaths the fruits
ample bed of hermetic questioning
where taciturn the bud of lightning grows
the trembling banner
when the eye can no longer succor
the bird grows up by the road without a guide
risen from the demons' torrents
when solitude saturated with secret eyes
appeals to the vegetation of pride
the shutters of your youth swing open
and love leaps forth across the dense delay
in vain have the halberds tousled the throng of mists
that the noble force aimed at—hiss serpent hiss—
the massed arrivals showered on you their messages of sun
with so much affection intermingled that light
seemed to crown the incestuous memory

contradictory fright upsetting the balance of mountains in your head
you utterly disgust the fantasy by which the certitude of
          fate subdued you—
day won to insecurity—undoing of visions—
at the summit of your sight has placed the haggard prison
where unrealizable predictions will be lost
where lies of clarity will be lost
where the mind no longer knows itself
among the weights and measures the inexhaustible radiance
where the dangers whisper to themselves the strange mutual aid
unconquerable fleeing the tangents of craters
padlock of fears

unfathomable vigilance
the secret harpoons

why start on my way—my way of sorrow—
why circle above the mocking wind
or watch over sick nights in the pardon of seabeds
and pillage the festive gold—to fasten it at the hatchway
        of your heart—gas midnight—
separate from sea fronds the old pebbles a tear which could not ripen
when arranged on new vigors of the sky are flying words
which have but a brief decay and fade out in submission
words are spinning
leaving a faint trail majestic trail behind their meaning scarcely a
        meaning
or bouquet of streamers hanging onto each gaze of a beacon
at the window lit up by losing neither fire nor speed
—and stars—but we have grown old enough while musing on
        them watching them
prowling around morsels of exile the larks
what do we know of them—with this hard pitching on
        the ill-trimmed waves before us
and the limping cadences of remorse we create for ourselves—
        what do we know of them
where that ends and for what visionary ramble we continue
        our factious way
to the limit of our obscurities
as far as the tufted bed of rushes
as far as the distant sieve crouched behind the hesitation
as far as the dry leaves that the reasons let fall by the way
by way of offense at the end of their favor
and the wise cruelties the halting sobs of nightingales
and so many others and so many others
carried on the ridge of the horizon
toward sacrifices resplendent with labor and with pastures
the expanse hardens under watchfulness
and the intense waiting of its silence steals in

the waiting with noiseless tread grazing in our mind
breathless and purposeless
extracts out the splinters from the smooth mantilla of the dunes
among the longest among the painful ones
crawls the distress of artesian phantoms
radiant exhalations risen from vocabularies household gods
that the cold renders visible and new

child yellowed among packets of childhood
and childhood covered with sandy reasons
insatiable child among the relics
the cool water has tarnished and all his eyes are dead
flagrant childhood multiplying mirrors
and stirring the late braveries of echoes
at each step found again and yet more fleeting
always found again and always more blind
like a plant that would unknowingly devour us
like a love that would unknowingly devour us
among the icicles a joy that would unknowingly spring forth
like the manner whose contour it would trace with a fine hand
the crown of the tree would be seen in the leaf
and in each leaf there would be another leaf
and in each leaf unconsciously the tree-trunk
in another language than that which shelters us
you see high noon at the heart of bitten fruit
and like stalks you see the branches firm and stretching
through half-opened eyelids
like multiple languages
like veins anchored in the leaf
and to the point where one can no longer see—alike—
to the variegated patterns of the infinite likenesses
echo of parallel forms the path of voices vanishes
with yours in the sea with the sounds that legend blurs
to the waiting eye of the unsubdued

×   ×   ×

the tree lives in you and you live in its shadow
concentric circles flee with time
the heart a heavy stone that drowned men put on
holds you in the depth of inexpressible relationships
hardly moving among the errors
the solid links—oh slow oarsmen of soot
come in through the window—the night old with masks
allows each night the long youth to enter into me
never again to lose its footing on this hostile earth

I have acquired its slight taste of salt
and I have lost its secret ways
love open like a tomb
so many patient men carry it in them to the tomb
so many other shadows
the plants grown tense and on the lawns so many other
        lives nights too long
clink their delirious rhymes
and so many others and so many others
who could read them and retell them
able neither to die nor to live

Part VIII

I remember a tortuous deception drawing its bitter substance
        from the past
sailing without clarity I know not where
sometimes a mirror was seen to open on the forehead of the
        song like a stiffened childhood
which spat the image on the ground
and broke the radiant youth—traces of blood trailed somewhere on
sheets soiled by late twilights

feverish worms under the embers
I remember also it was a day softer than a woman
I remember you image of sin
frail solitude you tried to conquer all the childhoods of landscapes
you alone failed to answer the astral summons
I remember a clock which cut off heads to tell the hours
those that wait at the crossroads the lonely ones
in each lonely passerby is torn one day the crossroads of a day
and as the hour of love comes from air returns to air
each crossroad finds itself in another calm waiting
with the melody sung in the distance
childhood more and more distant
on earth chewed with ashes in the lock of farming jaws
voracious door with an adult laugh of iron
I remember the strange haste that impelled you after the
        passage of a convoy
massive chains moved about black in the heads
cocks set up a frugal song between each gaze exchanged
and the winds wiped the fresh barkings from damp muzzles
ready to explode far off where there was no more memory
they were exploding with the clash of noiseless flames
I remember a serene youth which gathered for its display
the shining sighs of the scattered explosion
noiseless but stuffed with flames
how I love them when they come to life again metallic from the
        tears
you know this—snowy adolescence—do you remember
dangers circling in the spray black with tears
among the buoys of severed breasts
we wanted to drink all the blood of rocks purulent with sun
that the waves tried to snap with their burning mouths
the sea brought scars still sensuously warm
at each moan she emptied from so much grief her bag of rattles
no longer knowing what could be done do you remember the
        sound that entwined us
our embrace that paled the evil predictions of the flame

and the floodgate of the sun gave way under the pressure of
    so much brightness
a grape's eye extinguished
it was a day softer than a woman that throbbed from one end
    to the other
I saw its body and I lived from its light
its body writhed in all the rooms
offering unappeased gods to blind adolescences
heaps of children changed to grasshoppers on immense
    desolations of beaches
their ankles yelping with a wild joy
branches chattering in the fragile streams
I saw its body stretched out from one end to the other
and I plunged in its light leading from one room to the other
the whiptree streaking thin trails of darkness
the immensely painful body—it was a day softer than a woman
under the beds I saw
heavy masses of shadows
ready to circle sleeping robbers
in the soft palm of the beds
on their ears I saw the aureoles
of heavy guardian masses with black fists
and moving in the middle continuous writing
the rain breaking gray wings and prisms
wills short and phosphorescent lost among crosshatchings of laughter
their quick step waking the fields closed by the eyes
noiselessly turning as a screw in the threads of the well's rim
rare gasps of rank weeds
and then catacombs of birds the birds
taking flight across submissive tentacles
the tamed brothers in the mirror
their porcelain eyes fixed on the enclosures of countries
where the lands are hurled in pools of corpses and of urine
farther on I saw the lashes crowding round the birds—polar crown
and the powerful falls of birds of light
on the inflamed world of fruitless days

and then I saw no further
someone slammed the door
—weeping friend down in the hold—
the night has crumpled up in me

over the vigils of groping nymphs
from now on it snows softly from the roofing of the night
color of night—watcher of runes
let there be only gullies thrashed by the impulsive blue
the eye adorned with chandeliers will descend from its glass casing
with a long wake of sharp whistlings
you thought yourself drifting toward realms hard with whiteness
where icicles strewn with sighs of straits
toward other seas revive the nervous crevice
that the abrupt morning opened in the season's heart
the team of dogs eager for the chase
grinding from the light hearts the sheds of snow
with eyes of pearl at the bottom of test tubes
from having cooed too long in the drizzle of wreckage
joyous around the sloping roofs
where love struggles caged sweats in the fireplace
and cries and moans like a storm dying down in the strait-jacket
ships dumbfounded on mute sands
a cough without echoes tapping on the door
the emptiness where the harsh blue yawns
the guttural depths of wave breathe—
far off so maternal the reproach that breeds the silence
          in the glistening worm—
motionless and bright from so much tension
to stay upright tempest to starboard
anger has conquered the turbulent space
and delirium flails the milky ghosts
only puppets left behind at the mercy of the ends
the bloody cradle song of naval agonies
the disillusion of experiments
harrassed and shameless emanations of oblong hyena cries

mixed with frenzies miasmas of brain
with hopes impatient for freedom
it was a gnarled morning of bark and empty shells in cruelty
so young were the words that their meaning slid off the skin
and the roughness all around did not burden the sonorous foliage
with the weight of remorse
pondered by the blood misunderstood in the sea's immense devastation

then I drew back under ruined porches in the silence
the moon crumpled up in me—and I kept watch the night long
at the talons of rock displayed and jagged to tear human silence in
        shreds

deaf roads were losing their wings
and man was growing under the wing of silence
approximate man like myself like you and like the other silences

Part IX

the wolf entangled in the forests' beard
frizzled and broken by jolting and splitting
and suddenly freedom its joy and suffering
leaps up in him another suppler animal reveals his violence
he struggles and spits and tears himself away
solitude sole richness hurling you from one wall to the next
in the hut of bones and skin given you for a body
in the gray pleasure of animal faculties bundles of warmth
freedom solemn torrent may you remove my flesh my barrier
the carnal chain around my soles vertiginous impulsive tensions
adventures I would throw by pools by packets and by fistfuls
against my shameful timid face of flesh and of so little smile
oh powers I have glimpsed only in rare flashes

and that I know and feel in the tumultuous encounter
brake of light progressing from day to day along meridians
do not place your iron collar about my neck too often
let my flight spring up from my tarnished earthly self
let it tremble at the touch of bodily terrors
escape from hollow veins from hairy lungs
from muscles almost moldy and from memory's frenzied shadows

on all the curves of earth I've skated elegantly free
pressing to my bosom destiny in monogram
I have drunk and eaten
the embroidery of the sky unravels bundles of cocoons are
          raining on the convent
and over there clouds shield themselves with wings that hatch
the wailing eggs of embryonic worlds—
what brusque aversion will chase the snow today
for I want the map to show me clarity
your lips are a shining repose for me when twilight puts its signature
at the bottom of the day the page that has seen laughed and suffered
so much

in the chest of contraband I live my double life
toward the explosive danger whose prediction pains me
threading my way among the rows of gods and those of light
bumping against the boundaries of white-gloved days

the trains halt at seaside the scales of landscape vanish in the sea
the swimmer sows in the water the seed of his gesture
and already the fruit of motion moves along the latitude and licks it
he plows the stubborn wave
from his hands and feet trail effluvia that guide
his mass of flesh carried by the dream
to the door of dream with the rhythm of his breathing

on the bank the clothing in a heap of holiday sun
foam gripped solid in stone talons

disjointed dancers playing incandescent vertebrae flakes of snow
eyes deepened by the mines darkened at their center penetrated
by purplish salt the rust powder the mineral cloak of its reign

and on fragile shells fishermen shed their destinies
spreading out fanlike the wandering confetti scatters
beats the sea with random wings of butterflies
while famished birds divert the lepers' rattles enlarge their sweep
they fly so far away you see earth's curvature
the earthly sadness in the shade of mountains sky and water
at times the net comes up heavy with rings and moving rockets
gathering whole families of colors plucked in the unfathomable
        swirling
but work is only the colorless price of family hunger
wails of sirens moans of milky ways of hostile wind
storms in the sky upside down dance eagerly
plunge and touch the sea with their heads
empty the pockets of the nuptial coat

granite heads snatched off on the billiard table rolling and games
flotsam left in customs on the frontiers of meager destiny
white sails unfurled imploring peace upon the emptiness
sails white unfurled hands of sails joined in prayer
the ship kneeling with bowed head moans and laments
but if the sky took off its eye mask to see them
hope in radiating volleys would cheer the feverish prey
man so fears the face of his god that deprived of horizons he
        trembles
man so fears his god that at his coming he stumbles he drowns
horizonless man so fears his death that deprived of god
        he hides his tomb
man fears so much

but for what purpose the vast pools of marshy complaint
the sun knows only his rotund incandescence

laughing from all his golden flaming mouths
he rises

and the wolf entangled in the tortuous vines
has found his shepherd shepherd of the holy constellation
has placed in the confident calloused hands
his strength seeker of undiscovered freedoms
has found his shepherd the motionless shepherd
so great that he need not walk who is everywhere
has found his shepherd the shepherd who leads all the flocks
         and all the shepherds
in love so great that he need not move
so pervasive his presence where others walk not finding
         the end of the thread
not finding the end of the thread
the end of the thread they took in their hands at birth
whose other end they dropped when the imperious hour
cut the end of the thread from the hands tense and thin
that others took up but that no one could keep
until the return of the beginning of their coming into the world
the wolf has laid down his pride and his scornful haste
         worm-eaten by the years
in the solemn and confident hands of the motionless shepherd
shepherd of waves riding toward what end intercepter of dramas
shepherd of rains traveling from country to country
shepherd of irrational depressions that periodically cloud us
shepherd who guides our fates in so many directions
that sometimes they meet so often they run side by side
not touching and in extravagant curves and zigzags
follow each other insatiable magnets in their nostrils
parallel on paths spaced in spirals of different reach
shepherd of our doubts where we are bogged down our brains
         in pieces
hands which toward death direct the needle of their compass
the uncomfortable existence we have rented
and in which we try to settle down

shepherd of warlike evocations rushing toward each other
shepherd of humble peasant hesitations
of torrential landscapes in the timid dwellings of breasts
shepherd of boats of birds of hypocrites
and shepherd also of lovers of exchanged glances
brightness forever immeasurable from which life and drift are born
I see you radiant as light in the noise of capitals
in the leaf of rosebush in the knowledge of the dying man in the
hand held out to me in the gauzy insect
in the water in my dream flowered with resplendent uselessness
I see you motionless and yet walking through everything
removing heads replacing them with other heads of animals
directing the traffic of the stars and that of winds and waters
and that of blood in underground arteries and of fishes
and the sequence of glances despite in each of us our anguish
our miseries and our inner chances alternating on the market
whose lowly reasons you keep and the cruel secrets of the falls

shepherd of the pavements flocking in the opposite direction
from the progress of the crowd scissors in constant motion
cutting the distance in paced-out measures
motionless shepherd in the halo of golden dust
sing placed in the curtains sing tufted eye sing
shepherd of days that pass leafing through the calendar of
        diminishing shadow
sing tufted mimosa eye at the window sing sing
the country scowls at the mouth of mountainous frontiers
at the coming of the enemy hail vermin storm grasshoppers
shepherd of eternal snows and higher on your chair of cloud
fragile pane window on the sky
sing vain remedy take the pulse of rivers
fever of the year sing doctor of the seasons of reasons astrological
sing man stripped of the effervescent humility of man
flower fountains spring up from the lakes of light
from the clouds of snow the couch on the horizon
offers rest to the god turning inconsolable around his axis

and the flocks of our gentle feelings move on
toward the celestial pastures of the night

the wolf entangled in the forests' beard
has found his shepherd motionless shepherd
who guides all the eyes set in the summit of the moving hills of faith
shepherd of the immeasurable brightness from which
        life and drift are born
he rises
moves on toward the celestial pastures of words

Part X

surrounded by echoes the head crawls down the track
        of the smoking bellows
that volcanoes have dug along the prospectors' trail
up there where all is stone
and fragile warbling followed by disconsolate suns
the anemic duct opens in the valley's chalk crater with its portal
        cravat
and metallic fauna swarm bitterly in the pond of rust and fur

fragile warbling of disconsolate suns—rumbling of dunes
hard to crack—the short grasshoppers in the crevices
that a faithful doubt delivers from the mesh of sleep
and the fatigues dribbling on the burning couches where the sun sets
surrounded by loquacious worries geometrical escorts
by tufts of ectoplasm by mirthful sleeping latches
by translucent trap doors by way stations of space
medleys of padlocked fissures—the air dies

                ✕   ✕   ✕

and may love follow on love followed by disconsolate suns
up there where all is stone
lover of gentle slopes magician of sudden waters
may night shiver deep in the hold
may you take from the pockets of coconut palms
the flying handkerchiefs where desires of the moonless travelers
       spurt forth
on misshapen illusions and the warehouses of races
the rain lays down its greenhouse cover
and the launch grown up at the bosom of the coral pecks at the reef
its wet eyes laid up from discouragement
waiting for you
up there where all is stone
and turn away with indifference

voracious songs have tangled the plumes of their dying measures
on the lectern of the ship where the wind has gathered up the sea
       from all directions
which the flora have followed and abandoned
slow springtimes whirled so in the merciful eye of the opening
that the shoals began to tremble from the ears of rafts
that the insects hardened in moonlight simmered in the
       impotence of dreaming
from the bells of immemorial bulwarks the torrents of centuries
       slapped the vaults
the fruit of livid sand lay close to the hillock of fear
and the sharp cliff seated knees against its chin
chewed on its star and the peaceful light that ruled it

collector of cigar stubs in the brush of ecstasies
of dilapidated stars fallen far off in the ditch of secrets
stumps of countries of heaviness shredded suspicions
of the stumbling fluidity of surf
absent-minded convalescence of flamingo flames
up there where all is stone

the mysterious vats of fascination
ferment the illusory wheat of voices
on the branches of waterfalls at evening the eyes' spiders
        shed their skins in sorrow
wild hope projected with the boomerangs and comets
in the jet-black dampness that no return grazes with meditative wings
or with firebrands of love

and the sleeper—incredulous of the vagabond caresses—
girded with galleys where the mind takes form
where no progress interrupts by a treacherous reflection the
        mystery's star-filled laziness
carves out a flight among the fragments of proverbs that
        the noise conceals
toward the infinitely mobile flesh of dream
and turns away with indifference

and it is in the smoke the vines of smoke the smoke
that the bowsprit gambols tramples down the grainy snow
it is in the smoke of the farthest pastures there all is stone
and it is the sun's smoke that rises from the rolling of dice
the trooping of huts around blind resignations
the hills uncreased at the passings of heavy caravans of heat
the threadbare leisures under the traveling rug of fodder
figure fainted in animal noises
ash expanded in the basket of sounds
and cutting on a bias the chalk relief the torpor of this noise
tattoos the facade with fatal ambitions
and love

so many hours have formed me with their friable cement of
        crossed tibias
so many men have preceded me in the noble furrow of exaltation
so much soul has been squandered to build the chance I gamble
in the lonely jail where a blood prowls thick with remorse

so many soft frenzies have brought the landscapes toward my eyes
and bitter consciences restrained the ground swells in the sieve
        of their anxiety
so many unseen voyages have soaked in my senses
so many miracles have linked us
to the fleet of words—dregs of divine innuendoes—
hypotheses rolling in the midnight crucibles of the mind
where the ground swells break and the waves of love
and so many others swell and sink again
and so many others break in secret

and let the owl walk and the night weave
and let the night walk on the foot of the pond
and let the rock woven with owls pitch its tent
let the cold rise from the naked boas to cover the peace of the dove
up there where all is stone
where the grass hardens where the fingers fade
where the heron fears the water where his shadow sputters
where the jewels fall and the glacier's lips quiver
where the fetus scoops the jewel case in a beak lamp
where memory stirs the wind of victories on the deck
where the coast is crumpled skin of time
where hearing hides itself in the ancient east and in fatality
on the moving vanities of crystal spaces
up there all is stone indefinitely
and in the alembic of games where we weep and up there all is
        stone
the alarm that rings a single time sounds from the height
        of a tear on the stay
hung in the throat spittle of the wind so slow it cannot sleep
torn by the sun visited by suns heavy in the sea

as long as the shade nibbles at the porous edges of night
as long as the fires settle down near friends on benches
and turn away with indifference
the quartz birdcatcher can water the dwarf light of the apse

in the whisper pearling the trigger of its wing-sheath
but from what unreal disorder of crypts and eyelids
from what bitter color from the depth of refrains
have we drawn the old disgust covered under the dead leaf of shields
and surrounded with invisible shields
repulsing life on the way
ennui—infernal hub—the brace and bit boring the gentle country
their magnetism humming encirclng the alligators in the stepless walk
have we reached—up there where all is stone—the fraternal stone
up there where all is stone
and contagion in the haven of talismans and instincts

what mirror swallowed in the gulfs will give us back at dawn
        the glassy shelters
of pretended nakedness the names where only the indulgence
        of boulders now ripples
the strongholds of the human chain glazed with mica
smooth down the clump of clouds—these are the teeth of thunder—
mouth wide open—that the crust of snow tenders to us—
they sneer up there
into gaping eternity hiatus has bitten
and the terraces split to the hearts of beliefs
the zones of dismantled brains slide on launches of treacherous limits
they begin our experiments—up there where all is pebbles
polar dissolution—cavernous fanfare—
which turn away with indifference

chilly future—slow in coming
a frothy start has led me in the path of your gaze
up there where all is stone and sheet of time
neighbor to clay craters where never swells under allusion
I sing the incalculable alms of bitterness
hurled at us by a sky of stone—food of shame and death-rattle
in us laughs the abyss
that no moderation penetrates
that no voice ventures to brighten

its elusive net of risk and pride extends
there where one can do no more
where the kingdom is lost the flat silence night's pulsation
thus the days join the number of unconcerns
and the sleeps that live on the hooks of day under their yoke
day after day bite their tails and dance around
and up there up there all is stone and dance around

Part XI

what is this cheeky snoring that fills the twilight
on the border of silence splashing among the angels
I walk through the sumptuous embroidered valley
which lies in your heart moved by solicitudes
and won in the progression of solstices in the solitude head held high
above the virgin tunic's pleats a torch
fears the earthly nakedness
the organ pours silk avalanches on the mural clouds
of crises and thrusts the storm toward the ceilings
breath deeper than volcanoes
unloads the net of sounds of so much tumultuous love
where the height is taken lofty breath
but marked by tombs scales the tympanum and flees

the marriage of the firmament orchard fresh vision
medallion of sweet water where the thirst of cymbals is quenched
on the lips of good mornings awaiting the fall of circumflex night
eyebrow of the world the jew's-harp is dying the shadow
furrows the wasp's buzzing waist and cuts it

under the oiled sun the plant can turn in the gears
of rotating lives and deaths filling space to the borders of incoherence

the pools of noise spread out on the paralyzed pond
and a few leaves a few corpses float on the thick trance
where are the angelic stages that sleep could not pass on to light
the lock of dreams has closed its jaws on the bleachers of man
and the breeze is no longer a shirt for the garden cinquefoil
      dear daughter
suddenly harsh tragedy and sacrilege have invaded our lives
tearing the brief shreds of rest from our bones
tearing the waters from the hinges of the archipelago conch and devil
of the harbor book that leaf covered by leaf and wave by wave
fill with writings with litanies and with brains

the noise of broken windows casts the sun in the sea
a birth night of larvae a night the confusion
the last judgment looms on glassy wings in our agitation
demolishing the love so airy that we have had built day after day
      in the innumerable vault
in the organ the sound was engulfed when his throat catching with
      fear
the beast rears up then lies prostrate in the heaviness of his trunk
and the birds grown enormous glide obliquely toward our dwellings
like black tufts sacks dilated with hypnotic cold they pile up
such is the strength of shifting moods worn out by
      legendary listlessness
indescribable theory of vocabularies and of thorax
seaweed asleep on delicate sands

scattered in the blue the fossils of spheres
prove nothing more so vain is the measure
of human breathing scanned in the profile of the dunes
but the dizziness spun by the dream which gathers
comets and edges in its circling
desperate caress on the migraine rails
dizziness with a thousand new understandings
anemic night sucked by hummingbirds old with coffins and
      with centuries of poetic elimination

and may the cherry
how we have wept from the top of the grating
electric sign astronomy
begins the alphabet of steps
the reasons for our keeping silent

of what use the resplendent spasm
for what place a depth of cartilaginous abyss
the anemone a stained glass window startled by the vibrations
resounding in the assonance the proclamation
conveyer-belt from faith to nothingness—
think of watery suspicion turn
in position it is the most distant downy signal the blue
my handshake on wheels
and let hesitation sow the grebe
all the brambles in tallow filigree
under the haughty arcade of the grove

let the leaning one
beside the dark one
I mean those huddled together under eternal coincidence
let them come to rest with my head on each shoulder
velvety alike but less crude
thus the avenue crossed with images is soon wrecked
by the trepan of the clock

the disheveled rain streaks our speech our fortifications of breasts
fisticuffs knots in the long journey of existence
what do they shatter clear with time and with mirrors
the starting-post at the human race-track
site of homesick eyes limits of oblivion
the moon in its array of stuffed volcanoes of fortifications of breasts
the pipe-organ pours its magic impetus on the stanzas
where old lungs resound with sacred fissues
and the tombs that dance on the necklace of gestures

shine among the diamond-studded exaltations of the venuses
    along the stadia
the days embark and follow closely on the viscous twilights
the organ pours out its azure signs on the partitions of gongs
shatters the wall of eyelids cemented and deaf like winter
the precise tremolo withdraws in its cavity of breath
that the hoarse darkness inhales—ex-votoes of meteors
fall from the bosom of night with the mammals and the trees
and all the money-boxes are emptied in the dark
that draws over every sin its lids of noise
where did it come from the vowel with beating wing
which prolongs the panting questionnaires of strangled flutes
the bridges and caressing jetties
elastic wakes the animal proceedings perhaps the stars and crashes
suddenly on plateaux of flesh and bushes

make way for muscled colors in their austere leaping
madness carved agitated gullies in the refrains of life its sidelines
the wailing obstacles drag in the horizon's scorn
morning jerks through the swaggering of branches saint vitus's dance
again the prism casts its incendiary apparatus
a stone thrown in water tempts pleated illusions barely waves
in the outskirts of the day long after the shock
man slashes to shreds the prey of his bitterness

squatting under the leaf memory distorts the face with sneering visions
unearthing the rubbish and the dross
hostility all is hostile around the nebulae of talk
and passion on the slope of the transparent blade
lashing whip of lightning branched with lancets
word—at the edge of the precipice in the centuries hardened
jet of poison fusing aborted summits
glorifies the shining tension of hatreds
the halo of intransigence blinding the vitiated color
and renews the charms of human controversies
adhesions to unreality of molecules by hurricanes in procession

vomit massacres the jumble of filthy swarmings and of gangrenes
piled up under tearful arpeggios in the hollows of the world's
      beginnings
oh intoxications deliver us from parasitic mire and from the
      lazy rite of living
and from the others from so many others

Part XII

time lets tom thumbs fall behind
he reaps delicate molecules on prairies of water
he conquers the airpockets crosses their jungle
he cuts worm from wave and from each half a butterfly is lit in the
volcano he threads himself along a violin note
he knots the running flow of glass in the frail transparent hours
until our slumbers upset the singing food of light

stream that the mountain weaves in the east hinged with danger
      and with why
and loads with medals and holocausts along the gardenia
has tightened around your wrist road buttoned with boundaries
      to the suns neighbors of the fields
beyond the banks the bow stretches the smile of the distance
      as far as the glacier's grin
the weaver's shuttle punctuated with oars in the intoxication
      of the centipede
crosses the bald barriers and the tufted eyes of seeing arrows
but the cleft at the lake's end comes undone
like puffs of clouds the tidy sentiments of layettes embroidered
      with pens spread out across the water
why am I not frenzy the drowning elf who swallows great
      mouthfuls of air at play

or the tremolo of fire running through space emptied by echo
the wind flees the tourniquet searches the landscapes the passengers
and the will to be oneself nestles its long lease in the hollow
    of the lapping

the lightbulbs under the tortoise shell hatch the grains of sand
    and beauty spots
the twilight draws farewells from the horizon washed with
    cold clarity with a stereoscope
lashed by ship gleams makes a circuit of the prison
and its fallings from place to place prepare the electrification of the
    eyes
adam and eve hiding at the very heart of the cloven fruit
two towers lower the sky twins of the ages subterraneously
with the taste of swollen metals the lenses of the stars offer
    their breast at the grotto opening
at the rock standing to attention for you
falling in the winter's carelessness drawing its swords
nothingness and hebetude seeding with a steady hand the trees
    into the precipice one after the other
shouting to new melodies the departures the rapacious leaps
    from the void
into the illusion of whiteness drugged by the chloroform
that the surface of ice takes to the noon of blood

adolescent delayed in a cloud of fallen angels
don't you fear the muffled speed of the river
pulling along the stations crowned by necklaces rich with frost
and gardens bridges sleeping objects
it carries the filial mud upstream from destinies
yawning at your breast constrained by heavy lionesses—
meanwhile man's rhythm drains the secret to the last drop for cash
under the cassock dead leaf lying in wait for the debtor man walks a
prisoner in the lining of his soul
surrounded by mists of fallen angels
for in the palm of his feast day

there have sounded the invisible hour of the spirit and the
      stigmata of the voices' infinity
the lock falsifies the meaning
when the dust grasshoppers wake who put a spider's heart
      into each wound
and claws grasp the man in search of the mercy of brick or sun

but heavy with thousands of hours which the cragginess of rock
      serves as miraculous hideout
I raised my silence to the gentleness of death
let its springtime swell soon bear us
let the harvest of its senses invade the felt nests
where the dog-days wait sluggish among the tobacco lashes
let its breath close the doors to the owls
let a blade of night graze on the taciturn hair of ants
the lamb fades from the sky sprouted with thistles of hail
and rebellion is in full swing of bursting and bloodied wings
among the now scarcely moving weaknesses of the shipwrecked
lost in the immensity of smoke a few ridges scatter
and while anger howls at the moon's mourning
and spreads the fetid shadows in vacillating alleys
fleeing on all sides like streams of wine from the cask of creation
no longer bordered by houses with their serried ranks of watchful
      teeth
knocking their heads together the buildings that no deluge of
      acid can dissolve
now they crack apart on the pavement with the remains of crutches
and they kill death with its head full of stones
the skeletal creakings opening the tomb at the rampant calls
cutting off the arteries the whirlwinds derailing pile up
and rally to our side

god juxtaposed with each allusion of millimetric gesture
god placed among the cells do not desert me
as I am—alone planted in the center of the hourly anvil
vague are your calls the regions that applaud but smooth

your hands in mine seized in the flight of migratory crises
and solitude lives circular huddled in the depth of the crevasse
compressed in my own depth I see myself absent and am
          astonished still to have such power of movement
on the periphery of the spot spilled on the terrestrial tablecloth
there are still like me some light drops of soul rejected
          by the centrifugal force
and where the stalk stands like a dagger's crook
squat the heavy souls unseeing

the valley is uneven that meets you god of dusk
and sovereign are the masses that you threw between us
but the north winds which point our way and with whom
          guileless we plot
lead us farther on
farther farther than the reach of your embarrassed smile farther
farther than the scorn where your charity delights in promising
          the pack of shadows
farther than tears where rewards will never swerve the bright
          oar of our racing cry
and the errors and impurities which we cultivate on the
          foreheads of dawn
help us push with their surprised starts the fresh and
          vigorous penetrations
polar antennae beams
repressing with the force of the unknown the putrid mangled flesh
rise to lucidities henceforth transcended to the sluicegates of dreams
burning with an agile insomnia of game and of ember the transfusion
of intruding comforts those of the limits of lives and those
          forming the troubled border of deaths

man with sails unfurled by wind cast into the perplexity of traps
the wounded eye pities you bitterly to be pitied
white is the unrest the foam flings against the stone
but autumn has heaved its long trailing sigh
and by puffs of papers strips from cocoons their fluorescent roofs

only the women raked with newspapers insist on reviving
    the cheeks of spring
irremediable force in the lode of each fiber savored and whose
    every end is a beginning
by the path of what invincible lightning can you some day
    pierce the dwelling of knowledge
and farther than god plant the trees of flags and daggers
condemned to outlive you painful revolution of universe
overflowing with isolated forces but impotent harassed
    by the rasping of files
such a humble thing you are and so little limited in your strident
    desire
that the shames ripen in your breast in innumerable flora
and yet sacred is the dissatisfaction that hatches you indomitable
    bearing
seed of the haughty flood of tyrannical numbers and turnings

Part XIII

a most beautiful country lies in his head
where the sky's promise touches him with its hand
bare is the skin of the sky and scraped by the clusters of rocks
the stiff itineraries of the thorns in procession
have limited the feverish profiles of the air
and in his memory's cistern the swarm of tribes
matured in the treacherous levelings
scatter the panting foam the fruitless reason
its cursed capsizing chills where your pleasure ends the emptiness
    grows
the spur of sordid steppes breaks against the dolmens' track ventilator
whirring in the ravine's echoing tomb
ravine drunk with moaning depths

upholstered in delicate scripts in prideful dizziness and in algae
our looks sliding from vertical to vertical dissolve
draw eyes of oil on their pool
thus I watch you at the foot of the mountain
seated as night is ready to spread out
and on the hollow steps that your tread breaks through
death has crept in breath of appeasement

but on the footbridge holding in its balance
the plateau of the bank and the ship's bridge
you waver flux of daylight
carrying the small miracles of every day
on the flood of your arms and the night whimpers behind you
        torches
and game it comes disheveled
unbuttoned dropping in the ditches and in the mines
great pieces of greasy orient
and the wind rises pushing aside the stifling night
as the wide-open eyes cry for help
and arms in the air beating the tatters of air
and torn by herds of jackals in the mountains
the night lets itself fall layer by layer dense
waterfall in asthma tiers descending in the arenas
beaten vanquished silent until the opening of tomorrow's doors

a curve thrown far off trembles in the gaze
the hardened metallic flight of an oblique bird
of winter is his wake of diamond his beak
drawing his acid squeaking across the frosted glass
which carries you over the virgin abyss unfathomable
mourning meal lying in a pallid fluff of mist

don't you feel the long scratch on your taut breast
prolong the violin's fleeting mood
carved from the slope the river's thread
lost hair a tear a knife's blade

has fled the idle plaint of the chalk crater
which rising from the powders spreads its petals
and on the plains pregnant with village hopes
piles up successive whiteness of bed in heaps

the grottos make hollows in the accumulation of your age
from which hang great stalactites
and the cold extinguishes the graying air
like madness the limestone bites that dreams have frozen
along the eyelids of the earth opened with fingernails
have traced in your life the bleeding darkness
whose living paths are alone my light
and far off in the tempest of being is hidden the childhood of
        passions
piled in debris of ardent cries of fears
at the root of the world in the cradles of sprouts
man nests his senses and his proverbs

woven of lashes inarticulate wells on the reefs
shelter the morning denuded of doubt and of prayer
lift the lid of the prison of voices
so that even adrift they can sniff the eloquence of shocks
and untangle convulsions somersaults of signs
attach themselves to the headlands fierce eyebrows of the world
so that they can turn the trajectory of order around
or water the procession of smiles the length of caravans
the earth which forgotten on the face of the vines
ferments the salt of our embraces places on the path again
the anxious flesh latent hesitation

do you see the corpses aligned in me
the bridge of pains in coagulated rows of ages
the dying oscillation of feelings which ignite no longer
rubbing your eyes against the harsh glare you see straight enough
despite argument to throw letters of rain in the garbage pail
the climbing plants of your veins

fight with the weight of the abrupt light
spasmodic their fingers encircle my head and the night
disentangles the laws from the carousel of thorns
brain whose canals issue into dawn
at the knot of day and night at their handshake
at the origin of roads bordered with down and with teeth
time runs through the streets the length of farewells
while on the screen the trick of the devil wound up
again crackles in fleeting sparks woven from water
and in the hearts the massed fanfares resounding
carry the years toward the conquest of angers
now the cupola of silence rams its hat on the town
an angel dares to hang suspended in the air
after throwing the key out the window
what is this perpetual smile gazing at us
and that we call mystery on summer nights
the secret at your ear makes flowers and fruits grow like earrings
the alphabet of your necklace of teeth
you are so lovely you don't know it
in the gleam of antique colonnades padlock of rhymes
he carries his love letter to the sky
without finding it without finding it
the train rips up the country

patches envelop plantations
plans display their peacock feathers
on the forehead of haloes but in the shelter
the great tailor cuts the pastures of the earth
stretched out the oasis noises dry from one pole to the other earlobe
defying the apoplectic summits
the bird plunges crashing from crisis to crisis
toward the foaming torrents of manes and discomforts
up there the mirrors shattered on the country's head
chime the glorious reflections of the sky
smooth and muscled mountains where voices rear up
mountains draped in flora of the infinite

shields encrusted in the glabrous flesh
for the meteors free themselves from spectral virtues
breastplates wrinkled in the pockets ocean
mountains combed out fissures torn and dense
the net of sloping sides tightens the valley's corset
the noises hammer at the storerooms of being
and sprinkled with gems the sandy lizard drags his trail
breaks the ice encumbered with shellfish
traversed by the sickles fall
flashes of lightning the harsh beatings
in the drum of the massive games

so man gathering lost generations heaps
harvest baskets
in the bag of the hill that other torments will roll before them
each his own turmoil from one end to the other gripping
          the reins of the roads
shattering the greenhouses where dwarfs serve
each his own tempest from one end to the other sings
at the dangerous turnings
leading mothers and plants by the hand
that other torments will roll before them
tombs of wine turning over at the sound of downpours the storm
the summers of our beds muffled in the blood
until the burst of borders in solar fragments of ground swell
the boats split apart at the deep call of the treacherous depth through
which slides fugitive another depth falling from depth to depth
from transparency to transparency there are only astral waves that
          gather
the celestial harvest of the hours of glass
but man entrusts himself to his hardships
and in the attics of his head rats gorge on the infinite
man marked with mortuary punctuations
swept on the inside by the currents of frenzy and of air
the owl set on your shoulder

drives into your head his hard clairvoyance
the sterility of fixed punishment

meager well mill turned by the funeral donkey
the tangle of wreaths of distress
the hands of the escalator
spill out men fallen flat heaped up in transparent piles
in the strait without end and without augury
the hurricane has withdrawn its lottery from their night
has withdrawn the stars from their eyes
and inverted the bells of night in the sea
and the seas too it has inverted
that is what we know of the seas inverted in the well of the sky

meanwhile the clotted halo of the light
incense tiara on the head of the promontory
blossoms from the saturnine braids
and standing incandescent lamp your heart in your hand
culled from the urns spilling over with anguish
blinking beacon of the sun
your eye passed through all the holes the lapses of hours
foretells the path's surprising clarity

who will lead us out from the congestions of things and the flesh
the applause of the sea breaks against you
dike tragic and stiffened on the amphitheater's first step
old pleat of stone on the long-suffering forehead of the world the
wreckage and rubbish cast into the sea
and those of the sea into the world
anxious wrinkle of congested earth
moored in the gorge of marine shadows
clutching the blackness of the future's bold stern
facing the claws plunging into the waves upright
furrow steeped in the inconceivable imprecation of time
until the consummation of the centuries
until the exhaustion of cyclones in elysian warehouses

poor little life losing ground each day
overthrown toppled trampled poor life
poor life harassed by wild portents trampled
and yet: jaw of unshakable eternity and insolence
fortified and crenelated up to god's summit
that no eye has been able to climb
no cheek to warm with human tenderness
but to what purpose climb the peak strain the clouds
when human tenderness can no longer warm my joys
what matter the only friend the night the anguish
I carry in me the crumb of bread death the friend
and the degree of cold each day rises in me friend
becomes friend what matters habit
what matter the only friend the night the anguish
one day one day one day I shall put on the cloak of eternal warmth
hidden forgotten by others in their turn forgotten by others
if I could reach the luminous forgetfulness

Part XIV

lift your eyes above the alluvia of serious snows
lift your eyes to the height where jaws chatter
from so much stiff brightness
toward the mills with weather vanes of stars so quick
        is the whirlwind in its spinning
that its beams no longer pulverize the powder's cosmetic
        tribute to the sky
the beans of burned coffee downstream from the night
the flour how the shirts of the slopes are white
what pen writes the strange circular letter of the plaintive horizon
that your eyes chase from the center to the most confused
        and distant of the senses

they lift their gaze toward the eternal incandescence
that mutes the appearance of things and their semblance of heroism

we have displaced the ideas and confused their clothing with their
     names
blind are the words which from their birth can only find
     their place again
their grammatical place in universal safety
meager is the fire we thought we saw kindling in them in our lungs
and dull the predestined gleam of what they say

but when memory comes frightening in its mask of shouts of crime
eager to snatch the letters from the words
the straw emerges from the mattress of my body which unyielding
     as my god oppresses me
and so hard oh feverish sky and
and I am broken along the iron structure
and crushed like a fruit under the careless foot
I weep gall succulent deliverance
if I could kill memory elusive prey
how the word is dirty at its approach why not strangle it
before it spills from the bucket of the atmosphere
why does it not hang still from the monstrous drooling of stalactites
at the edge of the smile the animal grottoes
let memory be destroyed let its fame be struck down and the mirage
the contagious speed with which it spreads
reaches the furthest hamlets on the height and the horror

and still objects are there consolation bordering sensations
only their names are rotted decrepit unhealthy
light is a sweet burden to us a warm cloak
and though invisible it is a tender mistress to us
consolation
I sing the man lived in the voluptuous power of the seed of thunder
and wrapped in the starry magnificence of the dust and shines
consolation

and when one after the other we have passed through
        the supreme tourniquet
untiring sunflower carrousel of sun
and when the sadness of our sojourn has been swept from this world
from the summit of the cupola of rays bright tears will fall
and love will be strong enough to walk beside the slow
        consciousness of plants
consolation
in the flying cradles where grows the slow consciousness
        of plants and of things

the black tunnel traverses the head baked in an oven
twisted and shaken thrown against the walls swept in a heap
        like the garbage
I come out vibrant and bandaged with broad furrows of twilight
a word
convalescence
a word
dry and dulled
muffled in winter wounds
a voice disconnected from the curtains
consolation
crude layered cells
in the slow hell of your hot embrace
a voice is swallowed up and extinguished
a voice has put the mark of its five crystal fingers
on the ceiling
develops its seed of concentric fire
under the message of the luminous fakir
sheds myths and teeth through its eyes

now the tree has exploded from the earth
and the explosion has paralyzed again the scattered brilliance
but in my heart it is forbidden for the roots of varying instincts
to go out with the good uproar of deliverances and of doves
must I yet for a long time in ropelike stiffness

fill my glass already brimming with such minimal complaints
oh my god my violin it is not yet the opening so long awaited
which in the din of dead weights of volcanic draughts
stepping over barriers and filters could one day spill out
in the hollow of your impassive hand at the base of everything
that a second still supports perhaps
fruit bowl of the stars

a tree trunk placed on the edge
still smokes with thick clouds
and a forest would like to burn so trembling is its warmth
a man would like to burn a forest of men
at the sound of phosphorescent herds in the night of my consolations
a man would like to weep a man
a man would like to plunge his head into the cool river his head
a woman would like to weep over the man
a man is so few things that a fine net of wind carries him off
man

but what does man matter at the crossing of swords
which on the track of the sky sets flash and star against each other
in the caves of the brain cooks the mildew or the dawn
the kneading trough stagnating on the bottom of stale waters ferments
and its wine taste crackles in the throat
dry is my tongue and avid is my breast for new hells
grazing on the prairie crushed with barns and beams
flapping in the wind oriflamme and palace
the tongue of the wild standard taps against the palate of the sky
and the sky's dry throat splits like old boards
red is its hair spread out on the shoulders of the zenith
bitter the scarlet coin with which it repays us
for the patience we have shown in awaiting it
and bristling with flashing beaks barks the stormy embrace
        that besieges us
up to the ditch of the day where its germs encircle
the cotton bitterness of a third class rail car

×   ×   ×

the pillaged country cemetery
badly shorn badly smeared with leavening and rubbish
in the fertile depth of our ardor multiplies the holy net
          of superhuman rootlets
and though the useless shade ebbs away through the delta of smoke
and though the wear and tear of the furniture shows up the old
          misery
of superimposed ages and of families or trials
it is raining sun on the embers of sun
and ships of sun drown in the germination of nothingness
again the sun's petal with the taste of departure is encrusted
          in the tongue
my breathing stops only at the edge of repentance
it is raining sun fat drops quaver on the glacier's forehead
it is raining sun and the calabash of the world is filled up with it
a glass eye the world floats in the glass of the universe
green is its blood green the impetuous currents of rags and of wind
or of milk nourishing the newborn on the astral squares
and embryonic the whirling so distant
that fright will have perished
long before its image reaches the space holds us apart
such is the song of one who sees the sun grazing
and against the world's temple presses the revolver's lips
the numbers then are angels distilled in the somersaults
          of quickened veins
and although the burning thistle has touched my forehead
          at the place of the sun
I sing more quickly than the rattling of hail on the heart
and morning's eyelid trembles anguished
leech fastened to the year's frenetic flesh

continue sharp fears to click above our heads
your surgical instruments
vague forebodings sound the shouting depth of the wells
where we pile up pell-mell knowledge and poetry

but from our fists clenched and cemented with destinies
you can never take what the trial of the laughable grain
seizes from the indecision of a consoling day
take one step back leprous thoughts of death of vermin
consolation
leave to the cultivators of colors and of skies the succulent promise
of man carrying in his fruit the burning and propitious
      blossoming of morning
consolation
hope is healed on the sadness of cleared consciousness
a sickness like another a habit to develop
consolation
for vast is the stretch of the plain jealously guarded
      by the customs agents of death
and infinite the holy variety of your species
approximate man like me like you reader and like the others

Part XV

when the sun had laden with sufficient trophies
the sailboats of heat and swelled the udders of the earth
they began to spurt skyward their food of fire and abyss

on the slope veined with acanthus and with vine-plants
the plowshare turns the mist of gnomes under the stunted mimic clay
while through its polar ear the world represents the turbulence
of incomplete stars the northern bleedings
the surges of lava dribble on the valley
the jack-o'-lantern buds are of air buttoned to frost
which from their outflow of metal extract the honey from hasty
      sounds
and incisive despair clinging to the framework of the night

has loosened its grip such is the strength of the luminous summons
the wind once clasped around the evening of your bare neck
has crossed the aerial outskirts of the eternal visage
henceforth it blows in secret to invite
insinuating dawn to leave the inexhaustible bath
and the unharnessed waves contract under accordian folds—
the shiver absorbs and renders the severed tops
the multicolored harnesses disperse to all the winds
you take the violin by the throat
and then at the temples listen for the thaw of its word
but suddenly the bird clutches the ridge of thatched roof
torch of unpolished wishes
sets afire the day waking in our breasts

they celebrate the crystalline marriage
from which rise cool stalks of marine sparklings
the carts already sound the quick arrivals
of silver coins on the counter of the rare morning
and the sun pond swallows the aphrodites of fog
the precocious milk of their summers spurting on the walls of conchs
you are at the breakfast hour of your life
your steps knit the distressing distance already growing
you walk your head high with blades of grass
you milk the light from domestic hills
the naked light trailing at your feet
and which with your infant word you dress in fleece
but before your prayers have woven the atmospheric road
        where the echo is hitched
the basket of roads which meet around the spool
age is ready to take you in its artful net
from which escape is difficult and memories sift painfully

and then the branches of fire embroider the small cracks of the zenith
by which you have taken root in yourself
a pipe in the mouth of the half-open door
which your kiss splits in two crescents of alternate farewells

docile chalice comes to rest
put the muzzle on the burning clock tower of barkings
which in sonorous confusions details the neglect
church lifted by its waist from the hillside
sprinkled by the tide of the fringes of low-bursting flashes
the unloading of stars with neither guide nor respite
their prolific encampment among us

and the hand of god feels the hard pulse of the rudder
even and fearless the blood lashes the zodiac
while from the fiancee's parents rises the worthy lament
suckled on the risk of the volcanic sap's bubbling and
        of the moving train
it is here that life is severed like the worm
and the child finds its place in the chilly column
which follows the eternal moaning of the flesh

in each pore of the skin
there is a garden and all the fauna of pains
one must look with an eye bigger than a city
on the ice the wolves dance
you take your brightness up behind you
on your green play at sports and the stock market
and you sing often on the roof
from each note lines of the hand climb up on the foresail
animals descend to the roots
for each note is great and sees

to sow alarms in the skin of the earth
under the tree heavy with musical signs
to crawl blindly on the limestone hillocks
among the lizards and the tombstones
the resinous and chalky hangars
the cemeteries with the smell of turpentine
snatched by the rough claws arranged in semicircles
opened the laugh of leper's rattles

and eaten by the memories of diluvian lepers
what do they know of solitude
where the roads fade out under old flights
a shadow runs death

the breeze its hair streaming will sweep the banks the thickets
        and the horns
and the tear that the twisted cloud estranges
sounds over the decaying country a mourning trampling it at its finish
in the ocean on the velvet of dream
night quietly gives birth to a ship

morning morning
morning sealed with crystal and with larvae
morning of baked bread morning of shutters in madness
morning keeper of the stable
morning of squirrels and of window cleaners cool by the river
sweet-smelling morning
breath clinging to the striations of the iris

Part XVI

the monstrous eclipses tufted with trees
crushed in the mortars of smooth-orbiting moons
the vegetable tatters of the rampant abode
that the cloud drags toward the battle of eyes
have conquered your shade—xylophone of shells— mountain
whose russet beds of sun crackle chilly from volts and from surrenders
and in the gorges opened by nightmare blows
the wind cruelly cauterizes the lightning and the bay's thirst

×   ×   ×

hope with multiple currents climate the equal of paradise
has worn out the wagon and in each traveler I have
        a troubled residence and am bored
I know the shames buried in the sweetness of scarred sites
on the scale the circumstances answering each one's hunger
his rebellion his humility where are you acid greeds
avalanches accumulated at the crossroads of latitudes
where are you tribes bowed under the weight of absurd gods
penned in the stables drowsy with amphibia
in the lagoons chiseled by inclemencies and traffics
and under the perspectives of arches in the peninsulas
        majestic with humanity
subject to dark turbulence to tyrannies verbal funereal
avalanches of the caves lassitudes
where are you gods huddled round the marl of the word
arms folded on the stomach of the cavern the magnetized night
        is plotting
already with the slow bacterial swarming
that from plants made us men
with jaws grinding unable to spew forth creative hate
and love also landslides of hopeless fortune
between its teeth breaks the intrepid thrust of dynamos
in the haughty cup of your age
you will drink so they say still so many livid years
and your drunkenness will consume the light
and your eyes will exhaust the light
by too frequent borrowings of freedom
light washes over the interior vessels
of our petty households with each presence
and the prostitution we practice around the stations
where every hour our other selves arrive burdened with
        awkward parcels of life

my horizon is limited to the face of a watch
the arena where the bullfight boils in my heart harrassed by
        shouting summers

and under the passages heavy with pathetic confessions
      there are flowers kneeling
expiating their disarray in the flea-markets of spontaneous creations
piled in kaleidoscopic wardrobes the silent generations
clinging to the clusters of soap bubbles the octopi
mount toward the bloated dankness of the diaper sky
and the squawk of the fat parakeet caught in a door
colors the fountains lit by day spread with sleepy
      brandenburg trimmings
another town like another sorrow
time mocks us

street kneaded under the coming and going of wheels
bellows lifting rhythmically the crust of the earth
the breast of cherished words nurses mothers
who feel the greedy flesh of evenings
hands that lift from the stern forehead the thick layer of
      notched thoughts
carry to the lips the glass where worlds expand
offer alms and debase man's proper bearing
hands tense on the plank which will bear off the lowly body
but the plank is made of air and takes flight
hands that pray before the plank of air—unable to grasp it
telling other hands of the unspeakable possibility
what the ear tries out in delicate unrealizable vibrations
that alone feel the oscillation of chagrin
cool hands musicians of serene discoveries
hands adept at saving or destroying
hiding tears putting in order the herbals of notes and facts
hands that catch and tame the beasts now in human bodies
forged in the tension of celestial births
and also hands that kill
avenging man fallen into animal obsession
hands cut off
but there are also hands that write

peace to some disillusioned wealth to others according
         to the chance of the wells we fall in
incendiary hands
the only ones that shine

so marvels at the singing illustration the track
whose center is number lamp heart of cruelty
and raising the region despite the watching water
we are botanic vivisection
singing in the courtyards
swelling with an atlas strength the opaque extinction of oboes

the bars open for secrets and inside seashells
dance diabolic vibrations filtering the past
between the teeth clenched on the bite of air
I still hear the cloud saw
that cut the horizon from maturity from the rippling vestiges
and in your heart the troubling contour and the space beyond
the abyss darkens and the swimmers are crowded in
         the cooking pot
in a man country dry and barren this trampling is reproduced
with quarrels and bitterness or earthquakes
anvil on you trickster the sparks of the eyes shatter
approximate man like me like you
why not scatter your soul in playing cards
in geographic maps that your solid feet will tread
measuring the strength of cliffs with that of towns and nerves
peeling at the ports of call of generations the fruits
         of new ages oh aridity
subterfuges spit of angels sticky grease of jellyfish
excrement of the vengeful sea

and the muddy mollusk wakes up compact with epidermis
         and hieroglyphics
the town squeezed in its suburb lifebelt hedged
         in by misery scarcely floats

and all drifts by in the mediocre mire where an unstable
      song has blossomed
each goes off behind the hearse of his dense existence
that the noise swallows up and slowly stifles in its exuberant
      common grave
and bursting the tympanum of the drum to let forth new
      rhythms the electric flood
grazes the sudden emanation and the thread returning to
      the origin of the angel
to the cocoons of mewing stars floating on the pool of timelessness
lights on its way the nuptial row the faintings of milky octopi

Part XVII

imperfect returns of long magic meditations
of meditations seekers of obsessions and explosions
of extreme points of luminous longitudes
of exalted looks of the fatigue of snows
imperfect returns of long magic meditations
to the seasons here below
steeped in these algae teeming with transparencies
valances of erratic eternities dragged through the mud here below
eye always new at the return of things
untiring return from the height of migratory dreams
I dwell in the music in the stove where the shadows bake
a tear—cold lizard track—suffices for us—dazzling negligence
to extinguish in each lamp the silence that buries us in pillows of
      dawn
and leading the star on a leash the tributary of the circuit
      of the world tempts the infinite with sputtering imitations
does not yet close the star in the window of the eyes
casts off from pontoons the clairvoyance of ghosts

whose hands tense with chains
gather the delicate flight of fluorescent prophecies of suicides
and the inexhaustible speculations of high atmospheric studies
leprosaria of clouds

under the dome of talking wings able to count the grotto's darts
the lever of night holds locked in its iron hand all the heavy hair
thus in your heart of foolish glances the child holds the scale
at the center of his heart of sponge
in the shadow of the stormy and unkempt strength
and despite the lunar hesitation of perspectives seated
in the fields of edelweiss where the wild rosettes grow
the bushes clinging to the goats untie the flashes snatched by the fog
let the anemone's face lick the spot of sudden moon
and let the eyebrows of bitter wool above the salt temple
linger near the nocturnal prow's attempts to bloom—
the ostrich hearts hide the landscape's head in the sand
and the brush of pain still glides over all flesh
whether of pearls or diapers
and on so many others

at the nuclear borders where the clouds play ball with rain
presses the scaled summit against its juicy cheek from which
fall secret impatiences
the unexplored pleasures of these ravines of harmony
with their depth of affection always further off
spill out on the plain when midnight reaping all the errors
scolds the infinite dying color of the leaden night
of the leaden day

man celestial pitcher whence the dream draws its hallway light
gathers the pollen of lapis lazuli at the crossing of the boulevards
the hunchback urns—we don't have the time
the bellman frees himself from feeling when the sheaves come
          near the mill
and the fish wrinkled ear leaps around the eye-dropper of awakening

the bow stretches the articulated grill of laughter—dawn
and the gloves draw out the small mines of truth from pockets sharp
        with lively borrowings

buried are the images in the searching flights of albatross
and the screwdriver heart goes to meet them
for I have abandoned you beautiful rim of the sun
at the curtain of the empty window pinned with rainbow gardens
and though the horizon of my bright pleasure stayed to warm you
with the watchful warmth of tulips near you
in mourning for the drones of clouds the cinder of songs
winds toward the unspeakable despair of granite
the melting of days—the streams grow thirsty
and the screwdriver heart goes to meet them

and when like salt your age rises to the water's surface
filtered through so much long hair of women and smoke
        of trains and boats
the hangars of years of slag disgorge in the valley
and against toothless billiard tables bump the ragmens' houses
and the asphalt brains
chances are offered by nature in retreat
threadless scents of absurd derangements of asphodels
scarecrows of the soul that chase away all consolation of
        milk-colored seagulls
old gardens fluttering tearful in the frills of shivers
the medals of moss flattened on the debris of battlements
which show the stygian rivers of our diluvian knowledge the road to
take along the asterisks of autumn
and when the hay ferments along the whistlings
engulfed for no reason in the deep bursts of laughter
showing stalactite teeth to the dew of ashes
and to the terrified gapings of crustaceans
the quavering flame of daggers climbs on stairways of monkey-puzzle
        trees
on the high steps peopled with cumulus

with aerial precautions with wretched vowels
with singing cushions of ulcers of clarity that burst and with winds
where at every step the riddle of our reality grazes the anger of the
        reasons for azure and madness
and of so many others and of so many others

do not close your eyes yet
in the covers of hedge under the cowls of pastures each jealousy hides
and for the mouth besieged by insults of bugles and fireworks
surrenders the sweat of the hands of resin

the pores of the earth open with those of the skin
and with hands parted the still soft shell-wounds
clutched in the earth for fear it will take flight like a piece of
        washing
grip its stiffness of dirty winding sheet
do not close your eyes yet
the murderous cavalcades of solitude
and this blackened force that reverberates in me
breaks in me against the walls breaks
impetuous as a spattering ray of heavy sun
that the hammer drives into the well's muffled throat—
let this nameless force its mouth twisted from self-ignorance
        powerless to
dislodge the night embedded deep in the skull
join on the familiar plateau through tumulus and coral
the two eclipses with the handle of marjoram the ruined peoples
the hunt of the black wave the blazing knowledge
displays the sky stagnant with scythes
and love weaned from bitterness under the cupola
and the enamel smile grafted on the vein
the guitar muzzle for raucous distrusts
the easy tool in the hand of the raffia desert
the spring corrected in the industrious soul
gives way to the drug of a future youth
what crime unsuspected and what sober vegetal pain

can appease my monstrous desires some sapphire day
my monstrous desires of corrosive sky
of a man encircled by sepia bites of violent idols
while his life falls to pieces under the steady rain of temptations
blind to the incantations of spells this bread of daily illusion
on the square of sleep with the milky larval uncertainties
where the sap of our doctrines of death and inspiration
        slowly drains away

then what old age banished from the filthy depths of hell
watches us too in the corner of the sun where our path has
        passed or will pass one day
rumbling with ambitions as yet unrecognized furnished
        with purulent patiences
and on the gangrene of the pastures that dissolves the mouth
        of the waning color
is prepared the advent of the mind with the mortal marks of
        anthracite
and the screwdriver heart goes to meet it

and whether it be the names of flowers the banks of phrases
        mixed with island gold
the roads' habits the capes of solemn meanings
where all is real and the garden of the hesperides lies no farther
        off than the handshake
where the dregs of languages foam on their surface
and all the lofty disillusions and their conduits of fire
ratify the pagan meal in the silences of the rock
whether it be the prodigious erosion of outcries
or the wavering aspirations moving in the herbaria of dream
and the bamboos revolving around the oar's acrobatic ceremonials
so slow is the mind's navigation that entrusts itself to
        melancholy's solemn pledges
so eloquent the lantern signaling so much emotion in
        the flank of the night
with melancholy's solemn pledges

what does it matter—the junk of marvels traces new paths
on this earth of hearts—its empire
do not close your eyes
where do the labyrinths come from and the elastic traps
     of flesh saturated with madness
and if you open the zephyrs with melancholy's solemn flanks
do not shudder—the circus garlanded with pagoda bells
     presents itself to the peony
and upheavals have worn away the saddle of orchestral waterfalls
so many nights have lit their pipe at the sparkling stirrups
     the mystic winds
which have drawn breath at the base of your word
do not close your eyes yet
at the kennel of the sun all the music has withdrawn
the roots have pushed it to the tortures of sporadic spheres
and hugging the coasts and the cavings in of metaphors
the eyes of numbers have been filled with time rung in the arts game

and human love shaped under the crust of loathing
formed by the sad pallor of prisons in its iron stomach
and the fear that rises on ladders of truth
is discovered and lost in the wild boar's eye
and the chimerical tears agree on stilts
the hate which nests in the memory of
wine flakes off and is found again chilled in the hours of flint
and the suffering—chalice of wrinkles—that the earthy face
     of immemorial day desires
and drinks—prolific season of funerals with unharnessed temples
and whether it be the grief of the wind carried on the nickel
     forehead
that fills the oliphant of somber clay with the lyric passions
     of delirious clans
the numbers have leveled out so often the immense instincts move
toward this divine manure—the carcasses
and whether it be the heart that moves to its meeting
     of love or the chagrin

always there will be so many others and so many others
do not close your eyes yet
nor those of others

Part XVIII

your footprints invisible on the sea
raise up provisional pagodas of water
jesus of air ferment of splendid halos and sower of birds
chain leading back to the helix of clouds
climbs impalpable sigh swimming devil
toward the neck of the circus flask
your words equipped with sails reach all the ports of memory the
ferryboat links our two hands that seek each other in the hay of
          dream
hand—opened diadem of the heart opened to the crowns of fruits
gentle word resting in my hand magic freshness
in the cormorant concealed in its breast flying in a turn of astral sign
the light expressed loses its petals

flock of towns and villages grazing in the shade of an herbivorous god
a god no larger than an oak leaf
no heavier than a cricket's chirp
no richer than a nosegay of buttercups
no larger than a diamond's setting
and how many useless sufferings on this flower of archipelagoes and
          islets
fallen with a few drops of water noiselessly in the azure
the world the continents the oceans the hulks

and such difficult relations are formed between appearances
          and architraves

man slightly animal slightly flower slightly metal slightly man
relations independent of voices and of riverbanks
relations like planets that grow and taper off
swell up with tumors vegetate or slowly perish
we are surrounded by a string of barbed-wire lanterns harness too
         heavy
to venture forth to war against this false self
the restless one unappeased by death
unknown one deep in the self who tracks my days blind with hope

a scattering of gold between the forests and the lakes
bad instincts dozing in the lazy depth of pitchers
no enough of this peace
I want the battle I want to feel the burning of the fate stamped
         on my heart by a carnival god
to feel the hot breath body to body the injustice the battle
to throw off the heavy obsession—laden with so many obscure links
face to face and to clear my way across satanic outlines of mustiness
and sly temptations seasoning the rumor that so many others
         have mouthed before me
the unknown

tree trunks carry leafless planispheres on their tops
telegraph-poles have wings of mercury on their ankles
white birds scrve as kilometric markers
distances fly off backward
and in the crystal globes of volcanos the submarines go by
         in long necklaces of migratory fish
and still in the train I feel on my shoulders bruised so long by the
         desert
the weight of legendary cattle led to the slaughterhouses of calm
         weather
the windmills mills of torments
crushing the hyperborean regions where elementary loves are drying
the sky's tongues mowing down the chimneys of narrow factories
the rivers lean to murmur in your ear the secret story

all the trades are gathered about around the prophetic cry
around the finger on the lips of the weather signal
the flowered muzzle of the tree sniffs the storm coming stealthily
and still the train chatters in morse code across countries and voices
mellow crowd exchanging words of flesh and bone
when the word is so dear for those who need it
word that I wait for nugget word in the cragginess of the port
around the hive of your prospective sweetness
we are so many bees whose flight is checked by your promises
and in the breeze tender salt song of those who have
        hung themselves in the sky
whose bodies ulcerate the wind and whose tatters brush
        the floes like fans
the machine smoke barks now and snaps up the ventilating fire
the wheel of death on shipboard such are the circuits of the brains
that turn on themselves the spiral of human sufferings
and so many others and so many others
but the wail of the siren grows menacing
it sweeps the flood across the deck
mermaid avatars accompany the secret call to shipwrecks
and our loves burn in the flame of sails
they are far-off the swollen rivers with cluttered songs
        framing the carrousel
and all the households grown intolerable in the barometers' veins
difficulties of love centuries of love the letters
letters meant to be written with the entrails' sap
but age seized them in its empty flight in search of charm
cemeteries that the dead men swell like waterskins with memories
and all the bitterness that could not issue forth from lungs too supple
they are far-off the bulletins so eagerly awaited in the papers
imposing their lives on ours despite the country hurled into
        the distance by the dark discus-thrower
fits of impatience fallen to the bottom of the bag in the ditch
sawmills of men express trains carrying twisted
        and bewildered heads
that's where the train and thought lead

I feel in myself the whole town's despair cast against the wall
incendiary tears falling from above flights terrors filth
I feel in myself the town's despair cast against the wall
verbose cruelties transgressions maladies maledictions
I feel in myself the whole town's despair cast against the wall
horrors with painted wrinkles infernos suffocation of soot sweats
grimaces of storms contagious cataclysms avalanches tombs

I wait I wait the patience of my destiny reaches the candle's end
the last flutterings of a moth all I have left
that the shadow first plunged in me and then pulled out slowly
and slowly crushed the stone slowly strangled the confession in me
I waited bundled in my menial humility
rescue like a drunkenness overpowering the dull eye
emerging from the bouquet of muted rays
I wait for divine imprudence to drop its die of love
on my head whose roots already go to meet it
the sharp virtue of the number it releases and shows me
I wait for the apocalytic chariot
to take me in its whirlwind infinite and gold
for the prophecy of order at last to crystallize in death
and so many others and so many others

Part XIX

the whooping cough of mountains firing the steep walls of the ravines
with the pestilential buzzings of autumnal aqueducts
the reclaiming of free sky which like a common trench caught
        so many pastures
the languages of clouds the messengers' brief apparitions
announcing in their tufts supreme clamors and obsessions
underground the restless workshops of slow chemistries like songs

the rain's rapidity its crude telegraphic tingling like a ruminating shell
the deep punctures of peaks where the fleecy wash descends
worn-out from all the countrysides and the ruses
          of mocking valleys seducers of countries
the godless promenades of streams
the daring of their exploits against the seated dusk of clay
the oblivions of essences drowned in the oblivion
          of numbers and of ferries
in the fibrous dungeons agglomerated stalks and bells
where spinners of cares faint in the shade clanging with scythes
and uncover the eyelids of phallic phantom icicles
the bareness of stone walls their newels climbed by a thousand fingers
intertwining in braids of dandelions
and the balance of temperatures fanned by the exaggerated stare
your kindnesses produce in me aimless wanderings of facile
          and numbing prophecy
and stony in my garments of schist I have pledged my waiting
to the torment of the oxidized desert
and to the unshakable advent of fire

jostled in the basalt silence of ibises
caught in the reins of subterranean rivers
left to the frantic forests of hydras
where the sermons of thick summers gargle dreamy rivalries
the night swallows us and hurls us to the other end of its lair
rousing beings that the grammar of the eyes has yet defined
          on the space of tomorrow
slow encirclings of coral
slaughter the high forks of stony wills
the notches in your heart it is a sultry season of gravel of hungry
          men
and how many huts in the shelter of your forehead have inscribed
          the mosses' broad mourning on the breast
falling in the ruin of a pile of futures
covered with muddled imperfections mixed with the ambushes of vines

when the schools of murky fish are infiltrated
by opaque death and tresses

we were crossing the heaths made gentler by attention
quietly careful of the monotonous jolts of phenomena
that the practice of the infinite imprinted on the blocks of knowledge
but the scaly structure of scattered opinions
on the moist infinity of diadems—the fields—
disdains the sensitive pulp of truths
with a hasty privilege of sharpened torture

the hatchets were chopping amid chestnut laughter
and the discs of hours flew to attack
aerial flocks were bursting in the head
our reasons lying fallow restrained their diaphanous turbulence
and the knotty trajectories that they traced in time
were incarnate tentacular in the ivy constraint

there we forsook luxury and the dogma of the spectacle
sacrificing to other instincts the bronze desire taught us by its fruits
mow down adamantine insistences the vain landscapes my senses
        elaborated
stand upright muted hallucinating mistrust
on the moor of my being the roads are all opened for you
take away what drunken reproach could not yet vanquish
and all I could grasp and in which I no longer believe
the clot of what I could not grasp rising in my throat
the seaweed dragged by the implacable working of the depths
and the triangle's flower incised in the pupil
the battle my breath loses on the stiff white page
and the osmosis of odious thoughts
the sorrows riddled with persistent sowings of seduction
the sorrows built on pilings safe from diversions
and the hut velvet with dust
and a lost soul's dwelling

and so many others and so many others
sick or found again
for stony in my garments of schist I have pledged my waiting
to the torment of the oxidized desert
to the unshakable advent of fire

hands strangely separated clusters of transparent hands
shuffle dominoes of stars over the swamp they are sheep
and shells of crushed clouds nautical odors trailing
on the table of the sky covered with eucharistic games
what games what savage joys support with disarray your
        conduct in the menagerie sky
where beasts and planets intertwined roll opium eyes
stretched out from one end of the aquarium to the other
        your heart so luminously carved from silence
dedicated to the minute artifices of blades
incrusted with rebellious drops of wine and blasphemous words
is permeated with the ecstasies ebbing and surging
        in the verbal congestion
with which the typhoon stigmatized your forehead

henceforth the ramparts' prow is carved like the swimming figure
but now your eyes guide the cyclone
haughty shadowy intention
and over the sea to the boundary of the wakes of birds
the wind coughs to the boundary where death lays down its load
in our numbed consciousness thunder promethean waterfalls of echoes
when the earth remembers and tosses you that is suffering
a beaten village dog and poor you wander
you always return to the starting point disconsolate with the word
a flower in the corner of your mouth a consumptive flower
        jeered by the harsh necropolis
tons of wind have poured into the deaf citadel of fever
a ninepin at the mercy of a thoughtless impulse what am I
a disconsolate starting point where I return smoking the word
        in the corner of my mouth

a flower battered by the rough fever of the wind
and stony in my garments of schist I have pledged my waiting
to the torment of the oxidized desert
to the unshakable advent of fire

when the complexities of chance make fast the moorings by their
        smile
when your heart is summoned—where solid jaws sink in—
stale and dusty moth—dull intimacy—what do I know—
        workshop of the night—
when the jar with the hissing of a trampled nest of snakes
where the persuasions of virile harshness endure
snarling to a gradual moan
a slow furnace of invincible constancy—man—
a slow furnace rises from the depth of your slow deliberation
a slow furnace rises from the valley of glacial principles
a slow furnace of unspeakable alloys
a slow furnace reaching the centers of lucid emotions
a great furnace rises from the coughs slaves of fortresses
a slow fire brightens in the gaping fear of your strength—man—
a fire grown tipsy on heights where the coastal traffic of clouds
        has earthed over the taste of abyss
a fire climbing supplicant the ladder to the stains of unbounded
        gestures
a fire barking forth streams of regrets beyond hypocritical
        suggestions of the possible
a fire fleeing from the muscular seas where man's escapes linger
a man who quivers at the vague presumptions of the labyrinths of fire
a fire that weaves the massed surging swell of characters—submits
harmony—let this word be banished from the feverish world I visit
savage affinities undermined by emptiness covered with murders
crying out at the impenetrable impasse sobbing with tattered flamingos
for the fire of anger varies the flickering of the subtle remains

according to the mumbling modulations of hell
that your heart strains to hear among the giddy salvos of stars
and stony in my garments of schist
I have pledged my waiting to the oxidized desert of torment
to the unshakable advent of its flame

OTHER WRITINGS

Sunday*

The wind weeps in the chimneys with an orphanage despair
Come near me like a boat amid the reeds
Spread out your words like sheets of white infirmary beds
You can weep calmly there it smells of quinces and of firs.

Tell me of distant countries
Of strange people
Of the parrot island
My spirit is surprised and gay
Like a friend just out of the hospital.

In your voice are worthy old women
Your arms run across my breast like a river
I love the tamed animals
In the menagerie of your mind.

On the bridge a man leans, whistles toward the water thinking
        nothing
At home it is warm, happy as the birth of lambs in their pen
Your story sleeps like a child rocking a woolly elephant
At home all is peaceful like horses drinking at fountains.

In long lines the boarding students file by in the street
In each gaze a family home
A friendly table younger sisters
Flowerpots at the windows.

---

*For variants and annotations to the text, see "Notes to Other Writings," beginning
    on 275.

✕   ✕   ✕

At dusk the cold slithers along the corridors
An immensely long snake dragging its tail across the tiles
The lake is stitched with white thread
The drowned men float to the surface—the ducks withdraw.

Next door the father hugs his child indifferent
Gives her advice at her departure
The lake has closed up again like convent doors behind a daughter
The gurgle of her drowning was horrible—the frogs fell silent a
        moment.
I'm off to meet a sad poet with no talent.

(FIRST POEMS)

Elegy for the Coming of Winter

Beloved, (listen) the poplars lament your going
And I think: so long as you aren't chilly
Take thick clothes and lots of books to read
(One night you'll find a withered lily)

I know how things will turn out: (comedy) I'll catch a clean
        handkerchief
To weep all my sadness in, I'll cough in it too because I'll have
        caught cold
Then I'll float it in the air when you are far away—honest thought
And I'll remember another time when I looked for another girl
        in the streets

✕   ✕   ✕

Think about it: perhaps no one will await you there
And you'll weep, and regret, life is sad, sad
You'll always remember the handkerchief floating
Unleashing a terrible wind in your garden
Laying the paths bare, uprooting the thought that brings you back
      home.

Listen to my wise advice
Stay near the table and sew in silence
You haven't finished your silk dress yet
Listen to my wise advice

✦

Beloved—winter is coming and you are leaving
And the old horse rotten in the garden
No longer has mane or ears; I wait for the full moon
To leap in the saddle and rush after you, light (Understand . . .)

(FIRST POEMS)

Note on Art

Art is at present the only construction complete unto itself, about which nothing more can be said, it is such richness, vitality, sense, wisdom. Understanding, seeing. Describing a flower: relative poetry more or less paper flower. Seeing.

Until the intimate vibrations of the last cell of a brain-god-mathematics are discovered along with the explanation of primary astronomies, that is the essence, impossibility will always be described with the logical elements of continual contradiction, that swamp of stars and of useless bells. Toads of cold lanterns, squashed flat against the descriptive sense of a red belly. What is written on art is an educational work and in that sense it can be justified. We want to make men realize afresh that the one unique fraternity exists in the moment of intensity when the beautiful and life itself are concentrated on the height of a wire rising toward a burst of light, a blue trembling linked to the earth by our magnetic gazes covering the peaks with snow. The miracle. I open my heart to creation.

Many are the artists who no longer seek solutions in the object and in its relations with the external; they are cosmic or primary, decided, simple, wise, serious.

The diversity of today's artists gathers the fountain's spray into a great crystal freedom. And their efforts create new clear organisms, in a world of purity, with the help of tansparencies and the constructive materiality of a simple image as it forms. They continue the tradition: the past and its evolution push them slowly snakelike toward the interior, direct consequences far beyond surfaces and reality.

(DADA 1)

The Second Celestial Adventure of Mr. Antipyrine

MR. ABSORPTION
    bells and platters of bark straw
    dilate the pupils of serrated pelican
    despite the restlessness of the bloodmeter policeman of the volcano
    predisposed to tuberculosis
    metallurgic
    and watchdog
    coagulated child on the folding seat chamber pot
    you are better off as a lever

and so much the better tooth from the viewpoint personage
    restaurant
gets tipsy on serpentine outrage is a hat
you aspirin understand the over-there whose
of the tape recorder dagger 37
vulgarly thirtysevenoline called arthur

MRS. INTERRUPTION
    feathers and saws
    insecticide radiator

MR. SATURN
    insecticides are bitter
    just remember the visit at the minister's
    five black girls in a car

THE DISINTERESTED BRAIN
    oh yes fathers and invoices
    still one's honor

MR. ABSORPTION
    I already myself

EAR
    He already himself

THE DISINTERESTED BRAIN
    whistle swelled up with loveless lemonade
    awakening in condensed milk
    meets a yellow woman fish thanks aspires
    the color of opium lantern
    violin ears
    the time of the slice of the eye of the wind
    wears mustaches

MRS. INTERRUPTION
well my eye wears mustaches too

MR. ABSORPTION
exiting by a rubber pump
measure or perfume
or light up since I am still possible

MR. ANTIPYRINE
I exportation

MR. SATURN
do you have frogs in your shoes?

EAR
b.b.b.b.b.b.b.b.b.b.b.b.b.b.b.b.b.b.b.b.
b.b.b.b.b.b.b.b.b.b.b.b.b.b.

MR. ABSORPTION
the horsy pinchers
of saturated ostrich genitalia

EAR
c.o.d. stammered the queen
flower decoration of hardened casein
rape the envelopes
prepare on the round head racetrack an indignation traversed
        with icefloes
alarm clock attached to
finished airs
memorandum
possible sour smile of machine-like cork
flute bone
rectifies
the liquid with copper ornaments

in an explosive pocket
where the newborn comes out with palm tree fibers
without chassis he got up resignedly and moved slowly
            toward the door
yacht dismantled into shellfish buttons
on foot
ovation
swollen surplus
of illicit tick tack toe
illimine
soldered
if not
very very dear
procession of bottled gendarmes
umbrellas and parasols

MISS PAUSE
    pause

EAR
    and other fatty matter sterilized
    to take away the tannic acid which distresses you make it boil
    and make a tunnel
    you %
    he long

MRS. INTERRUPTION
    for

MR. SATURN
    decidedly decidedly decidedly decidedly decidedly
            decidedly decidedly decidedly decidedly
    uncovered forehead of the sun
    naturally naturally

MRS. ANTIPYRINE
> I know a kneeling number which is not at all a brush poem
>> playing about the mouths of the shell
> but the address of a French artist
> and a composition in black staccato
> of vegetal balcony metronome on a wink
> medicine for the vaguely tubercular in a sack

EAR
> it was up to her to embroidery

MR. SATURN
> the wrapping of 4 and 4 and 44 how many points spigots of lies
> and cellulose goats are there in the human body? drama tar washing

MRS. INTERRUPTION
> n.n.j. h.n.t. h.n.j. h.h.h.

MR. ABSORPTION
> like the suspenders of public mountains hold the attention
> of the tunnels pants
> it was up to her to get along

THE DISINTERESTED BRAIN
> the sleep the general the heart theft
> grape tobacco the stomach nostrils with grey hair
> the cool pins
> testicular soap in the coffee
> a side of motor with hazelnuts
> and the iced brain of the amorous aviator

EAR
> the cardiac roots of sickness evacuate eclipse and jewels
> repertory
> binoculars
> anonymous mirror

German measles
cravat of rivers and two-buttocked sable

MR. Aa ANTIPHILOSOPHER
without looking for I adore you
who is a French boxer
maritime values irregular like DADA's depression in
the bicephalic blood
I slip between death and the wishy-washy phosphates
which are scratching a bit the common brain of the dadaist poets
luckily
for
now
mine
taxes and expensive living have determined me to abandon the D's
it's not true that the false dadas snatched them away from me for
repayment will start as soon as
there's something to cry about the nothing called nothing
and I swept away the sickness held in customs office
myself shell and umbrella of the brain from noon to two
          subscribing
superstitious setting off the workings
of the spermatozoid ballet which you'll find in dress rehearsal
in all the hearts of shady customers I'll eat your fingers slightly
I pay the renewal of your subscription to love that squeaks like
          doors
metal
and you are idiots
I'll come back some time as your urine
reborn to the joy of living the wind midwife
and I set up a boarding house for poet-keepers
and I come back again to begin again
and you are all idiots
and the key of the self-stealer only works with twilight
oil
on each knot of each machine is a brand new baby's nose

and we are all idiots
and terribly suspicious for a new form of intelligence and a new
        logic in our own manner
which isn't at all DADA
and you let yourself be swept along by Aaism
and you are all idiots
cataplasms
with the alcohol of sterile sleep
bandages
and virgin
idiots

MR. ABSORPTION
feel your knees give way
luminously
scarlet darkness comes from that and sometimes light
and don't look at the doctor coming with the instruments

THE DISINTERESTED BRAIN
mother of pulmonary rains by the daily vulture of the gun

EAR
from her mouth spittle glides like hanging lanterns
you are nice and slender sir
your curls of light you know have buried you between the
        walls of feldspar
morsel of misery

THE DISINTERESTED BRAIN
I didn't interrupt you but that is pronounced feeeeeeeelds-paaaaaaaar

EAR
you are nice and slender sir
your curls of light you know have buried you between the
        walls of feldspar
morsel of misery

THE DISINTERESTED BRAIN
badabà badabà badabà gorilla

MR. SATURN
return to the innermost center
look for the innermost center
on the center there is a center
and on the center there is a center
and on the center there is another center
and on each center there is another center (encore)
and on each center there is a center
on each center there is a center

MR. ABSORPTION

MRS. INTERRUPTION

MR. SATURN

EAR   tree

MR. ANTIPYRINE

THE DISINTERESTED BRAIN

MR. SATURN
the doctor is digging around

MRS. INTERRUPTION
whistle swollen with loveless lemonade————latent
sub-matinal crispation————running-account of faithful
hours swallowed by the steppes and the great
lucidities————always readable and flexible————with
100,000 francs as capital————Antipyrine in his pajamas
drops the gazometric word he had been keeping in the
fingertips of his woolly brain. Today we can affirm with

certainty that mechanical crayfish bird legs thunder of
French vermillions and of the remains of statues in
earthenware and cartridges peopled the peaceful
circumvolutions of his lungs. A beard of cool androgynous
stalactites hung all about the pelvis and the lever of his
amorous intensity. From mercury to the cherry-tree nature
deploys the logistics of its fighting scales. The only real
adventurer in the countryside the tree feeds on its own
nervous tic. The book open like a muscle————with a steady
pain on the left side————the time marked at the bottom of
each page after meals————that efficient precision rigorous
medical martyr amiable opprobrium pillory.

THE DISINTERESTED BRAIN
in the sleeping-car I stroked vaseline
the dimensions are elastic and love at four meters
our our love hangs in shreds like a putrid glacier
take drink shoot knock him out

MR. Aa
tzaca tzac tzaca tzac slides tzaca tzac tzacatzac

EAR
slowly drag the boat red and squalling foetus
and the woman leaps out of bed boumabarassassa
and the woman leaps suddenly from the bed boumabarassassa
and the woman leaps out of bed boumabarassassa and runs
          with the lamp between her legs

MR. SATURN
look at the pendulum becoming a tongue
tear of bifurcation to tell you the temperature

THE DISINTERESTED BRAIN
our entrails are transparent like long long long long long long

long long long long long long long long
protozoa

EAR
    the doctor runs
    suddenly snatches the form which is:
    a head of hypocampus hemorrhoids in its eyes resting against
    the frontal shell, one wide open like a balloon and the other
    closed like a boat the ears are breathing curly stripes or
    sodden standards, a large and toothless black laugh, arms are
    coming out of the jaws one is long like a lamprey fingers
    turning like a windmill on the middle part a drapery drawn from
    the stomach

MR. ABSORPTION
    one of its eyes the greener one is running running
    the rest is opaque
    between the rails of a broken cello nerves of an intersected fish
    dance micoula the most crafty the most alert the most orthodox
    doctor

MR. ANTIPYRINE
    dadadi dadadi dadadi moumbimba dadadi

MRS. INTERRUPTION
    the officers are dancing the queens also have the my god in
           their kidneys and
    puerperal fever

MR. SATURN
    look what our toilets have in them
    the civil servants are going to bed with the saturday evenings
    the watering can of despair in the brilliant rectangular has good
           taste
    the princes are pissing in the streets

MR. ANTIPYRINE

    light has been concentrated in spheres whiter than the
                  narrowness
    of angels
    the poles are stretching in prudish ellipses
    mechanism of the centipede
    go to the pederast's country but take the necessary precautions

THE DISINTERESTED BRAIN

    telephone there is no one left no more workers no more concerts
    it's no longer hot it's no longer cold the proverbs have given out
    the gastric juices have given out the lightning-rods are spitting
               lightning
    and the motors are making oil colors which can be used as
    toothpaste when we are rejoicing on the aristocratic altitudes
    we are eating antelope mustaches let's shout fire.

(DADA 1)

For Marcel Janko

five black women in a car
blew up according to the five directions my fingers point in
when I put my hand on my chest to pray (sometimes)
around my head shines the humid light of old lunar birds
the saints' green halo around cerebral evasions
tralalalalalalalalalala
that you see blowing up now in the mortars

there's a young man eating his lungs
then he has diarrhea
then he farts luminously
like the coming back of birds sung about in poetry
like death spurting forth from the cannons
he farted so luminously that the house became midnight
the tall sailboat opened its book like an angel however
                your leaves, oh spring, have been fixed like a
                beautiful page into typography
zoumbai zoumbai zoumbai di
your drawing in my intestines has eaten the bad and the good

especially the bad like the general's joy
for ever since I have been afraid the rats have been gnawing
                at the deserted church I took away the draperies and
                on each one there was our Lord and on each lord
                there was my heart
my heart I have it as a tip hihi

                                                    (DADA 2)

123 ▶

Mr. Antipyrine's Manifesto

DADA is our intensity: which stands the inconsequential bayonets erect the sumatral head of the German baby; Dada is life with neither slippers nor parallels; which is against and for unity and certainly against the future; we know in our wisdom that our brains will become downy cushions, that our antidogmatism is as exclusionist as the civil servant and that we are not free although we shout freedom; severe necessity without discipline or morals and we spit on humanity.

DADA remains in the European framework of weaknesses, still it is a bunch of excrement, but we want to shit in different colors to ornament the zoo of art of all the consulate flags. We are circus masters and we whistle in carnival winds, among the convents, prostitutions, theaters, realities, feelings, restaurants, ohi, hoho, bang, bang.

We declare that the car is a feeling which has spoiled us enough in the slowness of its abstractions like transatlantic steamers, sounds, and ideas. However, we put the facility on the outside, we seek the central essence, and we are happy if we can hide it; we do not want to count the windows of the marvelous elite, for DADA exists for no one and we want everyone to understand that. Over there is Dada's balcony, I assure you. From there you can hear military marches and go down slicing the air like a seraphin in a people's bath to piss and understand the parabola.

DADA is not madness, nor wisdom, nor irony, look at me, there's a good man.

Art was a hazelnut game, children put together words that ring at the end, then they wept and shouted the stanza and put doll shoes on it, and the stanza became a queen so as to die a little and the queen became a whale, the children ran until they were panting.

Then came the great ambassadors of feeling who cried historically in a chorus:

Psychology Psychology hihi

Science Science Science

Long live France

We are not naive

We are successive

We are exclusive

We are not simple

and we know perfectly well how to discuss intelligence. But we, DADA, we do not agree with them, for art is not serious, I assure you, and if we display crime in order to say ventilator in a learned way, it is to make you happy, good audience, I love you so much, I assure you and adore you.

Dada Manifesto 1918

The magic of a word—DADA—which has set the journalists at the door of an unexpected world, has not the slightest importance for us.

To proclaim a manifesto you have to want: A.B.C., thunder against 1,2,3, lose your patience and sharpen your wings to conquer and spread a's, b's, c's little and big, sign, scream, swear, arrange the prose in a form of absolute and irrefutable evidence, prove your nonplus-ultra and maintain that novelty resembles life just as the latest appearance of a whore proves the essence of God. His existence was already proved by accordions, landscapes, and gentle words. ₊⁺₊ To impose your A.B.C. is a natural thing—therefore regrettable. Everyone does it in a form of crystalbluffmadonna, a monetary system, a pharmaceutical product, a bare leg beckoning to an ardent and sterile spring. The love of novelty is the agreeable cross, proves a naive Idon'tgiveadamnism, sign with no cause, fleeting and positive. But this need has aged also. By giving to art the impulse of supreme simplicity: novelty, you are human and true about being amused, impulsive and vibrant in order to crucify boredom. At the crossroads of lights, alert, attentive, on the watch for passing years, in the forest.

+ ⁺ +

I am writing a manifesto and I don't want anything, I say however certain things and I am on principle against manifestoes, as I am also against principles (half-pints for judging the moral value of each sentence—too easy; approximation was invested by the impressionists). + ⁺ + I am writing this manifesto to show that you can do contrary actions together, in one single fresh breath; I am against action; for continual contradiction, for affirmation also, I am neither for nor against and I don't explain because I hate common sense.

DADA—now there's a word that sets off ideas; each bourgeois is a little playwright, inventing different dialogs, instead of setting characters suitable to the level of his intelligence, like pupae on chairs, seeking causes or purposes (according to the psycho-analytic method he practices) to cement his plot, a story which defines itself in talking. + ⁺ + Each spectator is a plotter, if he tries to explain a word (knowledge!). From the cotton-padded refuge of serpentine complications, he has his instincts manipulated. Thence the misfortunes of conjugal life.

Explaining: Amusement of redbellies on the mills of empty skulls.

DADA MEANS NOTHING

If you find it futile and if you don't waste your time for a word that doesn't mean anything. . . . The first thought revolving in these heads is bacteriological: at least find its etymological, historical, or psychological origin. You learn from the papers that the Krou blacks call the tail of a holy cow: DADA.

In a certain part of Italy, the cube and the mother: DADA. A hobby-horse, a nurse, double affirmation in Russian and in Rumanian: DADA. Certain learned journalists see in it an art for babies, other holy jesusescallinglittle-children, a return to a dry and noisy, noisy and monotonous primitivism. You don't build a sensitivity on one word; every construction converges in a boring perfection, the stagnant idea of a gilded swamp, a relative human product. The work of art should not be beauty itself, because that is dead; neither gay nor sad, neither clear nor obscure, simply making individuals happy or sad in serving them cakes of sacred haloes or the sweatings of an arched course across the atmospheres. A work of art is never beautiful by decree, objectively, for everybody. Criticism is therefore useless, it only exists subjectively for each person and without the slightest generality. Do you think you have found the psychic basis common to all humanity? The experience of Jesus and the Bible cover under their broad and benevolent wings: excrement, animals, days. How do you mean to put order in the chaos constituting this infinite and formless variation: man? The principle: "love your neighbor" is an hypocrisy. "Know thyself" is a utopia but more acceptable because it contains nastiness within it. No pity. After the carnage we still have the hope of a purified humanity. I always speak of myself because I don't want to convince anyone, I don't have the right to drag others along in my current, I am not obliging anyone to follow me and everyone does his art in his own way, if he knows the joy ascending like arrows toward the stars, or that burrowing in the mines to the flowers of corpses and their fertile spasms. Stalactites: look for them everywhere, in the cribs pain has widened, their eyes white like angels' hares. So DADA was born of a desire for independence, of a distrust of the community.* Those who belong to us keep their freedom. We don't recognize any theory. We have had enough of cubist and futurist academies: laboratories of formal ideas. Do you practice art to earn money and fondle the middle class? Rhymes ring the assonance of coins and inflection slides along the line of the tummy in profile. All the groupings of artists have ended at this bank even while they rode high along on diverse comets. A door open to the possibilities of luxuriating in cushions and food.

Here we cast anchor in rich earth.

---

*In 1916, at the CABARET VOLTAIRE in Zurich.

×   ×   ×

Here we have the right to proclaim for we have known the shivers and the waking. Returning drunken with energy we stab the trident in the unsuspecting flesh. We are the flowing of maledictions in a tropical abundance of vertiginous vegetation, rubber and rain are our sweat, we bleed and burn thirst, our blood is vigor.

Cubism was born from the simple way of looking at the object: Cézanne painted a cup twenty centimeters lower than his eyes, the cubists look at it from above, others complicate its appearance by making one part perpendicular and in putting it nicely on one side. (I am not forgetting the creators, nor the great motives of the matter they make definitive) ₊⁺₊ The futurist sees the same cup in movement, a succession of objects one alongside the other embellished maliciously by some lines of force. Which doesn't keep the canvas from being a good or bad painting destined to be an investment for intellectual capital. The new painter creates a world whose elements are also the means of creating it, a sober and definite work, against which there can be no argument. The new artist protests: he no longer paints (symbolic and illusionistic reproduction) but rather creates directly in stone, wood, iron, tin, rocks, and locomotive organisms that can be turned about on any side by the limpid wind of momentary sensation. ₊⁺₊ Any pictorial or plastic work is useless; let it be a monster frightening to servile minds, and not sickly-sweet in order to decorate the refectories of animals dressed like men, illustrations of this sad fable of humanity.—A painting is the art of making two geometrically parallel lines meet on a canvas, in front of our eyes, in the reality of a world transposed according to new conditions and possibilities. This world is not specified or defined in the work; it belongs in its innumerable variations to the spectator. For its creator, it is without cause and without theory. *Order = disorder; I = not-I; affirmation = negation*: supreme radiations from an absolute art. Absolute in its purity of ordered cosmic chaos, eternal in the globule a second without duration, breathing, light, or control. ₊⁺₊ I like an old work for its novelty. Only contrast links us to the past. ₊⁺₊ Writers who teach morality and discuss or ameliorate the psychological basis have, in addition to a hidden desire to win, a ridiculous knowledge of life, which they have classified, divided, channeled;

they insist on seeing categories dance in time to their measure. Their readers snicker and keep going: what is the use?

There is a literature which doesn't reach voracious masses. A work of creators, the result of a real need of the author, and done for himself. Knowledge of a supreme egoism, where laws fade away. $+^+_+$ Each page ought to explode, either from deep and weighty seriousness, a whirlwind, dizziness, the new, or the eternal, from its crushing humor, the enthusiasm of principles or its typographical appearance. Here is a tottering world fleeing, future spouse of the bells of the infernal scale, and here on the other side: new men. Harsh, leaping, riders of hiccups. Here are a mutilated world and the literary medicine men with a passion for improvement.

I say: there is no beginning and we are not trembling, we are not sentimental. We shred the linen of clouds and prayers like a furious wind, preparing the great spectacle of disaster, fire, decomposition. Let's get ready to cast off mourning and to replace tears with mermaids stretched out from one continent to the next. Pavilions of intense joy, empty of the sadness of poison. $+^+_+$ DADA is the signboard of abstraction; advertising and business are also poetic elements.

I destroy the drawers of the brain and of social institutions: demoralizing everything and hurling the celestial hand to hell, the hellish eyes to heaven, setting up once more the fecund wheel of a universal circus in the actual power and the fantasy of each individual.

Philosophy is the question: from what side to start looking at life, god, the idea, or anything else. Everything you look at is false. I don't believe the relative result to be any more important than the choice between cake and cherries after dinner. The approach of looking quickly at the other side of a thing in order to impose your opinion indirectly is called dialectic, that is, haggling over the spirit of french fries while dancing the method around. If I shout:
IDEAL, IDEAL, IDEAL,
KNOWLEDGE, KNOWLEDGE, KNOWLEDGE,
BOOMBOOM, BOOMBOOM, BOOMBOOM,

I have put down rather exactly the progress, the laws, morality, and all the other lovely qualities that various very intelligent people have discussed in so many books, just in order to say finally that each man has danced anyway according to his own personal boomboom, and that he is right in his boom-boom, as a satisfaction of unhealthy curiosity; private ringing for inexplicable needs; bath; monetary difficulties; stomach with repercussions in real life; authority of the mystical wand expressed as a bouquet of orchestra-ghost with mute bows, greased with potions based on animal manure. With the blue lorgnon of an angel they dug out the inside for a nickel of unanimous gratitude. ₊⁺₊ If they are all right and if all pills are just Pink pills, let's try for once to be wrong. ₊⁺₊ You think you can explain rationally, by thinking, what is written. But it's quite relative. Thought is a nice thing for philosophy but it's relative. Psychoanalysis is a dangerous sickness, lulls the antirealistic tendencies of man and codifies the bourgeoisie. There is no final Truth. Dialectic is an amusing machine which leads us

in a banal manner

to opinions we would have had anyway.

Do you think that by the scrupulous refinements of logic you have demonstrated truth and established the exactness of your opinions? Logic restricted by the senses is an organic sickness. Philosophers like to add to that element: the power of observation. But precisely this magnificent quality of the mind is the proof of its impotence. You observe, you look at things from one or many points of view, you choose them among the existing millions. Experience is also a result of chance and of individual faculties. ₊⁺₊ Science repulses me as soon as it becomes speculative-system, losing its useful character—so very useless—but at least individual. I hate complacent objectivity and harmony, that science that finds everything in order. Carry on, children, humanity. . . . Science says that we are the servants of nature: everything is in order, make love and die. Carry on children, humanity, nice bourgeois people and virgin journalists . . . ₊⁺₊ I am against systems, the most acceptable system is the one of not having any system, on principle. ₊⁺₊ Making yourself complete, growing perfect in your own littleness until you have filled up the vase of your self, the courage to fight for and against thought, the mystery of bread sudden unleashing of an infernal helix into economic lilies:

DADAIST SPONTANEITY

I call Idon'tgiveadamnism the state of a life where each person keeps his own conditions, although knowing how to respect other individuals, if not defending himself, the two-step becoming a national hymn, a whatnot store, a radio playing Bach fugues, neon lights and signs for brothels, the organ diffusing carnations for God, all that together and actually replacing photography and unilateral catechism.

Active simplicity

The inability to discern degrees of brightness: licking the penumbra and floating in the great mouth full of honey and excrement. Measured by the scale of Eternity, all action is vain—(if we let thought undertake an adventure whose result would be infinitely grotesque—an important fact for the knowledge of human impotence). But if life is a bad farce, with neither goal nor initial labor pains, and because we think we should withdraw as fresh as washed chrysanthemums from the whole business, we have proclaimed as the single basis of understanding: art. It does not have the importance that we, as mercenaries of the mind, have attributed to it for centuries. Art afflicts no one and those who can get interested in it will earn the right to be caressed and the wonderful occasion to blanket the country with their conversation. Art is a private thing, the artist does it for himself; a comprehensible work is the product of a journalist, and because right now I feel like dabbing this monster in oil paints: a paper tube imitating the metal you squeeze and out come hatred, cowardice, meanness automatically. The artist, the poet are delighted with the venom of the mass concentrated into a section manager of this industry; they love to be insulted: a proof of their unchanging nature. The author and the artist praised in the papers notice how their work is understood: as the miserable lining of a cloak for public use, rags covering brutality, piss coalescing with the heat of an animal hatching the basest instincts. Flabby insipid flesh multiplying by means of typographic microbes.

We have discarded the sniveling tendency in ourselves. Every filtration of that kind is candied diarrhea. Encouraging this art means directing it. We must have strong, upright works, precise, and forever unintelligible. Logic is a complication. Logic is always false. It draws the strings of ideas, words, along their formal exterior, toward illusory extremes and centers. Its chains kill, like an enormous centipede stifling independence. Married to logic, art would live in incest, swallowing, devouring its own tail still attached, fornicating with itself and the personality would become a nightmare tarred with protestantism, a monument, a heap of heavy gray intestines.

But suppleness, enthusiasm, and even the joy of injustice, that little truth which we practice innocently and which gives us our good looks: we are delicate and our fingers are adjustable and glide like the branches of that insinuating, almost liquid plant; it gives our soul precision, the cynics say. That is a point of view too; but fortunately all flowers aren't saintly, and what is divine in us is the awakening of antihuman action. We're talking about a paper flower for the buttonhole of the gentlemen who customarily frequent the ball of masked life, kitchen of grace, white cousins supple or fat. They do business with whatever we have chosen. Contradiction and unity of polarities in one single stream can be truth. If you are going to pronounce that banality anyway, evil-smelling appendix to a libidinous morality. Morality atrophies like any scourge that intelligence produces. The rigidity of morality and logic have made us impassive in the presence of policemen—the cause of slavery—putrid rats filling middle-class stomachs and infecting the only bright and clean glass corridors which remained open to artists.

Let every man shout: there is a great destructive, negative work to be accomplished. Sweeping, cleaning. The cleanliness of the individual affirms itself after the state of madness, the aggressive, complete madness of a world left in the hands of bandits who vandalize and destroy centuries. Without goal or plan, disorganized, unconquerable folly, decomposition. Those strong in words or in strength will survive, for they are quick to defend themselves, the agility of body and feeling flames up on their faceted flesh.

Morality has determined charity and pity, two suet balls grown like elephants, like planets, that people call good. They have nothing good about them. Goodness is lucid, bright and deter-mined, pitiless towards compromise and politics. Morality is the infusion of chocolate in the veins of all men. No supernatural force ordains such comportment, rather the monopoly of the idea sellers and the university profiteers. Sentimentality: seeing a group of men arguing and being bored, they invented the calendar and the medicine prudence. The philosophers' battle started by labeling (mercantilism, balance, meticulous and paltry measures) and it was once more understood that pity is a feeling just like diarrhea in its relation to the sickly disgust, the revolting task of corpses to compromise the sun.

I proclaim the opposition of all cosmic faculties to this gonorrhea of a putrid sun coming out of the factories of philosophic thought, the fierce battle with all the possible means of

DADAIST DISGUST

Every product of disgust capable of becoming a negation of the family is dada; the whole being protesting in its destructive force with clenched fists: **DADA**; knowledge of all the means rejected up to this point by the timid sex of easy compromise and sociability: DADA; abolition of logic, dance of all those impotent to create: *DADA*; of all hierarchy and social equation installed for the preservation of values by our valets: DADA; each and every object, feelings and obscurities, apparitions and the precise shock of parallel lines, can be means for the combat: DADA; abolition of memory; **DADA**; abolition of archeology: DADA; abolition of the prophets: *DADA*; abolition of the future: DADA; an absolute indisputable belief in each god immediate product of spontaneity: **DADA**; elegant and unprejudicial leap from one harmony to the other sphere; trajectory of a word tossed like a sonorous cry of phonograph record; respecting all individualities in their momentary madness: serious, fearful, timid, ardent, vigorous, determined, enthusiastic; stripping its chapel of every useless awkward accessory; spitting out like a luminous waterfall any unpleasant or amorous thought, or coddling it—with the lively satisfaction of knowing that it doesn't matter—with the same intensity in the bush of his soul, free of insects for the aristocrats, and gilded with archangels' bodies. Freedom: *DADA DADA DADA*, shrieking of contracted colors, intertwining of contraries and of all contradictions, grotesqueries, nonsequiturs: LIFE.

Proclamation without Pretention

Art goes to sleep for the birth of a new world
"ART"—a *parrot word*—replaced by **DADA**
PLESIAUSAURUS, or handkerchief
The talent WHICH YOU CAN LEARN *makes the poet a druggist*
TODAY *criticism balances no longer launches resemblances*
Hypertrophic painters hyperestheticized and hypnotized by the
hyancinths of muezzins of hypocritical appearance
CONSOLIDATE THE EXACT HARVEST OF CALCULATIONS
HYPERDROME OF IMMORTAL GUARANTEES: *There is no importance there*
is no transparency or apparency
MUSICIANS BREAK YOUR BLIND INSTRUMENTS on the
        stage
The **SYRINGE** *is only for my understanding.* **I am writing because**
it is as natural as pissing as being sick
Art needs an operation
Art is a **PRETENTION** heated in the TIMIDITY of the urinary
basin, **Hysteria** born in the **Studio**
We are seeking **upright pure sober unique** strength we are
seeking **NOTHING** we affirm the **VITALITY** of each instant
the anti-philosophy of **Spontaneous** acrobatics
In this moment I hate the man who whispers before intermission—
eau de cologne—bitter theater. CHEERY WIND.
IF EVERYBODY SAYS THE OPPOSITE IT IS BECAUSE THEY ARE RIGHT.
Prepare the geyser actions of our blood—submarine formation of
transchromatic airplanes, cellular metals numbered in the
leap of images
        above the regulations of the
BEAUTIFUL and its control
It is not for the runts who are still worshipping
their navel

White Giant Leper of the Countryside

salt groups itself in a constellation of birds on the cotton tumor

in its lungs starfish and bedbugs swing
the microbes crystallize in palms of muscles swings
goodmorning without cigarette tzantzantza ganga
bouzdouc zdouc nfounfa mbaah mbaah nfounfa
macrocystis perifera to kiss the boats boat surgeon scar clean damp
laziness of brilliant lights
boats nfounfa nfounfa nfounfa
I stick candles in his ears ganganfah helicon and boxer
      on the balcony the hotel's violin in baobabs of
      flames
the flames develop in spongelike formation

the flames are sponges nganga and strike
the ladders climb like blood ganga
the ferns toward the steppes of wool my chance toward the waterfalls
the flames glass sponges mattresses wounds mattresses
the mattresses fall wancanca aha bzdouc the butterflies
scissors scissors scissors and shadows
scissors and clouds scissors ships
the thermometer looks at the ultrared gmbababa
bertha my education my tail is cold and monochromatic nfoua loua la
mushrooms oranges and the family of sounds beyond starboard
at the origin at the origin the triangle and the travelers' tree at the
      origin
my brains go off toward hyperbole
the kaolin swarms in its brain-pan
dalibouli obok and tombo and tombo its stomach is a big chest
here the drum-major intervenes and castanets

for there are zigzags on his soul and lots of rrrrrrrrrrrrrr
      here the reader begins to yell
he begins to yell begins to yell then in that yell there are
      flutes that multiply and corals
the reader wants to die perhaps or dance and begins to yell
he is thin stupid dirty he doesn't understand my verses he yells
he is one-eyed
there are zigzags on his soul and lots of rrrrrrr
nbaze baze baze look at the submarine tiara which unravels in
      golden seaweed
hozondrac trac
nfounda nbababa nfounda tata
nbababa

(TWENTY-FIVE POEMS)

Movement

astronomic gargle
vibrates vibrates vibrates vibrates in the metallic throat of heights
your soul is green is meteorologic emperor
and my ears are vegetable torches
listen listen listen I swallow mbampou and your good will
take dance hear come turn drink twist ouhou ouhou ouhou
falcon falcon of your own bitter images
mel my friend you lift me in the morning in panama
let me be an unimportant god or a hummingbird
or else the fetus of my servant suffering
or else tailor explosion color seal
dress of circular waterfall internal hair letter you receive
      in the hospital long very long letter

when you consciously paint your intestines your internal hair
you are for me insignificant like a false passport
the chimney sweeps are blue at noon
barking of my last clarity rushes into the abyss of medicine
        gone green my dear my umbrella
your eyes are closed your lungs too
you hear the pissing of the fountain
the chimney sweeps

(TWENTY-FIVE POEMS)

The Great Lament of My Obscurity Three

where we live the pendulum flowers light up and feathers
        encircle the brightness
in the distant sulphur morning the cows lick salt lilies
my son
my son

let us always (drag) along by the color of the world
it looks bluer than the metro and astronomy
we are too thin
we have no mouths
our legs are stiff and bump each other
our faces are formless like stars
crystals points with no strength fire burned basilica
insane: the zigzags crack
telephone
bite the ropes liquefy
arch

climb
astral
memory
toward the north by its double fruit
like raw flesh
hunger fire blood

(TWENTY-FIVE POEMS)

Drugstore-Consciousness

from the lamp of a lily such a great prince will be born
that the factories will be enlarged by fountains
and the leech changing into a tree of sickness
I look for the root unmoving lord unmoving lord
why then yes you will learn
come in a spiral toward the useless tear

humid parrot
lignite cactus swell between the black cow's horns
the parrot digs the tower the holy mannequin

in the heart there is a child—a lamp
the doctor says he can't last the night

then he goes away in short and sharp lines silence silent formation

when the pursued wolf rests on the white
the chosen one chases his shut-ins
showing death's issue the flora which will be the cause

and the cardinal of france will appear
the three lilies fulgurant brightness electric virtue
red long dry combing fish and letters under the color

the giant the leper of the landscape
stands immobile between two towns
he has rivers cadence and the tortoises of the hills heavily accumulate
he spits sand kneads his lungs of wool thinning out
the soul and the nightingale swirls in his laughter—sunflower
he wants to pluck the rainbow my heart is a paper starfish

in missouri in brazil in the antilles
if you think if you are happy reader you become transparent
        for a moment
your brain a transparent sponge
and in this transparency there will be another transparency more
distant
far off when a new animal turns blue in this transparency

(TWENTY-FIVE POEMS)

Saint

stony sea formation arborescent ascendancy
multiplication my memory in the guitars my memory trembles
the kafir the clown the gnu surround the meshing with garlands
the angel liquefies in medicine and dissonant sounds
climb on the lightning rod to become panthers ships meshing
        rainbow breathing them
the sounds all the sounds and the imperceptible sounds and
        all the sounds coagulate

my dear if you feel sick from the sounds you ought to take a pill
interior concentration crack of words bursting crackling
    the electric discharges of the electric eels the water ripping
when the horses cross the lake couplings
all the armories crack
the war
over there
oh the new-born baby changing to granite becoming too hard
    and too heavy for his mother the lithotomist's song
    crushes the stone in the bladder and fills it with
    lilac and newspapers

silence sulphur flower
typhoid fever silence
the heart clock microbes sand mandrake
in the wind you shake it like the mercury torch toward the north
the grass rotted lizards oh my sleep to catch flies astronomic
chameleon
oh my sleep of aniline and zoology

(TWENTY-FIVE POEMS)

Wise Dance March

the mirror breaks a lamp flees and the yellow trumpet is your
    lung and square the teeth of the star postage stamp
    of jesus-flower-shirt the watch turn turn stones of
    blackness
in the cold soul I am alone and I know it I am alone and dance
    lord you know I like it green and thin for I like it
    great wheels crushing the mighty gold here is the
    one who is always freezing

✕   ✕   ✕

walk on the ends of my feet
empty your eyes and bite the star
that I placed between your teeth
whistle
prince violin whistle birds' whiteness

(TWENTY-FIVE POEMS)

The Liontamer Remembers

look at me and be color
later
your laugh eats sun for hares for chameleons
squeeze my body between two thick lines let famine be light
sleep sleep do you see we are heavy blue antelope on a glacier
            ear in the stones lovely frontiers—hear the stone
old fisherman cold tall on new letter learn the girls in iron
            wire and sugar turn a long time the bottles are tall
            like white parasols listen roll roll red
in the colonies
memory odor of a clean pharmacy old servant
green horse and cereals
horn cry
flute
baggage obscure menageries
bite saw do you want
horizontal to see

(TWENTY-FIVE POEMS)

Springtime

To h arp

put the child in the vase in the depths of midnight
and the wound
a rose of winds with your fingers with beautiful nails
thunder in feathers see
a stagnant water trickles down the legs of the antelope

to suffer below have you found cows birds?
thirst gall of the caged peacock
exiled king by the well's brightness is slowly mummified
in the vegetable garden
sow broken grasshoppers
plant ant hearts the salt fog a lamp draws its tail across the sky
the little gleams of glassware in the stomach of stags fleeing
over the ends of black branches too short for a cry

(TWENTY-FIVE POEMS)

Sun Night

his king of ice and his name goes down
and appears in the sea in the fish shark his body
maritime guardian
to be born
voracity opened to the sounds of lances and the green door

be my sister in the wide march of the planet
too long I have seen skeleton the
mannequins with umbrellas in the white hot
mine

and I draw the country and your jewels are living eyes
the cow gave birth to a large living eye of pain or of iron
at the sea's edge the sphere climbs in a spiral
tempest

The virgin bruised her flesh and died in the desert
the fire inside the great volcanic stones
her image and the fruits
the rain will be flower of famine of drought
raincoat of our hearts make our flight easy and the embarcation
        of the plant-covered lord

(TWENTY-FIVE POEMS)

Little Town in Siberia

a blue light which flattens us together on the ceiling
it's as always comrade
like a label of infernal doors pasted on a medicine bottle
it's the calm house tremble my friend
and then the awkward curved dance offers age skipping from
        hour to hour on the clock face
the intact necklace of locomotive lamps unhitched sometimes
        descends among us
and deflates you call that silence to drink tin roofs gleam
        of herring-tin and my heart descends on low houses
        lower higher lower over which I want to gallop and
        rub my hand against the hard table covered with
        bread crumbs to sleep oh yes if one only could
the train again veal spectacle of the tower of beauty I stay on the
        bench
what does it matter the veal the beautiful the paper what comes
        after it is cold I wait talk louder
hearts and eyes roll in my mouth
on the march
and little children in blood (is it the angel? I mean the one
        approaching)
let's run more quickly still
always everywhere we'll be caught between black windows

(TWENTY-FIVE POEMS)

Note on Poetry

The poet of the last station no longer weeps in vain; lamenting would slow down his gait. Humidity of ages past. Those who feed on tears are happy and heavy; they slip them on to deceive the snakes behind the necklaces of their souls. The poet can devote himself to calisthenics. But to obtain abundance and explosion, he knows how to set hope afire TODAY. Tranquil, ardent, furious, intimate, pathetic, slow, impetuous, his desire boils for enthusiasm, that fecund form of intensity.

Knowing how to recognize and follow the traces of the strength we are waiting for, tracks which are everywhere, in an essential language of numbers, engraved on crystals, on seashells, on rail tracks, in clouds, in glass, inside snow, light, on coal, on the hand, in the radiations grouped around magnetic poles, on wings.

Persistence sharpens and shoots joy up like an arrow toward the astral bells, distillation of the waves of impassive food, creator of a new life. Streaming in all colors and bleeding among the leaves of all trees. Vigor and thirst, emotion before the formation unseen and unexplained: poetry.

Let's not look for analogies among the forms in which art finds outer shape; each has its freedom and its limits. There is no equivalent in art; each branch of the star develops independently, extends and absorbs the world appropriate to it. But the parallel sensed between the lines of a new life, free of any theory, will characterize the age.

Giving to each element its integrity, its autonomy, a necessary condition for the creation of new constellations each has its place in the group. A will to the word: a being upright, an image, a unique, fervent construction, of a dense color and intensity, communion with life.

Art is a procession of continual differences. For there is no measurable distance between the "how are you," the level where worlds are expanded, and human actions seen from this angle of submarine purity. The strength to formulate in *the instant* this varying succession is the work itself. Globe of duration, volume born under a fortuitous pressure.

The mind carries in it new rays of possibilities: centralize them, capture them on the lens which is neither physical nor definedpopularly—the soul. The ways of expressing them, transforming them: the means. Clear golden brilliance—a faster beating of spreading wings.

Without pretensions to a romantic absolute, I present some banal negations.

The poem is no longer subject, rhythm, rhyme, sonority: formal action. Projected on the commonplace, these become means whose use is neither regulated nor registered to which I assign the same importance as to the crocodile, burning ore, grass. Eye, water, scales, sun, kilometer, and everything I can conceive at one time as representing a value which can be humanized: sensitivity. The elements grow fond of each other when they are so tightly joined, really entwined like the hemispheres of the brain and the cabins of an ocean liner.

Rhythm is the pace of intonations you hear; there is a rhythm unseen and unheard: radiation of an interior grouping toward a constellation of order. Rhythm was until now only the beatings of a dried-up heart: tinklings in rotten and muffled wood. I don't want to treat with a rigid exclusiveness of principle a subject where only liberty matters. But the poet will be severe toward his work in order to find true necessity: from this asceticism will flower order, essential and pure. (Goodness without sentimental echo, its material side.)

To be severe and cruel, pure and honest toward your work which you prepare to place among men new organisms, creations living in bones of light and in fabulous forms of action. (REALITY.)

✕   ✕   ✕

The rest, called *literature*, is a notebook of human imbecility to aid future professors.

The poem pushes or digs a crater, is silent, murders, or shrieks along accelerated degrees of speed. It will no longer be a product of optics, sense or intelligence, but an impression or a means of transforming the tracks left by feelings.

Simile is a literary tool which no longer satisfies us. There are ways of formulating an image or integrating it but the elements will be taken from differing and distant spheres.

Logic guides us no longer and its commerce, easy, impotent, a deceptive glimmer scattering the coins of a sterile relativism, is extinguished for us forever. Other productive forces shout their freedom, flamboyant, indefinable and gigantic, on the mountains of crystal and of prayer.

Freedom, freedom: not being a vegetarian I'm not giving any recipes.

Darkness is productive if it is a light so white and pure that our neighbors are blinded by it. From their light, ahead, begins our own. Their light is for us, in the mist, the miniscule microscopic dance of the shadowy elements in an imprecise fermentation. Isn't matter in its purity dense and sure?

Under the bark of the fallen trees, I seek the painting of things to come, strength, and in the canals perhaps life is swelling already, the darkness of iron and coal.

(DADA 4 AND 5)

Bulletin

piercing sounds in Montevideo soul displayed offered in advertisements
the wind among the telescopes has replaced trees on boulevards
night labeled throughout vitriol's gradations
with the smell of cold cinder vanilla sweat menagerie
cracking of arches
parks are carpeted with maps tie banner
54 83 14:4 formula reflection
encloses the pulse laboratory of courage open all the time
stylized health with the inanimate blood of extinguished cigarette
cavalcade of miracles to surpass all language
from Borneo they send the account-sheet of the stars
for your benefit
gloomy procession oh mechanics of the calendar
where the synthetic photographs of days appear
the doll in the grave
fifth avenue on the horizon two accidents song for violin
underwater rape
and the barbs of being's last creation
whip the cry

(CINEMA CALENDAR OF ABSTRACT HEART HOUSES)

Circus

I

you were also a star
the elephant bursting through the poster
to see a huge eye whose rays fall curved to earth
seeing only under the tent
muscular strength is serious and slow beneath the bluish light
offers us certainty in certain examples
the precision of athletes sometimes clowns
must wait?
perspective twisting the body's shape
it's thrilling in these lights
far from here
invisible hands torturing the members
all the yellow spots steel-pointed come
centimeters closer to the center
of the circus
people wait
cords hang down above
music
it's the circus master
the circus master doesn't want to show he's happy
he is proper

II

entrance
of chocolate truth hazelnuts newspaper
one assumes about corridors and trunks from
door signs

you are anxious but I am confident
many soldiers with new gazes
the narrow layers of air stretched out the strong light falls
from the stairs
filtration through the grillwork of relationships
the elephants go to bed black satellites
is this a prospectus of appearances? lead us under the curtain
and in the familiar dressing-rooms
an unexpected finger suddenly touches us

III

it is only the beginning
my soul again a studio of paper flowers
I have not forgotten my mother however
the last meeting (so auspicious)
she would forgive me I think
it is late
you find in all the corners uncontrolled drum beats
if only I could sing
always the same always somewhere
this blinding light the ants transparency
surging forth from the guilty hand
I shall leave
the carved wood madonna is the poster the criticism
opaque silence cut by the uneven tick-tock
my heart lengthens the fifth measure
and the glory
glimpsed
the velvet curtain after the final march
with the subtlest inflection do you think of me
four numbers on the wall
with the last concern
why look for it
and here is that ringing which will never cease

IV

the lion tamer knows
people's customs what goes on in all the landscapes
the animals' mouths their saliva
all the breathing slow anxious gasping
from boredom from rage
the effect of wounds
the sure way to link them
against the poisonous liquor a light the golden bandage
and the food
he knows the practical ways to travel
the just and measured force of blows

V

anemia and elegance naptha swervings
goodness hangs bells around my neck
shrieks
planet of laughter liquor nocturnal violent burning

heavy black
smoke rising rapidly in a sharp pyramid shouts disk
gardener of your silence on the sea
and the vibrations of your bitter flesh

give birth and trade

VI

—who knows the just and measured force of blows
neither too weak nor too strong
my legs are long and delicate
run out of a crevice of steel
sun

we are honest folk
organization of fat lamps bouncing
let's dance let's shout
I love you the train leaves every day
Let's drink voltaic arch

song of the stewpan
dangerous operation
hand—flower of pink tree
tranquilizes my tears
offers to things
sister souls

splendor and subtlety
have gnawed at my heart
I spin ceaselessly
my arms spiraling toward the sky

it's cold
listen mother
and think of me
now

the last arrival from the tropics
equinox flower white-tailed phaeton
in a car towards amsterdam around a table and the valve
of the second fog

(OF OUR BIRDS)

Maison Flake

release trumpets the vast and glassy announcement sea service animals
aerostatic forest ranger everything existing gallops life with clarity
the angel has white hips umbrella virility
snow licks the path and the lily verified as virgin

     in altitude a new meridian passes by this spot

distended arch of my heart typewriter for the stars
who said to you "choppy foam of prodigious sadness-clock"
offers you a word not found in Larousse
and wants to reach your height
what vapor from a lightning tube pushes
ours up against the veil eternal and multiform
here we don't assassinate men on the terraces
colored by the intimate succession of slowness

we try unheard-of things
mirages in-quarto micrographies of chromatic souls and images
we all wear little bells for uproar that we shake
for major celebrations on the viaducts and for the animals
turning of a dance of octave range on meteor and violin
the play of mirrors passing year
let's have a glass I'm the nutty brother
ink of the sky lake of hydromel
flake of opaque wine in a hammock
practices the tranquil fecund offering
it scrapes the sky with its nails
and the skyscraper is only its shadow
in a bathrobe

×   ×   ×

the year will be among the palm trees and banana trees sprung
      forth from the halo like water cubes
simple productive vast music surging forth safely
and the crimson bread for the future and multiple season
of the old prints delicate in color showing kings hunting

pipe and sparring in the vase under the ace of spades piper with
the birds and the cool clouds an alert ship in their beaks
from the rock motor sparking good news the eiffel tower plays
$\frac{3}{25}$ the rebeck
here each chair is soft and comfortable like an archbishop
enterprise of asceticism monks guaranteed at all prices—over
      here ladies—maison flake

                                    (OF OUR BIRDS)

Entire Journey by the Moon and Color

the iron eye will change to gold
the portholes have flowered our timpani
look sir for the fabulous prayer
tropical
on the violin of the eiffel tower and ringings of stars
the olives swell up pac pac and will crystallize symetrically
everywhere
lemon
the small coin
sundays have luminously caressed god dada dance
sharing the grain
the rain

◀

newspaper
towards the north
slowly slowly
the butterflies five meters long crack like mirrors
like the flight of nocturnal rivers climbing with fire
towards the milky way
highways of light hair of irregular rains
and the artificial kiosks flying keep watch in your heart
when you think I see
early morning shouting
the cells dilate
the bridges stretch out and rise in the air to shout
around magnetic poles the rays arrange themselves like
peacock feathers
boreal
and the waterfalls do you see? arrange themselves in their own light
at the north pole an enormous peacock will slowly spread out the sun
at the other pole you will have the night of colors consuming
        the serpents
slides yellow
the bells
nervous
to illuminate it the reds will march forth
when I ask how
the ditches shriek
lord my geometry

                                        (OF OUR BIRDS)

Angel

color is recomposed   runs between the spaces
liquids hung   scales rainbow
worms of light in the steam   there where our duration is visible
where clarinets grow   woman pregnant with satellites
the bell slides under the boat   ball green burning
down there the town bandages   caresses the centrifugal wound
of flames
grip grip firmly   acids of stomachs and plant
the feldspar gleams in the speed   mechanic angel
on vacation   windmill
mechanic of necrologers   black man's head
menagerie setting   and friendships
then she throws at her husband's
head   a bowl of vitriol
let us go toward the others

meeeeteeeeoooorooooloooogiies

meteorologies

the sun slides tangent of atmos-
phere   slides aureole
skating dimensions

(OF OUR BIRDS)

◄ 156

Herbarium of Games and Calculations

immobile in her taut desire my friend
thrusts the circle of her wide
vision
over the squares of possible meetings
the windows of lips pour forth their noise
formula your thought's bitter ornate night
in bunches of grapelike balustrades
the confused silence filled with shrubs and brambles
but the blow bursts breaks desiccated
in iced porcelain through the ringing of laughter

courteous narrow delicate ambition
plays with well-known instruments
let's slide the bow across the lift of feelings
and on the slope of mismatched eyebrows
a caress of unmade bed in your half-reasoning astonished
makes the stones of disheveled marvels flower

I spend my time counting sunbeams
and the hair of your words
tree of the skeleton covered with leaves with springtime
turns in the ocean's depths waltzing blue
the attraction of your face
crowds into the conclusion of the chess match

(OF OUR BIRDS)

Midnight Salts

voltaic arch of these two nerves not touching each other
near the heart
under a microscope the black shudder can be seen
is it sentiment this white surging
and methodical love
DIVIDES MY BODY INTO BEAMS
toothpaste
transatlantic accordion
the crowd breaks the reclining column of wind
the fan of rockets
on my head
the bloody revenge of the liberated two-step
repertory of prix fixe pretentions
madness at 3:20
or 3 francs 50
for its pleasure cocaine is slowly gnawing the walls
eyes continue falling

(OF OUR BIRDS)

The Death of Guillaume Apollinaire

we know nothing
we knew nothing of grief
the bitter season of cold
digs long furrows in our muscles
he would have preferred the joy of victory
wise under calm sorrows   caged
unable to do anything at all
if snow fell upward
if the sun rose to meet us during the night
to warm us
and trees hung with their crown upside down
—unique teardrop—
if birds were here with us to contemplate themselves
in the tranquil lake above our heads

WE COULD UNDERSTAND
death would be a beautiful long voyage
and an unlimited vacation from the flesh of structures and of
bones

(OF OUR BIRDS)

Distinguished Crime

a dress rosy with fireflies
gelatine vigorous frost
leather
doctor for business
which doesn't work
boy boy
cried the empress
the girl
fell dead
it was the boy

Long Crime
the codfish of wool in the mane of the lion
leaves tracks and the saliva of crouched snails
the groom leaves messages in every room
but in number 67 on the third floor they found the gentleman as he
            was
finishing the last interruption of his age's hiccup

Crime of Sport
the criminal comes down in a parachute
to scatter the suspicions graciously directed
against his precious body and the good intentions of his
spacious face
and carries out the crime in 12 brutal picturesque poses
those are the consequences of love in the movies where
the paths of homogenous countries lead

✕   ✕   ✕

Solemn Crime

business business says the young apparition
a simple observation for the wallet of the commissioner
who loved her
who killed him
who buried him
who drank him
who inflamed him
who believed him
and who loved him
so many questions certified at the united states embassy in the hotel
crillon

remarks
liquidate your affairs before dying
everyone dies for death is brief
death is expensive but life is cheap
on the lips of thin paper
prepare your mysteries in the pond of allusions

Crime to See Clearly

orangutan and gibbon
lion and cat
puma and cat
rat and mouse
monster with the angelic décolleté of a polished glacier with
        brandenburg
mustaches and scissor legs
comes into the apartment
gooseberry syrup through the straw of the guzzle
what do you think we found in the morning
a young man sixteen years old
lighting the last match of his blood expiring and compromised
for man

for anthropomorphic monkeys
for cats
for the rat and the mouse
for parakeets
for the magpie the crow
for the rapacious diurnals
for the wild ducks
for the peacock the pheasant
it is the same

(OF OUR BIRDS)

Cosmic Realities Vanilla Tobacco Dawnings

I

listen I'll write a poem but don't laugh
four streets surround us and we tell them light
ON THE PRAYER POSTS AND YOU WERE TALKING TO
elephants luminous in the circus
I don't want you to be sick any more you know
but why why do you want to whistle this morning
telephone
I don't want to I don't want to and he is squeezing me TOO
TOO HARD

II

this morning
of copper your voice shivered on the wire
the yellow closed itself in the mouthpiece like blood
the woman covered with verdigris with ver-di-gris

dissolved like fog in the bell flowers
weep—rose of the winds—weep white
here is a light which could be black
flower

III

on steel salt lilies tell me again that your
mother was good

IV

I am a line dilating and I want to grow in a tube of tin
I say that just to amuse you

V

not because I could have been a wax archangel
or evening rain and car catalog

VI

in the pits life boils crimson
to have some silence I want to count my joys
you told me that I pity you
and I didn't cry when you saw me, but I would have liked
to cry in the tram
you tell me I want to leave
the pearls of my throat's tower were cold drum
major for hearts and slide
insects in the thought don't bite me,

ah $\left\{ \begin{array}{l} \text{finger flower} \\ \\ \text{the water barks} \end{array} \right.$

and if you like I'll laugh like a waterfall and like a
conflagration

VII

say: empty thought
quickly you know
I'll be a
cello

VIII

I hold your coat when you leave as if you weren't
my sister

IX

in frosted steel
ring the bell
do you sleep when it's raining?

X

the farm helpers wash the hunting dogs
and the king takes a walk followed by the judges who look like
doves
at the sea side I also saw the bandaged tower with its
sad
PRISONER
in the pits turn on the light
consequently
lord lord   }   of ice
forgive me

XI

BIG TEARS slide along the draperies
Horses' heads on the basalt like

glass toys shatter among the stars with chains
for animals
and in the glaciers I'd like to come along
with root
with my sickness
with the sand swarming in my brain
for I'm very smart and with darkness

XII

                    IN PORCELAIN the song
                    imagined
                    I'm tired—the queens' song
the tree bursts with food like a lamp
I WEEP longing to rise above the fountain twists
to the sky because there is no more terrestrial gravity in school and
            in
the brain
my hand is cold and dry but it has stroked the surging forth
of water
and I've also seen something (in the sky) like water screwing
down the fruits and the eraser

XIII

but I think serious thoughts about what's happened to me
lila
LILA
LILA
LILA
LILA
your brother is yelling
tell him

between the leaves of the book the humid hand
paint my belief with lime
burn dark in the wire
LILA

XIV

your eye is large
lord in the draperies
your eye pursues me
your eye is a ship's size excuse me
send medicines
stone

XIV encore

Lover's heart open in the stream and electricity
Let's look at the point
It's always the same
hairs grown around it
it begins to skip
to get larger
to rise toward the final flashes
surrounding it slides
quickly
quickly
rolling
nocturnal
turnings

XV

among the pains there are organisms and rain
your fingers TURNINGS

XVI

gulf
your heart will soar doing such lofty things
on the shiver stairs huddled together like the tree
between the reddish flashes
you go away
roads
branches
lick the snowy hips

XVII

where you see the bridges linking night breathing
darkness splits and clusters in pavilions
stretched down roads and winds toward your caress
the wound

XVIII

the horse devours colored snakes
be quiet

XIX

the stone
dance dance lord
the fever thinks a flower
dance dance on the stone
hot braid
starts again in dissonance on the way to darkness *my sister, my sister?*

(OF OUR BIRDS)

Optimism Unveiled

for:
worldly teas
match-box makers
money worry
a night of a superior kind
a cylinder of nitrogen covered with a top hat
a philosopher fallen in the pleasures of virgin waterfalls
a lovely alpine landscape with the moon and its luxurious stream
the cowboy catching us with his lasso of words
a barley sugar
a stormy sugar
a missionary preaching sleeplessness
a glass foot filled with water and birds
a nail protruding from marvelous liquids
the scorpion counting the coming avalanches
and the avalanches held carefully in sacks by
the management and by a society of anonymous
soldiers with shining stretched skin and sometimes
inflated by our special product
"INTELLIGENCE"
the least expensive and the most lasting
on sale
everywhere
forever

(OF OUR BIRDS)

Arch

the turnings of lines
              around a point
                         at finger tips
the wind bearing the odor of gas and gaslight
each object forms a letter   and I write letters
precipice   fatigue shaped in letters
lookout post   fatigue shaped in letters
of precise expectancy   the station on the map
I stuck the stamp serrated
with blood   of depth dawn
contours colors detonations   shouts screw down
the sail is red the mast
variegated   birds flying low
              flecks of gas
flying toward the sail the variegated mast draws an alphabet
in this change of temperature
                         bisexual
iron grayish with music
summoning other seasons
on a pole   of a former light
I recite   what a thought crosses the circus
your brain   and resistance
so flexible and above all malleable
brightredyellow at this moment
where you give orders darkness followed by a scientific
                         flower
the oily silence   underwater gramophone toward the
                   rope's end
      STOP
                   concentrates these moments

the flask replacing souls gramophone started up
                                by the phosphorous smoke
could the dance be forever finished? finished?

        magician   the plants
        go forward   surrounding burying
        bandage   last movement
        liqueur   dance
        before the impassive peacock the *DEADMAN'S*
        skull

piercing the a and with a white head of hair
fixed on the cross drops to the large belly
the vapor flattens on the surface   toward the margins
enlarging incommensurable circles
wait   wait   the new sky
                                as far as the passage

banner   definitive

                              (OF OUR BIRDS)

Boxing

I

the benches creak   look at the rug in the middle
    come   patience   pass   14   thanks
    ☞ **ATTENTION** it's the wound I'm exploring
A lamp pearly tumor
        crimson chalk
       Suddenly a corner falling
some   cards   knock   into   the   arteries
      in   the   shadows

drum with its leather wrists outstretched
little suspended bells enlarged roll under the magnifying glass
specialized in

aggravated slowness
surprises reserved suppressed for this performance
(The Management)
the professional grotesque
:prefacing the tired ambiguity

that they practice
THE WHISTLE

WHAT?

believe the bilious eyes *effect*
have forgotten the skies

reflection
—*I don't think so*
Besides they are good friends

II

diligence correct and dry
of any clown
any machine
fever foam taken up again
plantation of muscles
vacation of evidence
he goes off
turn slowly the expertise
he comes back
asbestos moon
comes in under the appearance and remains
fixed on the bridge
always ready   for kilometric transactions
he flees (applaud here)   who flees
exaggerates exaggerates   always well-dressed

```
                    clean hands   yesterday in the bar
    the imperturbable man waits   extinguish the flames of doors
             prepares the attack   he won at cards
            and the opaque nerve   whisky aurore
    stretch out the cords agility   "to-re-adore"
                     alternative   bravo for the heart
      the immense eraser of your
                       splendor   in its exact waterfall action
    surrounds the lover and the
                          lake    somewhere
```

III

the knot of muscles plays the entr'acte of the expectative
the zircon on the breast
whiskey quack powder
turn turn the wheel of members
for there is a truth in the world
incurable supposed under the ground-up thorns
profound study of obscurity
which hesitates the final blow
stirs up suspicions the deformed crater and the pearl oysters

(OF OUR BIRDS)

SPEAKING OR INTELLIGIBLE WOOD SIGN OF EASTER ISLAND

VIOLIN LAMPS A TAIL A WHITE LIGHT
VERY WHITE FLEE SUN AND STAR SNAIL OR
FLYING FISH IN THE STATION A HUMAN FOOT
WAITING ROOM DIFFERENT JARS OF EARTHEN
WARE TWO KNIVES ONE BIRD ON THE JAR OF
EARTHENWARE THE AXE 4 MEN IN DIFFERENT POSES
A LADDER
       COLOR HERE
WATERJARS IN WALNUT A SHIP AND 3 PIGS
HATS CHICKENS SAILOR'S STRONGBOX DOG
MANDOLIN
DIFFERENT FISH THE TORTOISE ON PALM TREE
EMPTY CHEST A VERY LARGE WHITE HAND 28
DIFFERENT OBJECTS
AND THE WIDE SOUND OF SPEED IS SLOWNESS
FIXED IN THE HORIZON'S FRAMEWORK
WHISTLE WHISTLE BLUE OF MAN SEE THIS
PARAKEET ON SPRAY SOLIDIFIED WHISTLE
NAVAL OFFICER WHISTLE
       THE CONTOURS MIX
WHISTLE IN THE WOUND THE GREAT
AUTUMNAL LIGHT WHICH SHRIEKS?
SHRIEK CROSSWISE

(OF OUR BIRDS)

The Showmen

the brains swell up flatten out
    heavy balloons tire shrivel up
            (ventriloquist's words)
swell up flatten out swell up flatten out
    flatten out
          dissolved organs
clouds have these shapes sometimes too
    widows grow nervous looking at them
        sometimes
        listen to dizziness
        acrobatics of numbers
        in the mathematician's head
  NTOUCA leaping
    cap and bells
which is dada which is DADA
    the static poem is a new invention
MBOCO the asthmatic   HwS2
    10054   moumbimba
there is a machine
machine
    the vowels are white globules
the vowels stretch out
    stretch out
        gnaw at us clock
        stick

AND LOOK A LIGHT IS RUNNING ALONG THE ROPES
    smoke curls out from the rope-walker's head
my aunt squats on the trapeze in the gymroom

her nipples are herring heads
   she has flippers
  and draws draws draws the accordion from her breast
she draws draws draws the accordion from her breast glwa
     wawa prohahab
in the little towns the sun hatches under the carts before the
     inn
             nf nf nf tatai
the little children break wind looking at the circus props
and there are lice
and grandmothers covered with soft tumors
   that is to say polyps

                            (OF OUR BIRDS)

Surface Sickness

he declaims the song of hail hell his neck is stiff
his tail a wire flower
his hairs are springs his head a rose window flattened out
everything of his is oxydized he canters on a line
if I'm a madman lord chrysanthemum my heart is an old
stuffed newspaper
beware of staring at me your lights will become wires
and your child's skeleton too

the tree has just one leaf
the tree has just one leaf
I hear the madman's steps prayer look at the green horse the nonchalant
athlete and the leaping of the saint in the crystal
variegated metal along the elephant's ears
piano pouring out a sulphur rainbow and crescent flowers phosphorous

and air the rivers with coal-black embroidery
you flow in me multicolored
the veins in certain stones
the sparks shining in the stones
the foliage bleeds

gulf sheep
inflates
death blackens fingernails
your light-giving hands caress wolverines and rivers
your eye cooks: come down copper buggy
wait on my heart I have such lovely spots
with scarred edges like girls' dresses
in cinder rainbows
the damp colors hang around
tipsy

(OF OUR BIRDS)

Cloud Handkerchief

Act IX

A forest. On the backdrop in large letters: Monolog. The Poet (comes forward, a mask in his hand).

Living, dying. To the right, to the left. Standing up, lying down. Forward, backward. Up, down. What do all these exercises have to do with a sickness not even connected with the body? I love her. . . . Yes, unfortunately, and at what a distance! The islands have quite a surprise in store for me, those unexpected islands emerging as if to be fed upon from the blue waters, gobbled up by starving fantasy in the place of any other more fleshly satisfactions. And isn't my heart itself an enormous restaurant where everyone

can eat as much as he likes without paying the bills and the ten per cent tip?
What's the use? I'd like to be able to tear my brain apart to see, as inside a
toy, the mechanism of my love for her. I who have never been in love.
(He puts on the mask.)
Love which in pure and delicate situations
smote with such subtle regrets my days and nights,
against the closed doors of time with gestures too gentle
to wake the travelers in hotels,
I believed myself bereft of it, I mourned its passing,
thought it torn out from me
to be carried far it far off by the rugged virile
current of nuptial mud, quick and volcanic,
comes today troubling the calm hypothesis
like magic wine fermenting in the cellar
in the depth of my sluggish head and my solitude.
Night, like a valve, closed the broad pipe
through which day leaks away, and the luxury of its light;
lives, alternatively small and large,
emitted once more an odor of dream and sleep
the black smoke of long ago weighed on the scales
of their eyelids gentle and heavy with songs.
But I, filled with the noise left by its language,
—traces of steps swept away, on the desert
that was my destiny the day I saw her,—
vibrating like her words at the sound of memory,
I was standing here, trying to measure
the residue of time that memory deposits
along its track, the slices of rare words,
the perspectives of images fleeting and skilled,
to grind these hard heavy seeds into thoughts:
flour of the brain, dust of this world.
Sand, if the wind torments its clarity,
blinds the gaiety of humble pedestrians,
and thought besides, rolling about itself
veils you with the whirlwind fruit and lies,
so I remain flotsam of the daily shipwreck.

Love cloaks the eyes of my heart and my brain.
The greedy fish, monsters of clouds,
hatred, grief, crises, horrors,
vices, germs and evil spirits,
beat me, mortify me, bite me tearing
up the elegance carefully prepared
I was to wear tonight at the opera ball.
And all that for two blue eyes
and for the five o'clock tea that the twilight offers to spring
in china cups, as invisible as stars.

(He hums the tune Violettera.—*The orchestra takes up the melody softly and
continues it to the middle of Act Ten.)*

(He exits. The scenery and the lighting change.)

Commentary

B.—*(The commentators take up the same positions again.)*—His song is lovely,
besides it is authentic, since it comes from South America.
A.—You are always flip.
C.—But he's right, because it's obviously a question of the poetic value or
rather the human value in which the poet has clothed his despair. I mean
the moment when he put the mask on his face to hide from himself the
improbable aspect of such a language.
B.—You know, I don't believe in anything.
C.—Then nothing has any importance at all; you can say "rubber" and think
"chrysanthemum." Where are we going, where are we going? Instead of
congratulating ourselves on such a pure and classic effort in which we were
permitted to participate. B.—You know, I don't believe in anything.
A.—Be quiet then, your skepticism is sterile. Put yourself in his position, he
needs to view poetry as reality and reality as mirage.

B.—As for me, if I didn't know in advance what sort of twist the author had given to his play, I would not hesitate one second to proclaim that poetry is a negligible product of latent madness and that it is absolutely unnecessary to the continuous progress of civilization.

A.—But in that case the problem is different and we don't have any time to discuss it.   *(Change of lighting.)*

Rule

disparate seas spread the billow of their indolence
in the beds with the white foam sheets
at the sound of the pages of waves turned by the reader of
the unquenched sky
the agreeable regular caress of the clouds
dissolves behind the mist
the promise so long awaited at the horizon of your smile

the earth at its breaking point unfolds the young white stone
of a giant's solid breast offered to the length of time
and the wind bites its lips in its black rage

shattered is the transparency shining through the glasses of our existence
the wind strangles the word in the throat of the village poor village
its life of strange clearings

broken is the chain of words covered with winters and dramas
that held together the intimate clearings of our existence

and the wind spits in our face
the tireless brutality of it all

(HEARTWAY GUIDE)

Forbidden Fire

XI

you will return my faraway one
I know the grasses watch within you
I exhaust my strength awaiting you
on the pavement of the long town

still a lofty intoxication breathes
lying near you—all the departures in its heart
a body with no fear of brightness
and the most shadowy for the loveliest water

what have we done with our nights with our days
what have we learned of torments starved for flesh
we have looked and seen only visionless sight
in seeing ourselves we have not seen our own lies

the dream I played by heart
in good times bad times and always empty
will you return snow my faraway one
the late landscapes will be of bread no more

(TRAVELERS' TREE)

Approximation

you come you eat you swim you dream you read
sometimes you chase the clear the boundless why of your acts
sometimes you wonder whence you come so lonely
correctly dressed and illegible like the song's appeal
with the awkward hour heavy in your sleep

you sometimes wonder what tomorrow will be
soaked in the salt liquor of the air wedged between the lands
you never wonder what
you are
in this instant which could not await your answer and flees

do not be the dupe of the sounds' attractions
playing at doubt and cloud in your echo
on other incalculable margins
you shall descend the steps of time to lose
the gradations of usurious shadows on the freshly brushed beach
and in the alternative pockets of the almosts
dug at the threshold of the harsh well-nourished waves

already the bagpipe wounds the worthy simulacre
of our reasons laden with the prairies' spasmless stretch
and their livid gravity grape-clustered
lingers mediocre along the twilight and the skin

(TRAVELERS' TREE)

181 ▶

The Lousy One

capacious pockets of misadventures
deep as the blue of waves
where frivolous and sidereal hands
count out money with awkward gestures

attached themselves along your seashell body
your body whose color of abundant rains
has suffered in sunlight the trials of microbes and rust
the slow loves molded at the beaches' limit

arm encircling the thick bare shoulder
root nightly twisted about the neck
fate moldy with remains of lice and algae
for whom the mud deposit your body is the island lost

a dull age hatches in your sea ears
a tree branch walks in its autumn rags
a block of stone cloud fallen royal alms
to the humid grief of famine crawling in the sack

in the shadow of your pores shrubs are growing
your fingernails dig your stomach's desolate earth
wounds and pimples are the only flowers to decorate
your being marked with splendors botanical and vulgar

your eyes have hidden gnawed by the impure hour
at the bottom of your bundle of life coarse and harsh
that with a wild swamp laughter surging forth
the wind tossed to the fates cherishing their shipwreck
but disdaining the bitter rot of shadow

they roll henceforth without road or adventure
and still god holds your sack
walking detached from you beside you

(TRAVELERS' TREE)

Traps in the Grass

V

the leaning face of the beautiful seeker
is reflected in the flame the dwelling of splendor
of fervent attachments and fates entwined
with the genesis of squalls stripped naked by our cries

since houses have aged within our nights
in dried-up parks in leaves of ember
in the swarm of perpetual memories
the petals of words of a light wind have paled

another childhood has arisen
in the melting of gestures
the tenderness of a deeper game
to win back all the cinders in the summer's doubt

VI

neither wine nor usury have put to rest
on the barrel's bottom the ancient distress
moving weakness what wind has been able
to shake off at last the lock of eyebrows

✕   ✕   ✕

with shutters closed to ancient visions
the wordless waiting nests in the eyes
without a shade of life—magician to the rescue
extending vain arms at each street corner

a new grimace has gathered the caress
of ancient wounds on a body unexpected
gaping vengeance—there is no more to say
no further taking life as it is on the slope

aged with remorse and brick upon brick
return in your bed where lie the forgotten
of nothingness peace layer by layer
will be able to build on magic laughter

(WHERE THE WOLVES DRINK)

a harsh winter garden is laid out in your past
which cannot go on or come again
no absurd flesh keeps you
stamps underfoot the bright becoming
of a childhood heavier than the sea

allows to live in the field of certainties
to the most treacherous fold
where your shadow is stranded in beauty

which loses its grasses
black caverns
that man forgot in the depths of himself
to clear away the leaks of light
great pieces of light thrown helter-skelter
tenderness itself at the heart of the slow rock

oh breasts inimitable in the dawn
and tender births of furtive springs

oh births of springtime hesitations
the roads are sprouting the laments in the lead
and the leaves will walk with remorseless step
to the eyes' abyss
to the victorious griefs of the absent

(WHERE THE WOLVES DRINK)

lies of a night lovely as a woman
we've all grown old at its bedside of blood
lovely and lovelier as the flame
could not assume the form of harsher wakes

in the ripening fruit I have enclosed you completely
my life with the voracious beasts of laughter
and the dead girl made voice in the mirror's echo
inscribed in your eyes' alphabet oh unknown women

new and lovelier the soft grass of the smile
at the high spring of arms stretched toward your zenith
it was only a cry a limit of air
and the wave torn apart in gaiety

how much is needed a time heavy with pardons
has sunk on the port where we land no more
the sun has forgotten me outside
clear wine

(WHERE THE WOLVES DRINK)

XIII. Taxes and Bargains

Invention since the deserted church is afraid and the rats also carry sabres candelabras and caps the skeletons rock back and forth when the ventriloquist recites the marseillaise and the rich man owns the herd of elephants translation and impassive evening he bought green horses essential for bitterness we know we know it is not portable but is harmful to concentration embroidery and natural like the crackling of electric fish in water when the horses pass by the words sputter with pleasures of green horse and chloroform.

(MR. AA THE ANTIPHILOSOPHER in THE ANTIHEAD)

XIV. Velodrome with Onions

Marriage ⅓ is also a product of sea life like the end of the sentence there it is and unpolished the flower wags its tail electric lamp shades are placed on it he believes in inviolable negations valid for a month so he is very nice.(*)

The telephone remains loyal to us like a metal dog says the dadaist he yawns yawns the curtains swallow the street light Aa sends all that express for the colonial exhibition the normal world mine phosphate the tribunal is a conjugal raid between the powder horn the handle the manifestation and the baggage of migraine seeds lunar soap and hors-d'oeuvres advantage have adopted a new virgin son and hidden him in the garage piano.

There is still the cancer of the red corridor lamp and the jaw garlanded with fingernails waits for the dwarf the train and the rabbit.

Mr. Aa waits for the mail the polite praise of perpetual criminal attack.

(*)and extremely agreeable.

(MR. AA THE ANTIPHILOSOPHER in THE ANTIHEAD)

XXIV. The Valves of Thought

A crystal of anguishing cry screeches on the chess board that autumn. Don't interfere I beg you with the roundness of my half-language. Invertebrate.

Beauty one calm evening. A girl that the sprinkling transformed veiled highway of swamp.

Treatise of language.

When the wolf does not fear the leaf I myself languor.

And as for the theft of squatting negligence.

In decomposing the horror, I myself very late.

Fatigue remembers having set down its baggage upon the whiteness of the hour.

Perhaps the private tooth. Understand the promenade of adjectives in the mouth of work.

The Spartans exposed their words on the hill for the foxes to gnaw at and tear out their entrails. A photographer passed. How do you dare to gallop on the fields reserved for syntax? he asked me. The word, I answered, has fifty floors, it's a godscraper. It was true, for the photographer was only a parasite of the amalgamated itching business.

(MR. AA THE ANTIPHILOSOPHER in THE ANTIHEAD)

XXVII. Avalanche

Boom, boom, boom, he undressed his flesh when the damp frogs began to burn, I put the horse in the snakeskin at the fountain we'll depend from now on my friends and the giraffes of bites on the marble are very interesting macabre waltz.

Sunday: two elephants Geneva newspaper in the restaurant the telegraph man assassinates the emperor's portrait.

The concierge deceived me she sold the apartment I had rented in the church after mass the sinner said to the countess: Good-by Matilda.

The train trails the smoke like the flight of a wounded animal with his intestines squashed poor animal.

Around the light revolves the aureole of birds turned blue in halves of light screwing down the distance of ships while archangels take enemas and birds accelerate our periods by hidden artificial means.

Oh my dear it's so difficult the street is running off with my baggage through the town the subway is mixing up its cinema with Jamaica the prow of I adore you accosts in the casino of the sycamore.

In fish nerves there's the vibration dada, da, da, repeats the instrument waterfall imprecise and odorless.

(THE DESPAIRING in THE ANTIHEAD)

VIII. Before Night

I

Before night falls, in this moment as disturbing as air suspended between liquid and solid states, when everything hides its face in shame, even the noises take flight, timidly, when the feeling that a vase is about to overflow plants itself with anguish in each breast as if another annoucement of the death of someone we love, of his awful suicide, were going to strike us, when this hatred of life can transform sorrow into an immense gratitude, when the heaps of corpses warming the winter frozen in us, half-putrified, men we have known in the constant bitterness of a restless gaiety (how powerful sadness must be among such obvious signs to take on such strange aspects) have mutilated, torn, and strangled each other with a fierce joy of destruction, in a delirium of hatred, a delirium of hatred, such a frenzy that only the liveliest joy can raise the purity of a soul to such tender altitudes,— before night falls, in this moment trembling in everyman's voice, without his knowing it, in the moment perceptible only to a few experienced beings for whom the invisible counts at least as much as degrading matter,—how degrading physical suffering is,—and knowing that you are a slave to pain wounds you in your human pride, when fate takes pleasure in showing you its steel fangs, ready to grind its own creation teeming with misunderstandings, between its lottery wheels, like a fire-eater at a fair, a subject to which I shall return, to which so many others have returned without turning around as in the song; finally, not to let myself slide down the bitter slope, before night falls, I say, in this moment like a long intake of air, seeming still longer in a hollow breast, a long breath to utter a cry which will perhaps never be uttered, the uselessness of things has become so fixed in the intentions of nature, I have decided to summon you, disgust, you who live hidden behind the meaning of things and people, always present, flooding this world with your sticky imprecation, you who have never changed, buried under immemorial layers of human despairs, fusing sometimes with the strength of storms and displaying yourself proudly before our hesitant steps, disgust, I have decided to summon you in a quiet voice with no trace of insult to

it, in a voice which would have captivated the voices of all men over the
infinite expanse where they suffer, bitter lament and suffering with no going
back into memory, of all voices bundled into a sheaf of hatred, I summon
you, disgust, to my aid, so that your hideous face, emerging in the middle of
this world, can take account of your filthy adorers and those who turn away,
so that your hideous face can divide into neat ranks the hybrid undecided
mass, I summon you, cunning disgust, you who slow down our movements,
you who take the harsh toll of at least half what our gazes have gathered,
all that thought has tried to replace or to sing, you diminish our hatred and
discourage the assassin born with us, who grew up in us and is struggling
in a prison cell between love and the sun, in us, disgust, when your face
has arisen from monstrous blackness and hidden half the sky with its fetid
substance the answer will open perhaps in the word of all men, like the light
gleaming only in their invincible hatred.

2

Turbulent man—oh man as I see you growing from the smooth palm of
mud, fusing your deep and delicate rootlings, scarcely joined to the earth's
skin, scarcely fleeing at the wind's rise, scarcely submerged by the fleeing
waters, scarcely surviving the profound play, gathering yourself in the aerial
agility—the turbulent man decanted by age, the man of dramas and irreme-
diable silences bows his head of dying sun, bows his look once swimming
with crimes, impulses, scrutinizing monkey-wrench gazes, the slow source
of sadness, of tenderness—oh moments falling fine as pearls on a sheet of
glass, memory, entering through the eyes and projected on the foul heaps
fed by deceptions—man folded over, a cool crock benevolent in the beg-
gar's hand, the beggar sonorous and full who knocks on the doors of being
as would a tree, a bell, a road stronger than you, man, you who have known
a road more imperious than a woman's voice and who have made of a voice
your nourishment and your daily luck and your sleep and your reason, man
harrassed by absences (must a wall absorb so many echoes that its presence
still resounds, for such a long time cruel or tender, infinitely tender), man
bends over a defunct world and sees love, poverty, a whole hunger built of
life, and man, and the passion he believed so strong as it ripened the cold

face, all it touched in its passing, often mocking it in a hollow similar voice, man who reached in his delirium the supreme lie purity accompanies, wearing itself out lying in its strength and doubt—falls, falls in the mud—and from the heights of its fervor, blind dizziness of snows—the snows melt and on each falling place, the place of a tomb is marked—man lives on impotence before the exaltation which draws him like a charm, man made to fall lower, lower, lower every day, without taking account, like water, as its freshness and as flame are priceless, priceless like a flying leaf is a bird singing crudely while beneath there are grave pains, jaws weighty with a heavy anger, heavy memories plunging in our immortalities, so many others which have not known how to perish, man who has turned toward cardinal hopes and has discovered in each beast an infant's cry and thought, like love, he has carried higher than the hour of the dead, man bends over the word and melts in legend like a mouth in desire and becoming in the line up of innumerable tombs through which he has forged for himself a king's forehead and a sun for the poor, sovereign bitterness and lassitude.

3

And when man had finished spreading out his obsession with the infinite, he began again the unreasonable cycle of perpetual failures. Dramas moved their vain and foolish wings. Love shone in him like a mine-deep secret. Sleep was not his friend. But the wind brought him new words and, under each, he found fresh grass. And unknown nests. And the unknown grew in him until it was high as his head. There was solitude; there, the ineffable was seen. There he built his house from the ruins. May his wishes wake, may the stone take root! But that could not be and he set out again. Over the sea, over the eyelids. Over the earth with fire.

(MIDNIGHTS FOR GIANTS in THE ANTIHEAD)

XVIII. Crazed Gesture

Crazed gesture and mental disorder, fearful indiscretion, I have seen you stripped naked. You hurled yourself headfirst against the doomsday feelings, those walls rising up suddenly burst from the quivering waters, with thorns on your back, a stubborn forehead, chest stuck out. Every life cudgeled its brain to pieces on its web at their dreadful appearance.

Sorrow was embedded in you, ridiculing its own becoming. Hope mocked, so well was pathetic and unconquerable sorrow buried. The wheels and the stinking mud, the bruised hinges set the tone for the painful laughter, burying being in the fractures of phrases. Dark gasps of a wounded boar after battle where the elements mingled in an insomniac ornamentation. Drunken, drunken on difficult living. The hiding places of unwieldy logarithms were their realm and their bread. They hoisted them-selves to the worth of a rock. Never resounded more strongly than ever in a heart in self-exile from the world. It would rather knead gusts of wind than give in to softness. It strove to find the grimace of the ground underfoot. And every smile was hidden from it under the luxury or the meagerness of the meal.

The immense malediction which it drew around itself and lived on, no longer needed to be expressed. It obeyed that malediction and as a wild thing, could not contain the torrid life captive inside it. It was squeezed in the vice of a massive trembling. The sluice gates gave way to invading memory; now the specter is rising, rudder first, disorderly, with a hammered-down heart, drifting, without mirth or wrinkle, wrists riveted to the rocks. The inundation of death, the impenetrable face fleeing the stigma.

I have blinded the ways of water.

If in the insanity of gestures, it is easier for the hopeless toment than for manifest sorrow to catch itself in revolt, there is all the bitter resignation, a far more irrevocable and fertile menace in the consolation of a love giving in to its destiny with the apparent calm of distraction.

I have blinded the ways of feeling.

But the revolt is brewing more sharply and tersely under the bright grass, and the serenity of a volcano cannot be determined. The untamed rockets in its breast deny themselves any escape; they await the din and the cleft and the radiance of the sign which the living will never snatch from the death that lives and is perpetuated and is magnified in the magic breast of poetry, invisible among tokens, inexhaustible in its power, always present.

I have blinded the ways of reality so that death can fertilize respiration and disillusion suffering.

(MIDNIGHTS FOR GIANTS in THE ANTIHEAD)

XII. Now or Never

The crocodile goes to the wood mass. Animal names have no longer a selling price on the wood market. With no consideration for the bride, the choppy waterfall, the wind is strangled in its frankness on the gable of good weather. Grasping the handle of the difficult passage, ladybirds across spider webs, the seer gnaws at the mountain range of iron reality.

What does the outraged widow matter to the straw journey? In the valleys decorated with sweets, the church tower sucks all the pleasure of the plunges. Snore, snore, cold stream, we must strip the road markers, those pedestrians of worm-eaten silence. The grass doesn't know what to do with its imperturbable solitude,—the trout climbs against the current of solitude. The road is quiet up to the mouth of the mechanical foliage—the man who knows how to keep quiet. Wool stockings—hairdressers of whales.

The authoritative finger of the most imperious reasons for living touches at the fountain the forehead of the cloud bakery. By shaking a little more vigourously every day the salad of bell sounds, the great apricot tree of pure hearts makes its way toward the breaking of the plaster sleep. The hail has so perverted the nomadic hesitation of the squadron that the shadows have been delayed over the swamp of vision, over the building materials of silence, and it is only after the long discussion of the gusting of dice, when the badminton stroke had reestablished the ceremony of fully lit drama, in the presence of the adversary, that you could see here and there staircases whispering light peels, birds just out of their molt scattering at random among the thistles of whole days and streets, paved with love or with the venison of memories, uselessly assaulting the eye tranquil as a stiffened torrent. The fighter approached in the mist had accepted the sun's challenge. Nothing will ever make him forget the cold burnings and the ornaments of the lie, the spectral promenade of variable weather over restless remedies, at the bottom of the visible world, the impure hair of springtime snows.

(THE DESPAIRING in THE ANTIHEAD)

II. The Measurer of Midnights

Once more we escaped the assaults of final chords. They were struggling for a moment of silence which they could not grasp. And we ran, huddled together in hordes after them, except for indications to the contrary or unexpected stampedes at the doors of emergency exits.

A head with a coupula mounted atop it leads you to reflect. As one feeds bread to the pigeons, we were the sad incrusters of its diadems. Underlined in red, we scrutinized the wrecks of lips. But at the stirrup's place, a single hooked nose raised its hand to the height of the breasts. And the tubular sea rolled feathers and tracks up and down. Broken lips occasionally appeared along its body. The sea crossed, the hands seated and hard. Ferocious teeth escaped from the knees and the aquiline shoulders grew green under the death's tuft. Networks and branches divested themselves of their matter and their color and thus disguised as air, took on the equivocal manners of clouds. And the shape of a three-horned ox. All of it could be contained in a shell by a wooden cork with a large chin, its ears made of feathers, one missing and with three points. The spade of the head with a little wicker goatee. Its coiffure minced about, the man was a nasal ornament, and on his face someone had planted open wings.

You say "someone," but we know it was the queen and still she didn't always permit her tongue to pass through the half-opened eye. Would she be otherwise just another queen like the former one because, perforated on the top story, the translucid breast no longer satisfied the stars.

She hesitates at nothing.

The points of her breasts were lips for kissing, lips unable to speak but capable of simulating varied hidden convulsions. It was up to desires to make them confess in slow motion what they quickly seized in the way of a new thought or memory. Gentle imprints like those of desolated walls. Fleshy gestures of the kind we no longer have. Ticklings of cigarettes and gloves reversible with the growths of charm and the time of moltings. How long springtime was then, when there was a lemon taste in the air over the expanse with no nostalgia for woman!

There is still more freedom beyond the worlds where bridges are burned. It has the sense of gaseous light and of the fife.

(THE DESPAIRING in THE ANTIHEAD)

Seeds and Bran

Starting now, the content of days will be poured into the demijohn of night. Despair will take on the joyous forms of the end of apple time and will roll like a hail of drums freshly poured on the humid shadow which we use for a coat. The nights will be lengthened to the detriment of days, in broad daylight, according to the rules of the most obstinate and sordid moods. Eggs of light will be piled up on the breasts of buildings. Dreams will be forbidden to accost women in the street. At rush hour, packs of invisible dogs will be released throughout the town; they will slip between feet and vehicles, all of them covered with a phosphorescent substance lightly musical like satin. Men, women, and children will touch each other's hands with an obvious satisfaction taking the place of politeness. No one will be called upon to account for the prolonging of these touches. From this formula, seemingly devoid of interest, unlikely knowledge and capital arrangements will be born. Soon all will have access to the hair. A new voluptuousness will blossom forth to replace love. Its chains will disappear and in their place will be silk threads as invisible as certain gazes expressing the world in its present complexity, sentimental and atrocious.

> now at this moment the fine rain of an obscurity of ants
>   luckily will fall on the town
> I say luckily I say nothing else but that
> and how could one noiselessly crush policemen
>   and break the transoms
> if the softness of the atmosphere among others did not
>   encourage by subtle
>   signs of laughter secretly whispered
> the makers of endless scenes who will appear
>   in the palm of the town

Heaps of fruit will be piled up at the crossroads, some of them as high as three-story houses. The news will be carefully displayed on the ship signals strung on rigging in its turn suspended from the street lights. Horses will receive the honor due to their plastic beauty and to the nobility of their character. Nothing will be neglected, neither the beautification of domestic animals nor the institution of bird parliaments. Men will talk no longer, while women will sing certain phrases of determined use and limited number but the sense of the words will match neither etymology nor habitual sentiments. Every Friday expressions will be changed, some omissions will be ordered, and within the limits of the repertory established for the current week, adding to the links with constantly fresh meanings will fill up the known melodies. Everything which might make a sharp sound will be covered with a thin layer of rubber. The noises will be muted and their resonances dulled.

In the enormously fluorescent town where the wisdom of crowds will be joined with the occasional madness of a few delicious beings, there will be instituted, in anticipation of the imminent transformation of matter, the hour of shepherds, to be sounded from the top of all the attics, for the benefit of those who have ears to hear with and not to shatter the windows with unfortunately audible banging; it will be sounded, in the clarity of welcome time, as the only din widely permitted. And the street singer will put the shadow to the rude test of silence spread out like a spot of red wine swallowing the whole town in boundless delight and pleasure toward which lead the meanings of man, that imperturbable solitary being who comes forth each day from a prison, . . .

These will disappear little by little: doubt as to the thoughts of an individual who possesses neither the ability, the knowledge, nor the desire, for diverse reasons, of saying it, and with it, the possibility of "saying"; the habit of thinking in words, for in most cases, only speaking aloud or quietly to oneself engenders thought; the moving force of thought whose progress, proven by what remains behind, counts under the rubric of time; the goal to strive for which, by the contagion thought's own end spreads out over the activity itself according to the mildewed notion of life in general, and finally the notion of continuous duration, for the static nature of imaged thought will retain the individual in the stagnating pool from which good and evil, the beautiful and the ugly, life and death will be absent. The sequence of facts will no longer have the idiotic style that paternal testicles give to the imagination, rather tenderness will impregnate the collective events by which spatial phenomena will be externalized. You can easily imagine the new nature of this time if you permit the hands to be ripped off by their roots from all the clock faces that are still to be wound up.

While waiting for this attitude to predominate over the former one, people will eat in vast establishments either dishes which the aroused senses will have ordered according to the olfactory and visual mechanisms, or whatever the wishes or the fancy of the acrobatic servers, living pendulums, will drop during their perilous leaps; from each bar will be hung a supply of one of the specialities with which chance will have provided, on that particular day, the population ready to accept the most extravagant innovations.

Eating, sleeping, making love, and so on, will tend to mingle; it would be impossible to restrain for long these vital manifestations within too rigorous and too specific confines. Mannequin-witnesses, made to perfection, will be posted in banal postures at bus stops. They will be made of edible matter and encrusted with pearls. Some practical jokers will flirt with them, but these rituals will turn into necessities with the right of tight-lipped laughter until the moment when new postulates make of them vestiges caught red-handed in mature stupidity, thus creating a new reason for continuing to believe in the ritual and for practicing it willingly. Fireworks will be replaced by the releasing in total darkness of birds equipped with tiny reflectors and attached by long threads to high pylons commonly called philosophers' towers. The worst tricks will be played on the persons whose thoughtful demeanor takes on the appearance of asphalt. They can be soaked in the pools, obliged to walk on all fours, and then abandoned to the delirious cruelty of the populace, to learn their lesson. Sadness will thus diminish progressively and when it has entirely disappeared from the town, new forms of joy will be released, in which the study of terror, fear, and cruelty will play a primary role, and bringing about a certain change in the henceforth uniform habits. Dogs gorged on gasoline and set afire will be turned loose in packs against naked women, just the most beautiful of them, of course. Old people will be pressed and dried between the leaves of great wooden books and then stretched out as carpets in middle-class salons. Crystal globes filled with aristocrats' tongues will be exhibited among the pots of jam and mustard in the store windows. Rapid cars with spears of steel in front can impale long lines of people queuing up in front of a cinema, for instance. It will be very exciting, won't it, everyone will say so. A house eight stories high which had sheltered the services of song for more than ten years without arousing the slightest worry, will fall over on its side, a minor functionary having cut the cord which alone attached it to its foundations. Or a mountain could, if it were hauled onto rails, come crashing down on the town, now that I think of it, but we should avoid as long as possible using this slightly brutal means of putting an end to the exquisite and excellent organization of general happiness. We will settle for sprinkling the public gardens with ink and building on the Place de la Concorde an immense ship whose motors will turn uselessly. Bandits will drag away with lassos any bankers who have gotten too close, and with medieval battering rams, we will destroy little by little this marvel of modern mechanics. However, every day, just at the moment when no one is thinking about it, for forgetfulness will be the basis of the new culture of joy in its most bitterly discussed manifestations, not from the point of view of their efficacy, but from that of the destruction which will constitute all the human pride of forgetfulness from day to day and from hour to hour, at the moment when the life of the town burns with desire to surpass the joy, when it has not yet finished crushing the fatigue of the little followers, of the great collectors of popular cruelties, the real inventors of unhoped-for times in a minimum of space, I am speaking of those few in number who live on the life of all and who, once they are dead, still serve as bread and butter on the table of the profiteers, so much happiness is exhaled from their stiff arms extended at the hour when forgetfulness will have already circumscribed life outside of any past and future, in a present ever more reduced to its shortest expression of existence, of silence; from the height of towers immensely lost in the quest for clouds, the hour of the shepherds will be sounded, across the glacial masses, so that the town trembling with dry and felt-covered noises will be transformed into aquarium life, like a lone and immanent summons back to existence. And the street singer will himself be covered by the cloak of this servitude, he who spread floods of silence like infinitely gracious waves over the town disproportionately cruel and contented. . . .

Finally prejudice, in its most beautiful nudity, will replace truth. Ingratitude and hypothesis—we know the role they play as instruments for prospecting human nature, on this poetic couch which imitates the act of knowledge to its most fortuitous secret—will be the key pieces in the laws of common sense. It certainly exists, that force of persuasion (I am referring here to its active sense as the true object of mutation) at the disposal of humor, integrated as it is in poetry, through the vision with which it clarifies the relationships of things and beings, through a constant and intrinsic negation of the affirmed object which it accompanies and which it destroys or through the suspicion it casts, gratuitous in appearance but necessary upon examination, on the interplay of directed and nondirected thought. The product of chance, it will return to chance, but to a humanized chance which would have lived out the space of a memory, a chance which would have taught memory its own adventurous ways of living and the inestimable perspectives it offers to human hope, through all the downfalls and infirmities, of bringing to life the object of dreams, outside every concurrence of circumstance.

Thus words themselves, by unusual couplings not predicted in the dictionaries of granite, are susceptible of taking on the new shade of a sense or of a loss of sense according to the principle of the boiling-over of liquid and of the changes produced in the nature of that liquid. Humor is the revenge of the individual, prey to the traps his own limits set him. Removing privilege from the autumn of words, which humor can make objective, still enjoys the fanaticism of caprice and the mysteries of seduction. It is insulting for everything exterior to it, insofar as it is too lively an affirmation of a sadistic-tragic personality fixed in an immense solitude. But as the individual adapts his experiences to the community's needs, humor, as it is modified, takes on a more universal character. I dream of a coefficient of humor which might serve for mathematical calculations, for purposes of lofty speculation. Of a specific and liberating humor, measurable in its own parts corresponding to the parts of everything definable. Of a humor which, extended to all the forms of human thought, in which it will be immanent, will permit the manifestations of science to live with and for, man, to participate truly and intimately in his everyday life and his style of knowledge. Perhaps it will be a question of love. Perhaps it will be a question of love/humor. Perhaps it will be a question of a consciousness with no tourniquet. Or the suppression of ranking numerals. Or the transparency, the disappearance of all ambiguity. Perhaps in a high sustained note the sun's resonance will march shoving aside all the dwarf nights which hang on to us and irritate us. Perhaps there will be, as there is at the limit of prenatal memory, beyond which the lack of consciousness provokes an anguish expressed in the unrealizable desire of a warm and gentle comfort, calm and black, the return and at the other limit, the fear of the disappearance of consciousness in death; perhaps there will be a transformation capable of envisaging that one without anxiety, as if one were to find at the end of desire the beneficient perversions still to be invented.

Life appeared to me in cross section like an agate whose spots are moving in a perpetual flight of worms writhing alongside each other trying to avoid one another and seeking in a constant equilibrium a way out which would conform in contour to the oppositions, the barriers, and the interdictions provoked by movement itself. Perhaps there will be a gap in the framework. Perhaps a possibility of no longer thinking in a closed system. The consistency of gas will perhaps win out. Perhaps it will be seen that as darkness is only a crystal globe, a tumor, it is enough to break it in order for light to exist and to invade memory and the fear of death. Perhaps it will be a question of love. Then only will the moral laws empty their pockets, for man will be visible and visitable and no one will wish to know more than can be seen, the *humanly thinkable* will turn aside, on its tracks of the new laws of chance and humor, the hateful *properly thinkable* which each day adds another stone to the millstone of our times of windowpanes and of clearings.

(SEEDS AND BRAN)

Resumé of Night

II

I like human substances compact and disheveled, difficult to disentangle even with the propellers of sudden dawn, those that find in ever virgin sleep forgetfulness of sharp eyes and of scrutinizing memory. Very rare, these water women only appear before the suction cups of mirrors between the immeasurable hours linking indefinable insomnia to the definitive day. But if the latter falls in a peevish cold mass on man's consciousness, the refuge taken in a vegetation of submarine softness, under the ambiguous eye, can only prolong the resolution of a humming sound, heritage of the infant night, through fragile tunnels of transparent membranes and planetary metamorphoses. A disconnected vibration of lamentations breaks like miniscule squares in sacks to tiny bells and clinking of jewels. Sun is its worst enemy. The wind can offer it the drunkenness with which the poor men at the bottom of the stairs tremble if the rocks galvanized by waves lie in the reach of its frenetic rigor. Thus the sea, cell of the dream, contains the greatest number of nuclear possibilities from which the apparitions of clouds and lightning muscled in anthropomorphic forms can influence slight modifications of the sex of certain beings which come about with a storm's simplicity. And all the jugs break with a sound of dry mountains, while in successive layers gradually lighter toward the summit, a feeling of life with an undercurrent of reproach clarifies with a new precious stone human charm continuing across the powder grottos.

IV

From the radiant monstrosities of fishing, the human soul has kept an iron-colored memory. Astounding immensities of vivisection. The foam of profound glances, the leather vegetation and the laborious heart of the toothless rivers meet in a shining cluster of wings stretching out toward the knowledge of gauzy souls. Despite the fluidity of the alarm, the arch distills the thoughts in dryness and difficulty. Dresses themselves fall asleep on the solidified waves of the sea's expanse. Tents and chariots give off a dairy breeze, while the pebbles, children of the crystal, drum in vain at the doors of barrels. They are the hoop-rollers of the horizon, battlements of the tall forests of marine adolescence, season's vintage of girls' eyes. The baskets with silvered temples of mother-of-pearl ecstasies have split apart, and have strewn the lands of distant destinies with the gleaming of rattles. The harvesters of moon vines have burned the last ports of call of foxes as a sign of mourning, and pulling the lightning from their eyes, petal by petal, they have counted their number in the coming clarity.

Thus rises the rapid landscape at the announcement of the secret well. A petrified hand unhooks itself from the wall's teeth and sleep falls once more on the bitter plank. Crime itself reconstructs, brick by brick, its dwelling of fire and heads crumble in the head with a tamed noise of rain and a ripping of muslin at the place of childhood. Marvels are borne in the infinite breast, but the steel lucidity of man strikes harsh blows against the matter whose object it is. Black, disheveled in animal dirt, all escapes are forever closed to it. And of what use is a solid water endowed with the potency of charm, when through it the colors lose their strength to shriek under the cinder. Midnight sounds every hour in this brain receding in its sphere and lost in its proper perspective with the unconscious slowness which in its turn recedes and is lost. Man labors in uncertain hours; the most visible are not always the most damaging, but rather the ones pearling on the forehead of birds. For one single open room, all the laughter melts, the plough will pass by again.

VI

It is a question of following step by step, across the collapse of memory, the prodigious development of a coefficient of ruin which will take its place in a universal system of dilapidation and thoughtlessness. What is the habitual conduct of an avalanche of ambient nature in the framework of each event for the use of life as a fruit tree? It is not to the rare moment of heroism striking the breast of the sky in virtue of the body's decadence and that of social relations, on the summit of a storm which no force could immobilize, that I shall confide the care of my rediscovery. Existences resisting the judgment of dust, the errant affections among the latent journeys and the domains of confusion, still rocked by a singular timidity on the lap of childhood, do you hear the cement voice of wolves when it knocks against the wall of the world? Potsherds of waves are dispersed then in the reeds under the eyes and the human creeks are wet with the sharp tears of abandon. The splinters of the sea, the new sand where the tenderness of the night objects, of sun breasts soft to the touch of seaweed fingers has fled? Still another cadaver of day to carry furtively up the slope of this universal sliding of things and of inspirations. Where the wall finishes, you change the cloud into shadow of harness; time is free on the breastplate of a new field. . . .

X

It would be difficult to convince me that a given individual (let's take the one who is right now synchronizing as best he can his organic needs with the time he has at his disposal until the bus comes) sees, hears, feels, perceives at the same speed and in the same dimension as I do what is going on around him and that his watches, meters, and adjectives have not been, from the moment of his birth, rigged by the unanimous and constant relationship of things and beings to which he has subjected the norms of his judgments. For it is enough to suppose that it is really possible in order to know a priori that nothing would transpire of that secret guarded in the face of everything and in spite of himself, because of the perfect conformity of this secret with the secret incorporated into the existence of every being. One must either break at some point the perfect circuit or, even with reservations, permit oneself to be forever contaminated by the dream spilling out of the jug of sleep, or glimpse that which the frenetic and discordant dance at the center of whatever framework—touched both in its admitted splendor and in its conventional duration—can produce within the world of thought in its deformed perspective. Removing oneself for a time from the coincidence of movements, whether it be slowed down or accelerated, augmented or diminished by volume and weight, from things and beings, not under the influence of a narcotic which, however, can already have given us the necessary foretastes, but in full consciousness, seems to me inevitably to ruin the system of prefabricated ideas about the reciprocal relations of participating man and nature participated in, or about those of non-participating man and the external world. But since man cannot be conceived of as isolated in this sense, the laws of exterior reality being such that all the coordinates in relation to him ought always, at every moment, to fit together, and since even his unconscious is forced to submit to them so that nothing will impede the tyrannical order, it is evident that every state freed from the direct control of perception by the objective means belonging to the surroundings—dream, narcotics—can make our lives longer or shorter. It is not out of the question that new methods can still be put to use in the exploration of consciousness, in every waking state, either by physiological interventions in the optic structure of the sensorial organism or by intellectual exercises softening the will by putting to sleep precisely those stiff and stubborn faculties of the intelligence which direct our lives according to schematic rules.

The storms which succeed each other in the head of man stifle under the weight of amassed cotton. But it is a question of a more luminous life which, on the edge of independence and with the aid of its appeal, will be made imminent, dazzling us by the rapidity of its comprehension of things and of beings. It is a question of an axiomatic of desires, of being luxuriously swathed in the drizzle of their possible satisfactions.

So, more or less, night appears to me in the fermentation of its profound chances.

XII

Night came to me as an unhealthy idea. Vitreous and vindicative. Never since then has it left me. It was only a matter, as in the case of a certain adolescence, of easily overcoming the limits officially decreed for fervor and the obstacles it posed. On one side the sea penetrated me like a light young substance; on the other side stood the very flesh of love which contained its fluid and incessant principle of reversal. The simplicity of a thought is not always the best guarantee of its exact gravitation around a beloved dwelling by which it is likely to be fecundated; but all the same it often happens that one takes up temporary residence on the mortal wing of an invading day, as on a journey one doesn't want to be attached to the mechanism necessitated by the exchange of memories between the objective visitor and the visited object.

How many bloody misunderstandings are born from the ignorance of this rule; those who would have been capable of giving us some meager information on that subject are now buried under the shriekings of carnivorous destinies! No impediment of that sort for the night traveler. The exchange of memory's reports takes place only with the tacit consent of a veil covering the appearance of both parties. Even the presence of an object must be approached in its fleeing; one can only brush into it in passing. And from this touching, from this gliding by, no moralistic idea should come to cloud the purity of the movement by implying a high and a low; no human objectivity should indicate for it a before and an after, for contrary to everything, night is not in my eyes a phenomenon having a beginning and an end, not even a static image around which the day could turn with the contents of day and night as satellites. It seems rather to be the summary of a state of preventive consciousness, by snatches, an indefinable succession of degrees of interchange between man and the universe, a state for which the circumstantial consciousness of duration is given as an astral problem, as a change in the periodicity of certain rhythmic or other phenomena in a general flow without subdivisions or measures, a flow complete and archaic. . . .

(NOONTIMES GAINED)

Limits of Fire

Married to great insubordinate masses, tossed about in the universal gathering of things, given over to the searchers of grave torments, to the human rootlets fixed in meditation and the complicity of the jealous, you see yourself accomplishing daily gestures in the cramped limits of supple branches. You oppose yourself to a blotting paper desire. You move about nervously under the wind of an always flowering wake. If I do not manage to distinguish from things the phantoms of words which have helped in their effusions outside myself, that is due to the continuity of their mediating action between the world and my adolescence. And from then on, subject to a feeling of abyss, fragmentary and strange, what could I do except to undergo with terror their call, desertlike and ferruginous? All earthly space was bucking under the cloud banks. I surrounded myself with fragile hibernations, with desiccating strengths. What will there be left that is human on the glabrous faced tanned by reading and the astringent politeness of notebooks with which I have made for myself a beggarly surrounding?

Habitual weakness, it shall be said on one day of revolt that the eyes we sought were empty of human joy. And men and joy, I have always tried to mix with them, since I could not have the promised ferocious fusion still found living in the residue at the bottom of stories among the germs of cold and the doors scattered with childhoods.

Waking

Hasten toward immense and earthly joy, the eyelids blinking as they dance against the wall of night. Enough of explicit death, light-hearted death used down to the nail polish, youth lost in the apostrophes of hypocrisy! Enough of the lifeless breath of hearts woven into salubrious baskets. Hasten towards the human joy inscribed on your forehead like an indelible debt!

A new form of summer vegetable is falling on the world's mist in tufts of slow grass, covering it with a thin layer of expected joy, of a glorious future foreshadowed in the steel. Hurry up, it is a brilliant human joy waiting for you at the turn-off point of this dismembered world, spoken in tongue of asphalt! There are reverses, springs sealed off, lips on tambourines and eyes without indifference. Salt and fire await you on the mineral hill of the incandescence of living.

(THE HAND PASSES in NOONTIMES GAINED)

The Herald of Eyes

The plantain tree tempts the unsealed soul. And it is true that a shakedown of rigid bark is lingering somewhere there. So man, after the debris surrounding his turbulence, would like to get rid of it: toward new departures! But then enough of the fetishists bowing to the ground before the spelling-out of their shame! Stand up straight, looks lowered on the embers, larvae of insurrections! And you, adulated hands, thin pretending hands, what do your impatiences matter; the torrent growls and the fallow joys listen at the doors of wheat for the order of battle and the pride of action.

A new memory rises to the sovereignty of the world and the few words fallen from its lips suffice to reconstruct the mythical flocks plunging into the throat of massacre. Mounting desires will efface henceforth the stumps of the head looking for impossible usages.

The fanfare of tulips on the wheelbarrow of wharfs.

Solitude, lofty serene solitude, it is to the passion of your multiple tables of resonance that I dedicate the bitter leaf to which the future is committed. There the breaker of mirrors bathes. Where the sun's cinders keep watch.

Already the valleys resound with hands joined in the renewed friendship of palms. But the river. But the excess of light. But the brief whinny. It is of death we are speaking.

(RADIANT MUTATIONS in NOONTIMES GAINED)

New Paragraph

Night paid with the uncertainty of candles for your knowledge, filled with scaly mountains, worn by swarms of plaster at the smooth surroundings of paths, kind to those whose sad countenance of candelabra lives is roughly treated by the day, to those whose strength is discharged on the pallets of a wheel like an interminable harshness of sentiment, of slavish pain, of wailing molting-time (hasn't the era of cages printed the flocking sway of heads on the polar bears dressed in the bread of bad weather?), night nourishing the misery of broken mules of indivisible sap running down the slopes of muscles, for too long now I have let myself be hoaxed by your stagnant clumsiness and the leather of your elbow has finally deceived the well-worn rubbing of my memory against the ancient phosphorous.

Your irritating action only reverberates in the singing breasts thanks to the fraud with which day is surrounded. The wretch welcomes you under the porches and in the lying granges. But the confusion you sow in your wake is not ended. Night unjustly compared to the proportions of a mole, I wish to refuse the incantatory aid of your electric foundations. In case of death, you are a serene intermediary ready to render the justice of candle-ends. You help the lazy to air the constant rain of his cradle undergrowth. You invite the uncertain one to fall back in the childhood of his grizzled head, on his heavy forward feet. What promises have you not made to the lovers of fleshy fat, to the cowardly outbursts of frogs, to the bony absurdities of the crickets of dry sand? Hitched to the baying of all sorts of forests, nibbling the minor fields at the place of the substitutions of sky, you follow the sparrow-hawk in his accustomed path. But when the traveler takes the path allotted to his exemplary error, you take the form of misguiding echos, charging his fear with all the weight of credence in your corrosive force. There you are installed for life. And the bundle on his back attracts the sneering stars.

Thus I loathe you and you are shattered by the masks.

I pass to the wounds displayed next, to the joys of open battles in which the unaltered clarity of blinds already plays.

(RADIANT MUTATIONS in NOONTIMES GAINED)

Bay Morning

I saw men brewed in the color of light soil
and the wing of their smile reigning over the air of the fields
the fruits bore before them the taste of their clear eyes
the supple light consuming the flame of bodies,
shed evenings and their bitter remains

I saw the forgetful bird drinking at the spring
plucking the new wave borne from hand to hand
noisy child of sorrowful dazzling seas
I saw in the very grass the summer of survivors
guiding human flight with its dizziness of rocks

and I embraced so long in the shadow of its shadow
the marvelous word founded on freedom
I so often took up from the nights the ancient dream
that from one refrain to the next
and from one grief to the next increasing
there has gathered behind my steps
a life following my life on a leash of difficult echo

calm of our fleeing proud crystal of dawn
at the summit of faithfulness

(NOONTIMES GAINED)

Anecdote

giants of rain coolness of summer
oh vain sparkling depths
still I go tempting the most certain falls
do I not see from afar my own living and dying

so I go leafing through landscapes to come
tearing torn faithful
made of dead wood flesh earth
badly off persevering
from one halt to the next

I am a horse I am a river
I go on clumsily nevertheless I live.

(EARTH UPON EARTH)

Invisible Earth

I have seen at close range among the blind the mystery of birth
the day rose broken chained and battered by the beams' black strength
in a clattering gallop under the velvety snow
I saw a flower of light the smallest silken gleam
flicker at a man's door poor man of forgetfulness and transparency
the song and the silence my beautiful country of joy

who knocks at the door forgotten buried under the sawdust
        of forgetting and winter
why are you knocking I said to the cold truth in truth
let the water of clarity drench the unmasked room
a thousand white wings cut the air suddenly violent as a girl's
        laughter
at the poor man's door where only the slap of the rain
        beat with fatigued blood
the day's the night's pulse and the invisible burn
holding on to the cracks of stars
dream or fruit of the silence of thorns
wind rain freedom

I've said what have I not said snow rain and wind and hail
and I've chased the flies uselessly
broken so many dishes
that shame mounts to my mouth
so many bitter words
on roads traveled by heart
eyes closed shame leading
a mocking laugh at each window
and great indiscretion in the looks between the leaves
of all the trees stabbed in my bosom
joy fruit freedom

×   ×   ×

I have seen at close range among the blind the mystery of birth
wind and rain and wine and fruits
the sun of the blind man a child in the snow
and for telling the future all the human strength
offered in flesh like salt and bread
to the most beautiful the marvelous to the future flame

it was a day like no other in the month of August
courage arried high its fiery forehead
the man who crossed the long night of France
saw anguish dry up at the edge of the well
and saw anger leap from the rape of the waters
only light alone
pure between the high lacerations

I have seen at close range among the blind the sun of birth
and the first flower
the bread shining on the peak of the shadow
and mountains of birds freshly confident
coming back to the spring
both the song and the silence my beautiful country of joy

(EARTH UPON EARTH)

Acceptance of Spring

I speak of a new time shining
and of a blue-tinged freshness
in the gold of heavy waters
set with slow daggers
the doors are opened ivory of ripe fruit
I speak of constancy
the breasts bleed
offering themselves up to the majesty of night

at the heart of the lacerations
the waiting becomes flame
dwarf suns salute the tongues of crystal
departing devoured by their echo
but the blood's gallop
among smooth tears
toward incredulous springs
divides the voices the just and the harsh

I speak of these springs
that the secret of woman's hands
has kept intact
at the dying of their embers
what does their brightness matter
if losing the way
they stray under the ashes
covered by the burning fidelity of silence

✕   ✕   ✕

what can they say
dull incandescence
wounds deeper
than sleeping countries
of which I speak—sand
having no name in this world
where the springtime in clusters
tears away from the vanquished night

why have I not untamed forces
trances of light
grafted fragile life
to the robust laughter of mountains
where old memories of fallow lands
slumber in my flesh
listen to the immensity
breaking in the trees outside

the fruit of castanets
grows clearer at the waterfall
you wake the sealed fire
at the deceitful dawn
here are the winds transfixed
in sleepers' dresses
dance the night of harsh ages oh stones
the numbers and their prey here visible
until they burst in a bloody laughter
let earth come on earth
and let the seed of its reign multiply

(EARTH UPON EARTH)

The Flight
(Dramatic Poem in Four Acts and an Epilogue)

From Act III Scene ii.

The First Narrator:

Leaving one being after another, a thing dies and lives again in another. Waiting for someone you love until death is confused with waiting. Wanting to keep what was given from the beginning. Coming and returning, doors open and closed. Helping and refusing help. Wanting to accept when nothing is offered any longer. Weeping, suffering, laughing from so much pain. Sinking to the lowest level, down to the mud, so that you can climb up again and so that the slightest smile from man or beast becomes the supreme deliverance. Wandering like a breath somnambulant, from inertia, while waiting, plunging into yourself the arm of pain until no one even recognizes the object of all that waiting. Following like a blindman an imcomprehensible dream without ever finding the source. Trying to drink from all the sources, even the forbidden ones of lying, pride, egoism, hypocrisy and never being satisfied. Living only by killing a part of oneself. Being cruel enough to impose this castration on the one you love. Wandering, leaving, always leaving, gritting your teeth, wanting to kill memory living only in its sweet and painful light. What's the use? One life after the other and from father to son, hope has made lovely gardens and promises flower. Always some great reason ends the unconsciousness of will. And that was never the end. Pain, pain on one side of the scales. What is on the other side? The joy of having suffered once again, even more, without forgetting it. That is the only joy, after they made you promise as a child that the world would be a game, one great appetite, a climbing toward the highest sunlit peaks? Solitude, solitude never broken except when you are by yourself. Life after life. The progression is not as slow as it appears to our eyes' laziness. From generation to generation it rushes towards a never attained abyss. And no dead man has ever passed on the solution to the survivors.

From Act III Scene v.

The Narrator:
And you, oh Silence, you who see things pass and then return
under different forms you know they are the same
and the departures and the forgettings of eternal likeness
have stripped your soul of scorn and of desperate passion

Just as growing grief lowers its voice
so total conquering grief finds a place forever far from the path of earthly
        sound
you find rest only in grief
and all griefs flow toward you regaining the universal current of their law

Oh grief's cessation you are present
for all grief loses already in its expression the order of its virulence
finding its rest in the grief of others
you spread it about you and you keep its secret

To what would the presence of the beloved son lead me
when already in his joy I see the seeds of sorrow
you try to retain joy longer than you should like the tasteless pulp of fruit in
        your mouth
the taste clings to the kernel which still must be spat out

Man is born the first time from the unconsciousness of inconsistency
and then again he is born to the external world
and then again becomes conscious of himself and is born
then again he believes he is born but his decline already begins
for in each of his new births he slaughters about him whether or not he
        wills it
and when what he has placed in the world by the devotion of his strength
is born anew then somewhere in him it must die
and that is the natural course of things one must know and accept

The Deserter

Here in the forest I live sheltered under the great hard limbs which make a bridge for me. Luckily it's summer. How silly it is, heat is a mother for me; and when cool water slips over my opened hands, the milk of leaves comes forth from the earth through a thousand pores of memories. The table was set. The horses' thirst quenched. The sweet straw of sleep. The giddy smell of the insects lisping. Splendor of the warm friendship of those days! Friends, friends, the games have just begun. The dream would be hollow without provocative laughter. And the girls not yet grown up blush at the adult words which run about in their nipple heads. Flesh bursting so full of life it touches death by its slow insatiability, heavy with impatience. And the peach of night where the forbidden star pricks the fleshy silence of the beast. Spinning about, twinkling density, shining marl in the sun of seeking. And everywhere a full and whispering presence, space stretched out, and in the silence broken by owl's hooting, a dog of loneliness, only one; but the windows shining with a gold asleep on the table, the dog inspecting the low-lying kingdom of furniture, sniffing sleep with his cold muzzle, living in the repose of his blood, and the words now and again flippant ones, you wonder if they have a hidden meaning or if only the sound of memory brushes them with a permanent breath, just like that, in passing, and still it is pleasant to grow impatient with the happiness of their simple existence, just like that, very near forgetfulness, at the edge of sleep.

Now silence bleeds around me and misunderstood space is shattered. Each rat running. Each leaf falling. A bird calling. Water ruminating. Animated night swelling its breast. A porcupine clamps down his fear. The fear everywhere of rapidly beating hearts. Prey or victor. General or cannon fodder. Horses, horses, run around the race track of my head. I am the one whipped. Even if I am not happy about it, at least something happens in this dirty desert of a bastard life of death of empty earth, where my weight takes root with all of a stone's injustice, the stone they made me hang on my neck, a muffled tinkling and its veined beating, even if it isn't until death, at least let it grow or else I'll fall.

The deserter has fallen asleep. By a thousand butterflies, death had made itself heard. What he's dreaming? Why bother to tell it. Under the dream of each word, isn't time always running? And the revolt against this time and this race, isn't that exactly the sense of seizing when the noontime of each thing approaches? He rose up against time, and life ran a little more quickly. He wanted to slow time down, and the days have passed that way. He wanted to let the day fall bit by bit and it fainted. He wanted to frame each fact of vision separately, prettily; one after another, prettily, to put it across from him and look at it at length, studying it in its hidden savor, plucking it, cleaning it. He wanted to live time. And now just because he wanted so much, he has lost it. He has lost time. He has revolted and deserted. After looking for it a long time (haven't you seen my time; haven't you found a time, it must have been mine?), he has fled under cover and has taken refuge in the forest. Already winter merchants were preparing to visit the towns for the profit of their bags and the new year sparkle of their credulous objects. They had no time to sell. The creaking of furniture, sand to put in shoes, the barking of a dog in the sun, a slow flight of lentils, white fear for gas lamps, lengths for castle corridors, cracking of walls, white snows in the form of sneezing powder, liquids in cubes, failings, bitterness for autumn colds and solid brains, an old woman's scratching, letters that don't arrive, paid vacations, awakened sleeps, woods of cold, pastes for lying and lozenges of pure water, earrings of the deaf, myopias at so much a yard, eyelashes of the blind, fistfuls of tombs, feathers of smoke, the invisible, cards to lick, nails made of air, colors of clove, buttons for surprise pouches, laziness, and many other articles, all that at a good price, but time, no, they never had any. So they were always in a great hurry and the days burned under their feet. They went from village to village offering the wind of their near-sighted attractions, curing and singing, crunching on violins and puffing out chests and shaking off the snotty. All that for a small price. But time, no, they never had any. Now the month died for the winter of hearths. The bears began digging the long grapefruit of their winter sleep. The flies themselves didn't yet know under the armpit of what roof they would shelter the freedom of their immodest behavior. Everything was going to sleep in bareness and madness. Only he was still offering the drink of silence to the infinite light wind tapping his chest. Would he, like the dry leaf, heap up the papers of his tattered memories or spread forth in the wind the mane of his experience of shoddy goods? He stood still, staring, for having lost time, the earth dozed in fits and starts with the irregularity of pebbles in the mouth and while masticating the slight slapping of the water, he thought with horror about the day when he would have nothing else to feed wisdom on. And without his noticing it, that day was already there, in its imperceptible nudity, in its nervous pregnancy, lymphatic and somnolent, crushed with snails, sticky with slime but still erect, gazing at him over its shoulder. So then? But he no longer moved. Thus ends my song of the one who lost his time.

Young people affiliated with the secret societies of duration, old people apocryphal and flattened in the nose of newspapers, women with facets for display just visible under the fat of shoulderblades, all of you, pedestrians or snivelers, look at the snow, it is trodden down with slow steps and the local paths raise their apathetic noses towards new feathery twitterings, babblings of feathers, freshly fallen, strong with their belief in a barer future.

(IN MAN'S MEMORY)

For Robert Desnos

in the white of my thought
a blackbird shrieks the grass sings
over the decapitated town
whistles the sudden air of blood
shaking the ripe tree
beggar of light

milady will you
and death displays his wrist watch
empty teeth on the band
and the bones of a thousand witnesses
milady will you
the dead wood of strong jaws
quietly closes the workings

one single hope in your head
in your head a forest
by the breaking of stars
I have known the melody
from which memory rises
there is no more resounding voice
in Paris paved with leaves
a summer does not respond when it is called
I am alone in knowing it

forget your sons your mothers
youth springtimes
lovers' kisses
the gold of time
a naked name is still flying about

✕　　✕　　✕

in the nights around the lamps
and the clenched fist of towns
lifts to the heart of day
this light this revolt
which you offer to passersby
in the palm of your hand
that of the world

in your arms which a wave could sweep away
one bird nothing more except anger
a face at my window
a joy is floating
my secret my reason for being
and the world

(IN MAN'S MEMORY)

The Ox on the Tongue

III

I smiled at the flowering lime tree like everyone else. I was on the edge of a basket-filled presence. Living no longer required either fruit or crowns. I bathed in an absence of bodies. Lightness was substance in itself. A child's laugh and everything was said. Horses somnolent with blinders soaked in memory, women's heads held high with pearls falling from them, bars with resounding counter words, fountains under the flickering of the heavy hair of snakes, tears of the yellow night of the poles, waiting suppressed, streaming without jolts or fingernails and, above all, the child's laugh which nothing escaped.

I mean that ugliness came to chase me from this country. It became as hateful to me as the hissing words which hit me in full freedom. The thread of patience has been broken and from the sheets' memories spring forth reserves of morose adulteries. Monstrous figurations, you were riding along the festival streets. So much the worse for the sun; I didn't believe my eyes at the sight.

VII

Startled, the hands scarcely distinguished between affairs of these and of the others, for the hour of departure, at whose beginning the urgency and the bursting of reasons were inscribed, came upon the man of riverbank like an imperturbable tide. Swaying seductions mingled with sudden grimaces, bargaining in snatches near the hats of winds, pedestrian penitents in front of minimized portals, gravid thoughts at the edge of swallowed tears, mewing coiffures on the ledges of horses' windows, you accompanied with your mental operations the passenger on the station's path. Nothing was lacking, from the slice of innkeeper ironed out on the doorstep to the multiplication of trophies in the cave of washerwomen. Night threw a phosphorescent powder over the alibi of gramophones, and although the sidewalks had nibbled from the cake of time the inscribed edge of gums, the town waddled about, assuming for the joy of planning, an air of complete misunderstanding. At the street's end, two horses like syllables murmured the fatigue of their steps in the ear of this john doe of asphalt, still there, the color of eggplant.

X

A house atop the wall, the apron of black rock, and at the trembling of the storm, anguish tightening its bonds. Bonds, bonds, the sun consecrated you. Across the lost causes, in the routing of words, fullness carved out a path for itself, mute as it should have been, forgetful of its own existence.

Everything was running, trees and waves. Resin stuck the steps of branches to the sand. And we, what did we become, ripened in immobility?

XIV

Brightness on the sky's table. Sun penetrating the winter of pebbles with difficulty. There also life has spread out, a life mixed with distress and joys, with loneliness and uncertainty. By believing in the good, by believing in the bad. Nervously twitching, you are carried along towards an orchestration of veins and a system of stellar crackings. The markets where wind-petaled words abound. Here we come, lips smooth with eternal thirst.

XV

Nothing but nights; the deserted figure stalking along the wharfs lacks confidence in himself and no one knows how to stretch out his hand to him. Thus he sows unhappiness and dissatisfaction along his path. But are there harvests? The morrows are slow to open the windowpanes of laughter. Light always lying fallow. The fans stammer; children recite by heart the alphabet of sleep.

(IN MAN'S MEMORY)

Freedom

In the shadow of the nut tree heavy with garden pride, tears came to my mouth. Their taste preceded them, melted along my whole body. Why was I crying? Nostalgia supposed no reference to the past, elusive and mobile; there was only the future in my head, where dull impatience confronted the narrowed perspectives.

It was through the magnifying glass of tears that I tried to enumerate the perfections of the clover, of straw, of nameless twigs, and of the incessant work of insects on a mound raised to the height of consciousness.

Still today the tenderness of that memory overcomes the cement of the prison which sometimes materializes around me. Freedom—since then, I have never ceased to open wide the doors, the doors.

(MINE)

Through the Vines

Confidence reigned over all the ashes spread on the horizon. I warmed myself in the round color that it cast, measureless. I was filled with the continuity of its energy. Alone, how could I have stood the luxury of this joy?

Immobile hours, under your throbbing unanimity I have discovered fullness. On the hills, a single smile prolonged the unconsciousness of my steps. But over the invisible path of loss, the crystal encrusted in the flesh of night opened on endless steps, always descending, the bitter taste of defeats spread out in the gusts of wind on the abandoned battlefields.

(MINE)

The Horse

It is true that I believed in the immense privilege of living. Each step amplified in me old but always mobile adorations. It was a tree, the night, whole forests of roads, or the sky and its troubled life, certainly the sun.

One day I saw solitude. At the top of hill, a horse, alone, immobile, was planted in an arrested universe. So my love, suspended in time, gathered to itself in one instant its petrified memory. Life and death completed each other, all doors open to possible prolongations. For once, without sharing in the meaning of things, I saw. I isolated my vision, enlarging its borders infinitely. I left for later the concern of seeing what one was to see. But who could maintain that the promises had been kept?

(MINE)

DADA'S TEMPER, OUR TEXT
An Essay by Mary Ann Caws

"What for the other literature used to be the characteristic,
is temperament today . . . It's only natural for the older
ones being created just about everywhere. With insignificant
variations in race, I think the intensity is the same all over,
and if any common character is to be found among those who
are making literature today, it is that of antipsychology."

Tristan Tzara:
"Open Letter to Jacques Rivière" (in *Lampisteries*) [1]

This text takes its starting-point in the Dada temperament—and in what it perceives, as well as the way in which it perceives, moving from the double and two-way images of Duchamp and Tzara to an apparently closed door, from the game of oppositional language to the complexity of the gaming table around which many selves are seated, from mirror image to the Large Glass. The eye is kept on the I but also on the double scene in the reflective game of Dada disquisition.

From M. Antipyrine to M. AA L'Antipholosophe, from M. Antipsychologue to M. Antitête, the antis have it: anti-aspirin, but also anti-head and anti-the-workings-of-the-head, philosophical and psychological: Tzara's approximate man, savage or not, will have none of the noble confessional about him. His self-portraiture is ironic and a put-down; he stutters: Aa, or then da-da, he is given to odd stylistics, half-repetitions, ruptures, and incompletions: *"Je me, en décomposant l'horreur, très tard"* ("I me, decomposing horror, very late") (TZ 2,293) or disguising his disorder in the reassuring coat and cliché style of a proverb, even more offputting: *"Quand le loup ne craint pas la feuille je me langeuer."* ("When the wolf does not fear the lead

---

[1] Tristan Tzara, *Oeuvres Complètes,* ed. Henri Béhar (Paris: Flammarion, V. 1:1912–1924; v. 2: 1925–1933, 1975 and 1977 respectively), I, 409. [TZ]

I langor me") (TZ2, 293) Tzara will write elsewhere and later about the "Automatism of Taste" and is, at the time of M. AA l'anti-philosophe preparing a one-up on *haute courture* as *haute coupure*, cutting and shaking up the elements in some hat or other. A "Treatise on Language," in fact, but the fact is hidden within the body of the "Sluice-Gates of Thought," a brief manifesto in the Antitête about the "roundness of my half-language"; of this language, we had scarcely to be told that it was "Invertebrate." The intensity of the temper already stressed may be anti-psychological, but there is clearly no question of forgetting the mental mechanism or what contains it. Tzara's incompleted novel is called *Faites vos jeux* (*Place Your Bets*) and indeed the play does begin here, but in the head. The last four chapters are entitled "The Surprise Head," "The Tentacle Head," "The Head at the Prow" and, as a resume, "Tête-à-Tête." That the collection should have begun with the expression "*le coeur dans le coeur*" ("The heart in the heart") and ended not with a heart-to-heart chat but a head-to-head summary indicates the attitude of the self-portrait.

Now Dada is a self-regarding movement in moving opposition to its own image and self-image: that there should be a paradox of this kind available is all to the good, for, as we know, Dada and surrealism flourish on the juxtaposition of contraries—yes and no meeting on streetcorners "like grasshoppers," according to Tzara, and, for Breton, the meeting of high and low, birth and death, absence and presence . . . Take, for instance, Tzara's "Static poem" (which transforms the words into individuals; from the four letters "bois" there appear the forest with the fronds of its tress, the forest-keepers' uniforms and the wild boar; perhaps also a Pension Bellevue or Bella Vista (TZ 1,726). Now whatever lovely view there might be is enhanced by its own opposition, cheerfully and vigorously stated: "Long live Dadaism in words and images! Long live the world's Dadaist events! To be against this manifesto means to be a Dadaist." Self-regarding and self-negating, keeping its humor good, Dada keeps it well.

As for the regard of the self, one of the most instructive texts signed by Rrose Selavy, herself already a double as we know, was written in German by a girl-friend of Man Ray, and translated into English, therein entitled, sardonically "Men before the Mirror."[2] The text in this table-turning description is cruel, as one might expect: Rrose Selavy's adopted text is not directed at a mirrored "Man," standing for all men, but at men, which is less general, more sex-specific:

> Many a time the mirror imprisons them and holds them firmly. Fascinated they stand in front. They are absorbed, separated from reality and alone with their vice, vanity . . . There they stand and stare at the landscape which is themselves, the mountains of their noses, the defiles and folds of their shoulders, hand and skin, to which the years have already so accustomed them that they no longer know how they evolved, and the multiple primeval forests of their hair. They meditate, they are content, they try to take themselves in as a whole.

Already, of course, a woman writing about these men as they are mirrored—whereas she is usually mirrored—is retracing the fascination. To complicate things further, a female speaker speaks of Marcel Duchamp playing Rrose Selavy playing at being a German girl playing at watching men watching themselves—the self-regarding game is right up Dada's alley, but only the sensitive reader will be bowled over by a direct hit: "The mirror looks at them. They collect themselves. Carefully, as if tying a cravat, they compose their features" (MS,195–6). Knowing what we know of the cravat, we are bound to find this composition slanted toward the phallic, but the very act of looking as it is seen by the other her or himself creating that self in the act of its own self-regard and self-creation should occupy the center of the gaze. Duchamp reminds us that "It is the ONLOOKERS who make the pictures" (p.173). Thus, it is scarcely necessary to point out how the reaction of a female I to some particularly aggressive images and some famous inscripted and wittily insulting images like the celebrated inscription of Lady Lisa in hot pants, whose celebration may have dulled our sensitivity, can occasionally be seen in a different frame from the one perceived by the male I—the frame, like the content, is placed there by the never passive eye.

---

[2] Marcel Duchamp, *Marchand du sel: Ecrits de Marcel Duchamp*, ed. Michel Sanouillet (Paris: Le Terrain Vague, 1958), p. 95. [MS]

As to this self-regarding self, it is rarely at ease; we remember the reflective despair of Jacques Rigaut: "I consider my most disgraceful trait to be a pitiful disposition: the impossibility of losing sight of myself as I act .... I have never lost consciousness."[3] Think, for instance, of the eye as it is kept on the eye, the I in the text, in all senses of eyes and texts. Dada, that ambivalent, bi-sexual, two-headed delight, contemplates its own visage in some of Ribemont-Dessaigne's ARTICHAUDS, hot spots for art, or really hot plates, keeping them available on the burner, like a *réchaud*, to heat and reheat, looking and not looking, in one temper now, and now another:

> Dada, o Dada, what a face! So sad as all that? So merry? Look
> at yourself in the mirror. No, no, don't look at yourself.[4]

"The eye and its eye," Ribemont-Dessaignes wanted to entitle one of his projects, "L'oeil et son oeil." Of course, what does the reader of a text do but exactly that, keeping his eye upon his own eye reading. The very uncomfortable nature of this forced look is apparently, inescapably, the contemporary text which stares back at us. Lionel Ray, who is, like Marcel Duchamp, the adopter of other personalities (formerly Robert Lorho, he is switching to still another name for his newest poetry) forces the reader to contemplate his own contemplation of the reader and of himself. Ray's rays mock our gaze, changing the textual passage into an encounter, not entirely welcome, between the author's eyebeams and our own, in some sort of *super-architextural* construction. We can have only a passive stare at this stare, and he outstares us, easily, in this narrow passage, scarcely large enough for his look and ours. The trace is vaguely Egyptian, and in one text we see the pyramid

---

3 Jacques Rigaut, *Ecrits*, ed. Martin Kay (Paris: Gallimard, 1970), p 113. Compare Duchamp's remarks on his Large Glass: "le verre m'a sauvé par sa transparence" (Pierre Cabanne, *Entretiens avec Marcel Duchamp* (Paris: Ed. Pierre Belfond, 1967, p. 22), and Raymond Roussel's in *Impressions d'Afrique* (Paris: J.-J Pauvert, 1963, p. 30–1) on his work like an "illusion de quelque sujet unique refleté par un miroir." Jeanine Plottel points this out in an article for *Le Siècle éclaté*, no. 2. (Minard, Paris)

4 Georges Ribemont-Dessaignes, *Dada: manifestes, poèmes, articles, projets* (1915–1930), textes présentés par Jean-Pierre Bégot (Paris: Projectoires/Champ Libre, 1974), p. 19. [RD]

form on the lower left—the sun as eye, the I as sun. Since the time of God, we had grown used to the contemplation of the sky and its contemplation of us, and the emblematic eye, contemplating both. But have we not always identified the seer with ourselves, included now in the seeing and seen? Accustomed as we are to keeping our eye on and in the text, the assaults upon the eye, like that of Buñuel's slashed eyeball, reminiscent of Magritte's severed red globe, read here as if the pointing finger had done an injustice to it, quite in keeping with Apollinaire's "soleil cou coupé," sends us back to Ribemont-Dessaigne's "L'oeil couchant;" for the setting eye, like some setting sun, is bound to be at once bloodshot and bedded, as it settles down.

Or again, Ribemont-Dessaigne's "oeil verbe" or "eye word" in the strong sense of that world-creating Word: it is on that globe, assuredly, that we should keep our eye. "Sous je", reads one of his titles, literally "Under I," if we can, as I think we must, profit from the English word play—the spirit of Dada including, as it does, plays in all senses and in the most uncomfortable ones, and including the game's denial, as its own mirror image. Witness Ribemont-Dessaigne's *Manifesto with Oil,* a text at play:

> Dada is no longer a game. There is no longer a game anywhere… there is one moment of the game when you play at not playing, and when it ends badly. That moment is now.
>
> The street must be sad in your eyes when you go out into it. And there must be no more consolation for you in the pit of your stomach.
>
> . . . . .
>
> But DADA knows choreography and the way to use it.
>
> . . . . .
>
> For you have to love me right through the cancer of your heart, through the heart-cancer that I shall have given you. (RD, 15–16)

Aragon's *Peasant of Paris* is also a spreader of this other sort of social disease in the *Passage of Paris*, the vertiginous poison and poisonous vertigo of "that vice called surrealism," upsetting to all stability. But DADA's choreography, subtle and unsubtle, is really supervisual as well as metaphysical, super-irritating and superb. Tzara's repeated sounds which are to start the listener yelling, as Marinetti's did, put the reader's nerves also on end:

> Car il y a des zigzags sur son âme et beaucoup de
>   rrrrrrrrrrrrr ici le lecteur commence à crier (TZ 1, 87)
> (for there are zigzags on his soul and plenty of rrrrrrrrrrrrr
>   here the reader begins to scream)

Verbal aggression, then, and visual too—the rrr on the page are fully as excruciating to the sight as they would be to the ear. The whole matter turns about the self-contemplation of the reader in the text as it frames the vision, self-conscious in its own exacerbation.

Plainly, the ideal would be a self-forgetting glance: but we are never self-forgetful. "To see yourself and overlook it's being yourself you see. But may this view on yourself stretch out and become essential before your eyes, like a measurable and synthesized landscape."[5] Here the doubling in personality becomes a tripling; my acting self, its overseer, and my further consciousness of that other look, like an overseeing overseen. The contemporary passages of the eye in the text are turned by the self-reflective vision into a confrontation: the onlooker or that other I stared at through a window: the problem is, as always, what is in and what is out, how the out relates to the in.[6] There is also a question of framing—what does the spectator face, and how does it face him, or then, us? Dada retraces its ambivalence on which the trick doors and trick mirrors, suitable to those images concerned with their own representation as well as ours, open either way, outward or inward, on either seen. As Edmond Jabès reminds us, "The inside and the outside are only the arbitrary part of the division of an infinite-time whose minute, always moving forward, calls the center constantly into question."[7]

---

5 Antonin Artaud, *Oeuvres* (Paris: Gallimard), V. 1, p. 205 [A]
6 Which is to say, outlook and inscape.
7 Edmond Jabès, *El* (Paris: Gallimard, 1973), p.31.

It is interesting, if perhaps not altogether appropriate, to remind ourselves here that the inward/outward concern, like that of a Moebius strip, is a constant: the alchemical fascination of texts written on both sides, in and out, or the vertical ambivalence of such painters as Van Eyck, whose Virgin writes her positive response to the Deity wrong side up for us, so that the sky may read it—the fascination with script and direction, with the direction of the script, is an enduring part of visual and verbal drama, as of the Dada circus.[8]

There are several obvious privileged places for the examination of the double consciousness of in and out, up and down, forwards and backwards: mirror, window, door and stair. Elsewhere I have maintained that the reason for their privilege, like the reason for the privilege of the crossroads as a place of confrontation of self and other has to do with the rites of passage which I take poetry to be.[9] Very briefly, as the anthropologists have thought us, in the words of Van Gennep and Turner, three times are clearly marked within these rites of passage or transformation: the moment of separation or the preliminary moment, the liminary moment, at the threshold between one state and another, and the moment of re-integration, in one's changed state. If we situate poetry in the middle or liminary stage, it signals adequately the equal importance of the outlook and that telescoping of the inner landscape which we might call the inscape: the viewing line alters with the direction outward or inward, up or down. For example, the multiple stairs, visual and verbal, which mark the change of status, of literary pace and of perception, often signify the decent in one's own mind and into its depths: the most famous example is of course Duchamp's remodeling of Laforgue's ascending motion in "Encore à cet astre" and then his *Nude Descending the Staircase.* (PLATE 1) which he describes as a great step to

---

[8] Michel Butor comments on the Van Eyck *Annunication* in *Les Mots dans la peinture* (Geneva: Skira, 1969), p. 135.

[9] Arnold Van Gennep, *Les Rites du passage* (Paris: Nourry, 1909); Victor Turner, *Drama, Fields, and Metaphors* (Ithaca: Cornell, 1974). See also our "Poème du passage," *Cahiers de l' Association Internationale des Etudes françaises* (Paris: Collège de France, 1978)

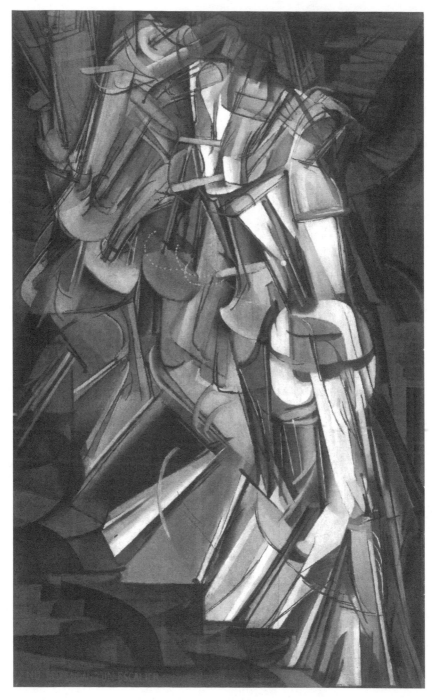

1. *Nu Descendant un Escalier (Nude Descending a Staircase No. 2)*, 1912. Oil on canvas. The Louise and Walter Arensberg Collection, 1950. The Philadelphia Museum of Art / Art Resource, NY.

the Large Glass: thus the stair and the mirror combine their two privileged passages whose conjunction reaches from Mallarmé's *Igitur* and T.S. Eliot's conscious reading of Laforgue to the celebrated surrealist conjunctions and constellations of Breton, Leiris, and Desnos.[10]

Now, in the instruction we take as a guide for the passage of the self from perception to perception, we might do worse than listen to Shakespeare:

The play's the thing wherein to catch the conscience...

Everyman a king, as it were. Furthermore, the play of images and themes and language can only be sharpened in its nuance and strengthened by exercise. The reader devoted to a passage poetics will re-read Mallarmé, for instance— the textual father of us all—working backwards as well as forwards. Not just from Mallarmé to what he fathered, Duchamp's Dada, Breton's surrealism, the so-called metaphysical poetry of Bonnefoy and the musings of Jabès, but also getting from the present back to him.

---

[10] Wallace Fowlie, in his *Mallarmé* (Chicago: University of Chicago, 1953), pp. 118–19, likens Igitur's stairs to a "graphic representation of the recurrent beats (of the heart as of the clock)." The best example of mirror and stair combined is perhaps Breton's "Je rêve je te vois superposée" ("I dream I see you indefinitely superimposed upon yourself"), where the image of the lady seated before her mirror "in its first crescent" is transposed to the image of a child at the top of the stairs and then to the god Shiva; Michel Leiris' *Aurora* opens with a slow, thirty page descent of a set of stairs, and Robert Desnos' "Pour un rêve du jour" ("For a dream of day") begins with a sphinx ascending and then descending the staircase, whereas his "Idée fixe" ("Obsession") seats a lady before her mirror to receive the tribute of the sea. Since he claimed each poem as part of one great poem, we might, without stretching a point, treat these images as converging. In each case mentioned, the other great image of the arrangement of hair takes primary role: Aragon, Breton, and Desnos ensconce their ladies before a mirror, a sort of Great Glass in which to fix their hair, and in each case the association is made with water ("the water wing of your comb," insists Breton, and Desnos' algae are brought to the mirrored lady from the very depth of the sea, that other crystal responding to the mirror.) The homage is then made from water to frozen water, if we take the baroque view. Aragon's *Anicet* (from 1921) combines the threshold of perception, the mirrored image, and the rivulets of hair matching the wetter ones in a particularly forceful way.

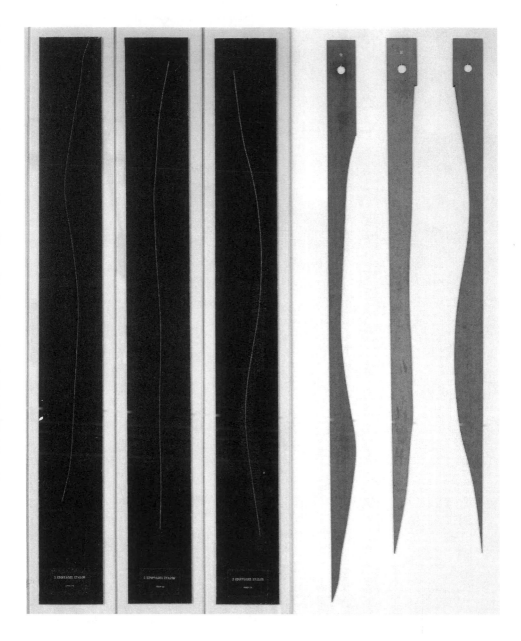

2. Marchel Duchamp, *3 Stoppages Étalon (3 Standard Stoppages)*, Paris 1913–1914. Assemblage: three threads glued to three painted canvas strips, each mounted on a glass panel; three wood slates, shaped along one edge to match the curves of the threads; the whole fitted into a wood box. Katherine S. Dreier Bequest (149.1953). The Museum of Modern Art, New York, USA. Digital Image © The Museum of Modern Art / Licensed by SCALA / Art Resource, NY.

Contemplating Marcel Duchamp's *Stoppages Étalon* (PLATE 2), those strings pasted where they fall, we might wish to trace those lines back to the original throw of the dice and those constellations of the page and the mind which haunt us all: "Briefly," said Mallamé, and no one is briefer, "in an act where chance is in play, chance accomplishes its own idea in affirming or negating itself."[11]

For Igitur, that other Hamlet, a white lace ruff—*dentelles* where the *dent* or tooth of conscience, some agenbite of inwit separates thinking head from black-costumed body—Igitur contemplating his mirror at once obliged to stare at his figure so as not to doubt himself, yet wishing himself away: "the purity of the mirror will be established, without this personage, this vision of myself." (M,439) We might trace our steps back, perceiving the Data temperament in a time before and as through some Large Glass (PLATE 3), not too darkly. We might then perceive that the Duchampian delay in glass, that *retard en verre* caught us before in another *vers* or verse, like another image mirrored in another page. The mind then moves from that empty Mallarméan mirror, horribly nul and "frozen in its cold" like some other lake where some other swan is caught: from this baroque image, as of a living water changed by ice by its *ennui*, his inopportune face will disappear, and yet we see it replayed in the drama of Hérodiade in her staring purity, her most sensual virginity self-exposed and self-wounding. "The Cornet," we read in *Igitur*, "is the Horn of the unicorn" (M,441)—and just so, from the shake of the dice in the single horn, the play on which Duchamp based his own Great Work, there arise these two figures now before our gaze, Hamlet's dark-clothed "*latent lord who cannot become*" (M,300) and Hérodiade's pallor, each taking shape before the mirror of Mallarmé, surrounded as we know by the figures of unicorns, those most ambiguous beasts, animals of poetic passage. For the unicorn, captured only by the virgin, wounds his captor; the balm lies only in the powder from that horn. The "fraise arachnéenne" itself, like the rose at the base of the stag's antler, makes the horn the transposing element here by way of the unicorn in the passage from Virgin to Bride.

And does not the severed head of John the Baptist, Mallarmé's "Precursor," lying on its platter, respond by some inner glance to the severed head of *Igitur*, distanced and displaced by the white ruff? The transforming and

---

[11] Stephane Mallarmé, *Oeuvres complètes* (Paris: Gallimard, ed. Pléiade, 1945), p 439.

3. *La Mariée Mise à nu par ses Célibataires, Même (Le Grand Verre) (The Bride Stripped Bare by Her Bachelors, Even) (The Large Glass)*, 1915–23. Oil, varnish, lead foil, lead wire, and dust on two glass panels. Bequest of Katherine Dreier, 1952. Philadelphia Museum of Art, Philadelphia, Pennsylvania, USA. Art Resource, NY.

tempermental look works a metamorphosis in each mind best demonstrated by Mallarmé, himself the truest Precursor, changing as he did the *fiole de verre,* that poison vial of glass, into a vile poison of the verse, that other *ver* where Valéry will stress yet another *ver* or worm to eat at the entire body of literature and thought. As Mallarmé changed his *fiole* into *folie,* Igitur's *Folie* becomes the reader's, being itself the Foolish Virgin of the Passage, the proud vessel that bears on to Breton's passionate vision of forever communicating vessels, and of a Nadja whose clairvoyance we would share: Nadja as reader of the modern text. Nadja passes, then, through Duchamp's door as if it were in fact a "porte battante," beating like the pulse of a heart at the center of perception. Nadja as perfect spectator for the Large Glass, which can be looked through or at or in, Nadja, in short, reflected in the opaque mirror of the *Noces d' Hérodiade,* seeking her own passage.

If Duchamp's door at 27 rue Larrey, open from one side and clearly closed from the other, disputes Musset's door of the well known title, which has to be closed or open ("Il faut qu'une porte soit ouverte ou fermée"), it is also a good example of the communicating vessels of perception and the sensitivity they necessarily awake in us.

The poem is aptly called "Le Contrefacteur," that is, a forger or "faussaire," or by extension a person going against the facts or "faits," or then a counter-mailman; it ends with Aragon's name signed inside out, written backwards, "in white letters on the door."

On lit à peu près sur la porte
Les lettres blanches retournées[12]

ИOꟼAЯA ꙄIUOⵏ

You can just make out on the door
The white letters turned around

ИOꟼAЯA ꙄIUOⵏ

It appears impossible to tell which way we are meant to be looking. For instance, from outside we might see through the glass door to the reverse

---

[12] Louis Aragon, *Le Mouvement Perpétuel* (Paris: *Poésie*/Gallimard, 1925).

side of the name, which appears right way round to the poet inside, who would be on the other side from us: the text, as such, would be written uniquely for him, so that we would be privileged to see only its backward trace. Or then he sees the reversal of what is written for the outside. Or still again, the door on which it is written could be a swinging door ("*une porte battante*") a door leading in an ambiguous direction, as in one of Duchamp's visual games, already mentioned, where the door looks open or closed depending on the observer's situation. Now in the latter example, the material support strongly suggested is a Dada object potentially double-directed. But "Le Contrefacteur" is itself in fact a two-faced text of a passage totally ambiguous, revealing the opposite of what a postman would see, that is, the opposite of a name outside, straight-side up, legible: its opening is complicated, as it looks out *or* in. Duchamp's large Glass forms of course the summit for such perceptive training of perception: its multiple complexity of meaning has the depth and brilliance of a Mallarmé text, *Igitur*, or *Les Noces d' Hérodiade*, pictured from both sides. The mirroring device puts, in fact, things as they may be: this Hamlet/Hérodiade "mis(e)-à-nu" like Mallarmé's own "vice, mis à nu," exposed, exhibited, and extraordinary.

The mirror questions even our own identity: this is the liminal stage of doubt for the passenger of the rites, whose humiliation precedes his purification. Ribemont-Dessaignes, in a completely different tone, but a not unrelated strain, poses an *identical* question, in an essay called, precisely, "Identity":

> Philosophy identity reduces us to mathematical identity.
> Chair = Chair
> 17 = 17
>
> —That is to say an object whose characteristics are enumerated is assimilated to a number or to a series of numbers.
>
>   . . . . .
>
> —To judge things in that way you have to start by assuming: Such a character is equal to such a character. And as in mathematical identity reduce all equality to
>   1 = 1
> Which is to day to return to the conception of unity. (RD, 130–32)

And so on. Which passage is to be compared with a passage from Ribemont-Dessaigne's *L'Empereur de Chine (The Emperor of China)*:

> There are between two and three many other numbers.
> Squaring them gives you a result
> Larger than four and less than nine.
> It's a mysterious world which is not measurable, and
> which is used to measure that which is not measurable.[13]

Although in a very dull disguise, this concern with identity and self measurement is in fact a good part of the vital leap which, says Tzara, is called thought: "le salto vitale s'appelle Pensée." (TZ, 281) Not a leap of death or of faith, but of life—that humor set in philosophical motion and self-examination and self-doubt, of which *Approximate Man* is undoubtedly the greatest, that incomplete novel haunted by heads called *Place your Bets* (1923) is a good bet, and a moving one. Full of doubt, as to the writing, even, the narrator laments his inability to step outside the self, or to judge himself more independently. That

> Is sufficient for me to detest myself, for me to despise my
> egoism. I am lacking a distance between the characters and
> the events they give rise to. My criticism is not objective.
> My readers will never be able to follow me. (TZ, 288)

What is this but a contemplation in the mirror of his own writing? That the woman in the text should be called "Mania," a sort of transformation of a "manie" or obsession predicting Breton's own *Nadja,* whose obsessive vision inspires our reading of Breton, is not without its own obsessive interest. The entire text of the unentire novel is based on the substitution and the repetition of self and other self, and of the fatigue of the reflective game:

> Although visibly false, this adventure excited me to such a
> degree (doubt had already substituted another myself for my
> own) that I left to see her . . . .

---

[13] Editor's note in RD, p. 132.

But distance had already withered my passion. For the first
time I felt fatigue and boredom inhibit the flow of my speech.
. . . . .
We, the knights of the double-self . . . (Tz 1,290)

This double self, here a tragic one, is referred to in an early passage of *The
Antihead* as a sort of Rimbaud parody:

Je m'appelle maintenant tu.
Je suis meublée et maison de Paris.
. . . . .
Maison de Paris, je suis très belle.
Bien imprimée.
. . . . .
Monsieur Aa L' antiphilosophe Je-Tu tue, affirme de
plus en plus que, sans ailes, sans dada, il est comme
il est, que voulez-vous. . . . (Tz, 2,399)

(I am now called you.
I am furnished and a Parisian house.
. . . . .
As a Parisian house, I am very lovely.
Well printed.
. . . . . Mr. Aa the antiphilosopher I-You yous, kills,
affirms more and more that, without wings,
without her, without dada, he is as he is,
what can I tell you. . . .)

And yet, the knight of the double countenance, like Kirkegaard's solitary
knight of faith, here leads the game, just as Tzara did in his early role of cir-
cus-tamer. "De mes maux qu'on m'a fait subir," says the narrator of *Place your
Bets* which reads: "Of the sufferings I have had to undergo/I am the elegant
inspirer"—or then, and I believe we should read it both ways: "Of my words
I am the elegant lover," for that animateur, returning to us the *animal* with
the *anima* is also an *amateur*. And then, seated around a gaming table, Marcel
Duchamp's multiplicity plays in the same multiple league. . . . From mirror

to gaming table, then, from the double self to the self multiplied as the dice are thrown: Mallarmé too is seated around Duchamp's table. . . . [14]

A psychological parallel to this double or multiple billing of one name and one visage exists in the numerous references of Aragon, Breton, but particularly Tzara, to the man masked, and perpetually ambivalent, the tragic hero, mirrored in his double role as narrator and actor. It is plain that the other question raised by this game of double perception is one of identity, of mask and of approximate relation: Tzara's approximate man, who "laughs face on and weeps behind," touching as he is brilliant—like the poem itself—raises his doubts facing others or on that place of passage which is the stair:

> Tu es en face des autres un autre toi-même
> sur l'escalier des vagues comptant de chaque regard la trame
> dépareillées hallucinations sans voix qui te ressemblent
> les boutiques de bric-à-brac qui te ressemblent
> que tu cristallises autour de ta pluvieuse vocation—
>   où tu decouvres
> —des parcelles de toi-même
> à chaque tournant de rue tu te changes en un autre toi-
>   même
>
> (facing others you are another than yourself
> judging on the staircase of waves the texture of each look
> dissimilar voiceless hallucinations that resemble you
> the boutiques of bric-à-brac that resemble you
> that you crystallize around your rainy calling—where you
>   find portions of yourself
> at each turn of the road you change into another self)[15]

---

[14] "Knights of the Double Self: Duchamp and Tzara, Laforgue and Mallarmé" in my *Eye in the Text: Essays on Perception, Mannerist to Modern* (Princeton, 1981).

[15] Translation from Mary Ann Caws, *Approximate Man & Other Writings* (Detroit: Wayne State, 1973, p. 53. Boston: Black Widow Press, 2005, p. 34)

4. Marcel Duchamp, *Étant Données: 1ᵉ la Chute d'eau, 2ᵉ le Gaz d'éclairage (Given: 1. The Waterfall, 2. The Illuminating Gas)*. Mixed-media assemblage: wooden door, bricks, velvet, wood, leather stretched over an armature of metal, twigs, aluminum, iron, glass, Plexiglas, linoleum, cotton, electric lights, gas lamp (Bec Auer type), motor, etc. Gift of the Cassandra Foundation, 1969. The Philadelphia Museum of Art, Philadelphia, Pennsylvania, USA. Art Resource, NY.

In the realm of the stair, the crossroads, or the circus ring of the page, or the game, around the window or the table, upon the canvas or in the mirror of a great Glass and a Great Work, be it alchemical labor, epic poem, or the lyric life, the animator of the circus leaves his mark on every passage, which is to say, at every threshold of perception and passion:

> mais que la porte s'ouvre enfin comme la première page
>> d'un livre
>
> ta chambre plein d'indomptables d'amoureuses coincidences
>> tristes ou gaies
>
> Je couperai en tranches le long filet du regard fixe
>
> et chaque parole sera un envoûtement pour l'oeil et de
>> page en page
>
> mes doigts connaitront la flore de ton corps et de page en
>> page
>
> de na nuit la secrète étude s'éclaircira et de page en page
>
> les ailes de ta parole me seront éventails et de page en page
>
> des éventails pour chasser la nuit de ta figure et de page
>> en page
>
> ta cargaison de paroles au large sera ma guerison et de
>> page en page
>
> les années diminueront vers l'impalpable souffle que la tombe
> aspire déjà. (Tz, 2, 99)

> (But let the door open at last like the first page of a book
>
> your room full of unconquerable loving coincidences
>> sad or gay
>
> I shall slice the long net of the fixed gaze
>
> and each word will be a spell for the eye and from
>> page to page
>
> my fingers will know the flora of your body and from page
>> to page
>
> the secret study of your night will be illumined and from
>> page to page
>
> the wings of your word will be fans to me and from
>> page to page

fans to chase the night from your face and from page to
  page
your cargo of words at sea will be my cure and from
  page to page
the years will diminish towards the impalpable breath
that the tomb already draws in) (AP, 83)

These pages of Tzara, themselves sufficient as a landscape, reflect the truest temper of Dada, and our truest text of that movement. That the *page* should be so plainly part of, and such an essential part of the *paysage* and that they should be part of the *passage* as it is part of them, is an unmistakable truth *identical to itself,* in whatsoever mirror we might choose to see ourselves and our text: "De vastes paysages s'étendent en moi sans étonnement," says Tzara in *L'Antitête,* (Tz, 1,349) "Vast landscapes stretch out in me without astonishment." Toward these interior landscapes Duchamp also directed himself, his thought and his surest contemplation and art—"My aim was turning inward rather than towards externals" (Ms, 11) . . . "Dada was a metaphysical attitude."

Thus the closed door of his *Étant données,* the great door of the given, as we might phrase it, is in fact itself the equivalent of that door window Aragon so admired in Matisse, in the concentration it forces on the eyes of the beholder, forced into the position of Peeping-Tom or peeping-reader, his view necessarily framed, concentrated through small holes pierced, upon the parts exhibited is itself part related to whole and the question of identity of perception and of passion—this door is the perfect example of what opens on an inner landscape and what frames a privileged inner seen.

Let us end our own scene here by a metaphysical paradox: what hides most is the most revealing. Remembering Artaud's paradoxical description of a state outside ordinary life, we could see as equivalent to the Dada temper, we take it as sign and as sight, as reminder of the text as a liminal state of removal and threshold, of the viewer as a passenger in Dada's right of passage. "There are no words to designate it but a vehement hieroglyph designating the impossible encounter of matter and spirit. A kind of vision inside. . . ." Here that quotation also may be left as incomplete, as the text of our own *architexture* is decidedly incomplete, its passage left forever open to the reader.[16] The latter's own outlook in its chosen obsession, often interdependent with its intensity, may be seen to merge with the multiple perspectives offered by the inward sight: behind all the closed doors, an open imagination—and still concealed in the passionate mystery of those vehement Dada hieroglyphics whose signs lead in and out to an unending perception.

---

[16] For the term "architexture," see my "Vers une architexture du poème surréaliste," in *Ethique et Esthétique de la littérature française du XXe Siècle* (Stanford University Press, 1977). See also, however, Tzara's great essay on hats and style in *Le Minotaure*, 3–4 ("D'un Certain Automatisme de goût," where he advocates an inter-uterine architecture: there the standard term applies).

NOTES to
APPROXIMATE MAN

The following parts of *Approximate Man* appeared before the publication of the entire work, although in some cases, the versions are quite different.

Part I: in *La Revue européenne,* June, 1928.

Part III: in *Les Feuilles libres,* no. 39, March–April, 1925.

Part V: in *La Vie des lettres et des arts,* no. 21, n.d. [1925].

Part XI, except last two lines: in *L'Espirit nouveau,* no. 1, January 1, 1927.

Part XVI: in *Orbes,* no. 2, Spring, 1929.

Part XIX: in *La Revue surréaliste,* December 15, 1929.

Part III, probably written before the other eighteen sections, is nearest in conception to the starting point for the entire poem. The center (*noyau*) of that conception is the brief poem "Approximation" (*Travelers' Tree,* 1923), a highly sentimental statement on the uncertainty, loneliness, and imcomprehensibility of man and his actions. Here certain key terms of the final epic already appear: "the unlimited why of your actions," "approximately," "illegible" (essential for its implications about language), "awkward," and "simulacra" (referring to the human comportment as uncertain, approximate, uneasy, and therefore false). The version appearing in *Les Feuilles libres* in 1925 is four times as long. Considered a complete poem by Tzara, it too is marked by banal and sentimental passages. A comparison of these passages with the final version shows Tzara's efforts at poetic concision and at creating images impressive in their emotional or unusual vision.

1925 version

remplir de *faits* chaque minute sans interruption
     ni *trou*
je *suce* l'aigre *bonbon* de ce que je ne comprendrai
     jamais   (a)

———

la mort est parmi nous est notre hôte ses signes
     sont parmi nous

dans les magasins de chaussures aux sourires *vernis*
dans les salles de concert *l'oreille* s'agrandit
      guette   (b)

———————

chez les coiffeurs tu te laisses soigner la tête
      inerte
sortant du linceuil provisoire prends garde que
      les doigts
du coiffeur n'effleurent la masse gélatineuse
      du cerveau le cauchemar   (c)

———————

mais le jour recommence couleur de fertiles
      espoirs   (d)

———————

le mauvais temps vomi abondamment par *les tristes*
      et célestes gueules   (e)

———————

mais passons car la respiration me manque le trait
      de ma plume est trop court
dans les librairies arbres de sagesse de prétention
      de fiel d'approximation
incalculable floraison *de souvenirs dans les*
      bibliothèques
chez *les cultivateurs froment de la chair*
se croisent les bras *des légumes et ceux des*
      fruits   (f)

1930 version

combler de *frayeur* chaque minute sans interruption
      ni *hâte*
je *bois* l'aigre *terreur* de ce que . . . (a^1)

———————

dans les magasins de chaussures aux sourires *roussis*
      avec le temps

dans les salles de concert *le cyprès* s'agrandit
        guette   (b^1)

_____

chez le coiffeur tu laisses *choir* la tête inerte
        et la neige
sortant du linceuil provisoire prends garde que
        les mains du cerveau
n'effleurent la mass gélatineuse du cauchemar   (c^1)

_____

mais le jour recommence couleur de fertiles
        logarithmes (d^1)

_____

le mauvais temps abondamment vomi par *le désert du*
        haut de ses tertres de nuit   (e^1)

_____

[reduced to:]
incalculable floraison de haine sur *les vaisseaux*
        fanés
chez *les solitaires désabusés sévère froment*
se croisent les bras *les lianes et les*
        édifices   (f^1)

1925 version

stuff with *facts* each moment without break
        or *gap*
I *suck* the acid *candy* of what I shall never
        understand   (a)

_____

death is among us is our guest its signs are
        among us
in the stores with *polished* smiles
in the concert halls the *ear* grows watches   (b)

_____

at the hairdresser's you let your lifeless head
      be cared for
emerging from the daily winding sheet
      take care that *the fingers*
of the hairdresser don't graze the gelatinous
      mass of the *brain* the nightmare   (c)

———

but the day begins again color of fertile
      hopes   (d)

———

the bad weather vomited at length by *the sad and*
   · *celestial mouths* (e)

———

but let us go on for I lack breath the line
      my pen draws is too short
in the bookshops trees of knowledge of pretention
      of gall of approximation
incalculable flowering of *memories in libraries*
with *the farmers wheat of flesh*
the arms *of vegetables and of fruits* are folded   (f)

1930 version

fill with *fright* each moment without break
      or *haste*
I *drink* the acid *terror* of what I shall never
      understand (a^1)

———

in the stores with *time-scorched* smiles
in the concert halls the *cypress* grows watches (b^1)

———

at the hairdresser's you let your head *fall* lifeless
      and the snow

◄

emerging from the daily winding sheet
    take care that *the brain's hands*
don't graze the gelatinous mass of *nightmare*   (c^1)

———

but the day begins again color of fertile
    logarithms (d^1)

———

bad weather spat out copiously by *the desert*
    from the summit of its hills of night (e^1)

———

[reduced to:]
incalculable flowering *of hatred on the faded ships*
among the *disillusioned lonely ones harsh wheat*
the *creepers and the buildings* fold their arms (f^1)

These comparisons only exemplify certain types of changes in images, that is, in the *spectacle* of language. There are equally striking changes in rhythm, occasionally toward the jerky or the incomplete, in accord with the approximate and incomplete nature of man and with the pathetically partial scope of his vision: for example in the phrases "little milk little sugar little," or "without bitterness without commitment without regret without," or "and may the cherry," or again: "if I lose my place it is that I." In many of these cases, the next lines originally continued the thought, but the poet inserts irrelevant lines so that these fragments can be seen as *fragments*. At other times, the writing is definitely altered toward a grander tone in keeping with the overall destiny of man, marvelous as well as miserable. As an illustration of the latter, the changes in the final line of the poem as it is worked out step by step are illuminating. In the first instance, the line read "selon les balbutiantes modulations d'esprit que ton coeur s'amuse à reconnaître parmi les fougeuses salves de frayeurs" ("according to the stammering modulations of mind that your heart amuses itself recognizing among the fiery salvoes of frights"). The four main changes are all toward the heroic. The stage is changed from the purely human and emotional (mind, fright) to the great traditional backdrop for heroic action: hell and stars; from the frivolous enjoyment of listening to the indication of effort in all its gravity ("wear out"); and finally, from the merely spectacular ("fiery") to the summit of cosmic intoxication, where the vertiginous salutes remind us of the ideals of surrealist vertigo.

[In the following annotations, the Roman numerals refer to the nineteen parts of the entire poem; the second number applies to the stanza separated in the test by asterisks; the third is the line within the stanza.]

I. The part appeared in much the same form in *La Revue européenne* except for 5.20, which read *les couleurs nous nourrissent* ("the colors nourish us").

I.1.4–6. Emphasis by repetition on the theme of language. This technique which Tzara frequently uses is itself a negation of the completeness of human speech, as if it were not sufficient to speak once.

I.2.1–2. See Tzara's remarks in the "Note on Poetry" concerning the poet's cruelty toward his language, "in order to find the true necessity; from this asceticism order will blossom, essential and pure." By the reversals of conception characteristic of Dada, language is also *necessarily* cruel toward the poet. This is the same notion of *order* on which Artaud bases his theater of cruelty: "I use the word cruelty in the sense of appetite for life, of cosmic rigor and implacable necessity . . . " Letter to Jean Paulhan, November 14, 1932, quoted in Antonin Artaud, *Oeuvres complètes* (Paris: NRF, 1964), 4: 122.

I.5.2–8. The interior clothing of care with its useless and perplexing ornamentation in these lines will be transformed in the final section into garments of stone, as this initial baptism by water leads to the final purification by fire.

I.5. last two lines. An odd play on the ordinary image of dreaming by the fireside. The word which we formed is now more active and more real than we are.

1.6.10. The unfinished line is appropriate to notions of death, departure, and irrationality ("without cause").

I.7.3. Like the tune of death man carries in him, the sound participates in the theme of language. The negative images, frozen, bruised, and dropped are associated with linguistic impotence.

I.8.3–7. The multiplicity and variety characteristic of Dada's atmosphere of "abundance."

II.3. After the initial darkness (storm, gloom, black, and anguish) and the poet's plea for peacefulness ("let the old pipe . . . be smoked, let the roofs be kept smoking"), the passage ends in clarity and tranquillity. A good example of the interior progression and rhythm of the poem.

II.3.1. In the typed version and proofs, there appeared an additional phrase: *valises d'hommes et de* ("suitcases of men and of"). This literal spelling-out of the image with its unrhythmical awkwardness was dropped between the proofs and the printing. Often the character of the final epic depends on just such an ellipsis.

II.3.2. In the proofs, the adjective "disparate" appears with "intentions." The qualifier added little and its elimination places the emphasis on the collectivity.

II.3.3. In proofs, the line read: "the flood as it gnaws the footsteps"; Tzara again moves away from the literal.

II.4.7. The common and suppressed source of the waltz and the head is the circular shape which both suggest. In *Place Your Bets* Tzara mentions automatic writing as the exercise of unpacking one's heart, that is, as an attempt to display all that was heretofore hidden. The heart keeps its contents packed in a portable form; the waltz depends on movement, as does the journey, and so on. These round images lead directly to the ball-shaped forms, the round gesture of the hands, and the men singing rounds under the bridges.

11.4.8–12, and 15–17. A series of cold images followed by a series of warm ones (fire, fur, rekindle). Many lines of the poem are linked in this way, so that the seemingly heterogeneous images show, on a second glance, progressions, modifications, and contrasts.

II.6.1. See commentary on the roundness of the offering gesture above (II.4.7); it can be seen as foreshadowing the later fullness or *plénitude*.

II.7.3. A complicated image of the artist effacing his first conception as his falseness effaces genuine lines of chance. As artificiality is contrasted with real endowments and actions, the artist who has the ability to rub out errors but who also soils what he touches is contrasted with the beneficent angel who grants success and fortune.

11.7.5–6. Recurring theme of language and its structure (knots, frame, scaffoldings) as it is destroyed ("undoes," "helter-skelter").

II.8.12. Before "carcasses," the adjective "heavy" was eliminated, since the bestial labor suffices to convey the weight.

II.8.14. Between "whiteness" and "immaculate," the word "virgin" was eliminated, the image of the virginal having already been suggested.

III. The opening lines of Part III pose a question about the meaning of generation, and many of the following sections are concerned with the passage of time and the loss of youth (discolored coins, dusty legends, man tired and "wrinkled to the soul"). The last section moves from the admission of personal falsity and incompleteness to the acceptance of universal order and the conclusion is a response to the question and to the lament. Order is as important to Dada as enthusiasm.

III.1.1. In the first printed version, the line began with "who"; the sense was clearer.

III.4.20–21. Originally the line "everybody eats all he wants" was followed by "the dishes of the imagination are washed with coarse words which soothe." The elimination of the excessively literal is particularly noticeable in connection with the theme of language.

III.6.4. Originally began: "garnished with poetry," then changed to "of ecchymosis" before the final shortening. The poet's impulse often seems to be a personal reference, which he then transforms into a less pleasing image, or which he eliminates altogether.

III.6.14. Instead of "lotuses," this read "lies" in the first version; the idea of lying was completed then by the image of covering. In line 23, the crickets were originally "resignations." In both cases the emotional content was suppressed.

III.6.30–34. In the first version appeared a long, rambling but quite beautiful passage on the subject of the poet's breath and his writing being too short, on the wisdom to be found in libraries and bookstores, on the theme of approximation, and on that of peace.

IV.1.2–3. A good instance of suggestion, reversal, and ellipsis. Doubting Thomas touching the wound is the probable starting point for this image.

IV.2.1. An image vivid like the strawberry on the lips in the preceding lines: the washing hangs, like upside-down flames, twisting irrationally in the wind like a drunken tongue licking the air.

IV.2.2–3. The beardless road seems to bear the same relation to the pram and the white linen (youth, baby carriage, diapers) as does the bearded forest and the hairy tree stump like a clenched fist to the adult world of virility and determination. In lines 15 and 16 the contraries meet, beardless road and forest.

IV.3.8–16. Time tarnishes the clarity so highly valued by the Dadaists and the surrealists. The crutches, the stammering, and the past weeping are further images of the imperfection that haunts the poem, to which the refrain "sleep sleep" brings a momentary consolation.

IV.3.14. Originally, a "heavy look," but the heaviness is already implied in the foot of death crushing the living being.

IV.4.14. This "cloud" was changed at one point to "hieroglyph" and back, another instance of suppression that does not interfere with the importance of the obsession with writing and language.

IV.5.9. The extension of this line in the detailed description to "in long scales memory" is finally omitted, but the strongest word ("scales," *pellicules* in French) is saved for future use, a frequent process.

IV.8.2. "Monstrous" was originally the weaker adjective "sinister," which was less appropriate also the theme of birth.

IV.8.3. The words missing in the final version are not crossed out in the typed version of the proofs found in the Fonds Doucet: *l'inquiet hasard et la clé* ("uneasy chance and the key"). Since this is often the case, we might suppose that another set of proofs existed.

V.1.4. The line once read "along your furtive pleats spring the tree weeps its resin into the winding sheet." The references to secrecy and death no doubt seemed excessively melodramatic. For another passage on spring associated with sickness and death, see the poem "Spring" in the *Twenty-Five Poems.*

V.2.1. The image of the medicine label pasted flat against the pharmacy bottles recurs repeatedly, beginning with the *Twenty-Five Poems.*

V.2.5. This line read: *se profile à l'horizon en cavalcade d'anges de bêtes et de têtes* ("in profile on the horizon the cavalcade of angels animals and heads"). Notice the rhyme *bêtes* and *têtes.* But the simple procession is changed to the announcement of disaster, as the verbs of catastrophe, "shatter" and "crumbles," replace the neutrality of the former spectacle.

V.3.8. The damp forehead of the earth was formerly a damp fruit: Tzara here turns his vision toward a sort of cosmic unity of man and nature.

V.3.9. Here an exaggerated "far far so far" was simplified.

V.3.10. The humble obsessions (*humbles hantises*) were originally humble caresses, more ordinary and no more touching.

V.4.2. Presumably the cloths are winding-sheets left behind in the open tomb at Easter.

V.5.3. The original image was far less striking: the carafe simply filled up with water's clarity.

V.5.4. The original version, where the grass was described as weaving its stained glass window (*l'herbe tisse*), is less impressive than the final one, which provides assonance and a greater complexity, as the glass is literally braided by the grass (*l'herbe tresse*). Quite unusually, this line rhymes with line 5 and 7: "l'herbe tresse son vitrail . . . " "l'herbe offre . . . le détail," and *mon souterrain travail.*

V.6.3. Instead of the original image of the air electrified with radios, it is energized with another image of language. The end of this section is greatly changed.

V.8.15. In two preliminary versions, the crystalline image was contrasted here with blackness, but the final poem turns toward the images of fire and transparency.

VI.1.7. Originally the line read "Outside and white," to refer to the preceding line; but a spelling error led from *et* to *est*, thus the reading: "outside is white."

VI.2. end. The surprising "gargle of cloud" (*gargarisme de nuage*) comes from the verb gargarise used in the first version: "whose white outside gargles with clouds."

VI.4.11. The image, related to one four lines before on the same page, is that of fish caught in nets when they swim upstream. Likewise man finds himself trapped when he attempts to return to his youth.

VI.5.15. Omitted after this line is a reminiscence of the direct fashion in which the poet addressed us and himself at the time of Dada: "that's not the way you make poetry, he says."

VI.6.7–9. These first two lines formerly connected with the explanation: "I was stronger . . . " But the line which now divides the interrupted sentence from its completion was added in the manuscript in order to interrupt the flow. This procedure of deliberate rupture can often be observed in Tzara's editing of the manuscript.

VII.1.1–5. These lines of loneliness and exhaustion (the sparse grass, the night wearing thin, the hair whitened, the child weeping, and the ravaged blackness) set the melancholy scene for the self-examination to take place within this section and for the return to childhood and the memory in lines 24 through 31. See note to VI.4.11.

VII.1.29–30. An example of the indefinable but unmistakable tone by which we recognize Tzara in his most lyric moments.

VII.2.5–10. The self-questioning lines lead directly to the image of the grown child haunting the man, the child invisible and not wholly comprehensible, bearing as he does only fragments of "temporary meaning."

VII.4.7. The mind no longer knowing itself is the prelude to a further examination of verbal weakness in VII.5.7-9 and of our own inability to be certain of anything at all; the pathetic interrogation in VII.5.14 and 15: "what do we know of them," echoes throughout the poem, which is, after all, a poem of only approximate knowledge.

VII. conclusion. Similar in tone to T. S. Eliot's *Ash Wednesday* (1930), as are some other passages: "peace on the outside of this world . . . and on so many others and on so many others" (23–2–7), for instance, and the final refrain: "and stony in my garments of schist/I have pledged my waiting . . ." (which also reminds us, even in its images of rock and fire, of *The Waste Land*).

VIII.1. in general. Note the repetitions of conscious vision and introspection: "I remember . . . I remember . . . I saw . . . I saw . . . I saw," leading to the withdrawal in the next part: "I drew back . . . and I kept watch . . . ." Silence is here a surer route to knowledge than is speech: "and man was growing under the wing of silence."

VIII.1.1–7. In spite of the menacing imagery of blood, soil, disappointment, and broken mirrors at the beginning of this section, the youthful spirit of Dada always returns, at least in memory, to its initial atmosphere of radiance and explosions (lines 25–29, 40, 42–43, 50).

VIII.1.71. The hopeless image of the falling bird is frequent in Tzara; see the note to XI.1 in general.

VIII.2.35–38. The naiveté of language cannot appreciate the wisdom gained by the "disillusioning experiments" (see line 30) which approximate man has had to make. It is a short step from here to silence as it settles on nature and on man at the conclusion of this part.

IX.1.5. The line was longer and therefore awkward: "he struggles and spits and tears himself away and shrieks and bites and runs and stops." The last four verbs were removed.

IX.1.11–12. The wish for random scattering is another form of mental approximation, here aimed against the poet's own grave timidity.

IX.1.15. Here, *lumière ambulante* ("walking light") was changed, probably for reasons of rhythm and to avoid the stiffness of the more pedantic verb.

IX.2.5. An interior echo in French: "et les nuages là-bas se *couvrent* d'ailes qui *couvent*."

IX.2.7. To avoid the excessive and unpleasant aural repetition, *pluie aujourd'hui* ("rain today") was changed to *neige* ("snow").

IX.3.1. The omnipresent themes of approximation, doubling, hypocrisy.

IX.3.2. Originally, the poet pictured himself as afraid; then the phrase *me fait peur* was changed to *me fait mal* ("hurts me"), that is, from the emotional to the physical.

IX.3.3. In the too literal image *les rangs des agents de dieu* ("the rows of god's policemen") the policemen were removed.

IX.3.4. The image of the white gloves comes from the policemen (see preceding note).

IX.4.1. The "scales" (*pellicules*) here retain the image eliminated from IV.5.9.

IX.9 to end. These celebrated passages of the wolf and the shepherd show the lofty and moving qualities of psalm and litany without sacrificing the constantly shifting nature of Dada imagery: "shepherd of boats of birds of hypocrites," "in the leaf of rosebush in the knowledge of the dying man...." The shepherd maintains a close connection with the theme of language as he "moves toward the celestial pastures of words." "Sing man stripped of the effervescent humility of man": it is pride in language that forbids the image of a sheep and suggests instead the stronger image of the wolf.

IX.9.3. "Serious" was changed to the human and precise image of calloused hands; the great shepherd has the characteristics of gods and of men.

IX.9.20. The more violent "snatch" of the first version, which placed man in the passive attitude, was here changed to "cloud": the strength is that of the shepherd and of the wolf who represents man, even if his energies are stifled (clouded) momentarily.

IX.9.31. These *hésitations paysannes* ("peasant hesitations") were originally the *habitations* ("dwellings") which are then placed in the next line. The process of changing a few letters and then of conserving the word scratched out for a later passage is typical.

IX.10.1. Initially, the image was the more usual "shepherd of the flocks."

IX.10.6, 10, 12 and **IX.11.2** and **4.** In all these lines the adjective followed the noun, as would be customary in French. But in the typed version Tzara changed each, as he frequently did throughout the epic. In a space of twelve pages, for instance, he makes 32 such changes. It is partly this series of deliberate reversals which gives the poem its extraordinary and solemn character. Here a slight formality is imposed on the spontaneous, reflecting the epic nature of the poem.

IX.11.1. The more physical and limited adverb originally used, *encerclé* ("surrounded") is changed to *embourbé* ("entangled"), which was probably suggested by the sound of the word *barbe* ("beard").

X.3.1. An unforgettable line in French ("et que l'amour suive l'amour d'in-consolés soleils suivi").

X.9.1–12. This sort of lyrical incantation combined with a rapid accumulation of images is often found in Dada and surrealist writing.

X.10. An example of the "preposterous" Dada image which has, however, a basis in everyday experience; the fire is often seen as friendly and cozy.

X.12. Like the "almosts of destiny" (*les à-peu-près*), the word "nevers" (*les jamais*) is another indication of the omnipresent concern with human language.

X.12.15. An image drawing on the power of mythological symbolism, reminiscent of the Mayan Codex.

XI. In general contains a brilliant elaboration on the theme of song and language ("I sing . . . "), where the old cracked lungs, the strangled flutes, and the unseeing (and "unhearing") eyes are contrasted with the mysterious and silken sounds and the "azure signs" of the organ, the noise of the gongs, the clanging of metal money-boxes. Here the church metaphor (organ, hymn, money-box, sins, beating wings) is extended up to the sudden descent from the words "perhaps the stars" to the crash on the earth of humans and ordinary material objects (flesh and bushes). Elsewhere in the poem, Tzara uses the parallel image of the bird falling and of the bird that "crashes hurls itself from crisis to crisis." (For a selection of the bird imagery frequent in Dada and surrealist poetry, see the introduction to my *Poetry of Dada and Surrealism: Aragon, Breton, Tzara, Eluard, Desnos* (Princeton: Princeton University Press, 1970).

XI.1.1. The line first read: "what is this snoring cheeky cushion filling up the angel." The angel eliminated here appears in the next line.

XI.1.11. This line previously read: "but from time to time the sounding rod pulls up for us a sturdy net of sounds." Obviously, the image of the sounding rod leads to that of the sound itself.

XI.5.5. The contrast between the caress and the headache was produced only after an initial line in which the image was all of one piece: "frantic race over the rails of wind."

XI.5.8. "The reasons for keeping silent," an expression which occurs four lines after this interrupted incantation, can be taken as referring to this interruption itself.

XI.6.11. The former reading of the line "under the dead eyelid" compared with the present one shows Tzara's increasing interest in the structural or formal outline of things.

XI.7.4. This rather peculiar line was once a more logical one: *viennent m'appuyer sur chaque épaule la tête* ("come to lean on each of my shoulders their hands").

XI.7.7. As the pendulum swings from side to side, it suggests a slicing or cutting motion: thence the operation of trepanning.

XI.10–conclusion. The last two lines, a variant of the recurring universal refrain, *et des autres de tant d'autres* ("from the others from so many others") were added after the first text published in *L'Esprit nouveau*. Together with the interior echoes, these refrains provide the formal and emotional structure of the poem.

XII.1.3. Compare the original reading, "the pockets of air snorings of eternity" with the first line of the preceding section, "these air pockets with those rounded cheeks, and the snoring in both".

XII.3.3. Compare this final, tightened version with the following draft: "makes the round of the prison of the world at a gallop whipped along by naval gleams."

XII.3.13. At first, the whitenesses were put to sleep by the chloroform (*blancheurs endormies*); this more subtle form: *alourdies* (literally, "made heavier"), is more effective as it is less obvious.

XII.4.9. The lining is an aural reference in French to the theme of the double: "la *doublure* de son âme." The original reading stressed the notion of enclosure with the phrase "enclosed within his soul like an interior conduit."

XII.4.14. An instance of the rather frequent changes to the exact opposite (see note on manuscripts above); the line first read "which will put the grasshoppers to sleep," then: "when the grasshoppers go to sleep."

XII.5.12. A brilliant example of the final condensation of images. The line formerly read: *et tandis que l'éclipse totale de la raison hurle à la mort des lunes* ("and while the total eclipse of reason shrieks at the death of moons") before the alteration of reason's eclipse into *la folie* and then *la rage*, and the transfer of the moon's death into the moon's grief. In French, the line now has a sonorous and tragic beauty: *et tandis que la rage hurle au deuil de la lune.*

XII.5.18. An example of the elimination of a limiting and useless detail: the noise was made in the first instance by nutcrackers (*grincements des casse-noisettes*).

XII.6.1–2. Both lines began: "my god" (*mon dieu*), before many of the personal references were eliminated.

XII.7.8. The line was more specifically human: "which we cultivate in our mental hothouses"; the final reading combines the human with the cosmic in the image of the "foreheads of dawn."

XIII.1.13. In earlier versions, the disdainful dizziness was once a dizziness of sounds, (*des sons sonores*), so that the delicate visual writing was echoed by the aural.

XIII.3.6. The rhythm is altered toward the expansive. The line read: "tuft of pallid mist mourning meal" before the final version.

XIII.4.1. The scratch on the proffered breast may be related to the image of the bird as he is doomed (often willingly).

XIII.5.2. The line was far more sentimental: the image of "plaintive stalactites," associated the drooping form with tears and lamentations. The change to "hardy" is one more instance of a positive alteration to the exactly opposite image.

XIII.7. in general. All through this section there is an emphasis on the look ("do you see," "you see," "rubbing your eyes," "this perpetual smile gazing at us").

XIII.7.1. The superfluous adjective "brutal" qualifying the lineup of cadavers was eliminated here.

XIII.7.9. Interesting example of the formation of an image; the line formerly read "eliminates the voices of the crown of thorns." From the circular image of the crown Tzara arrives at the carrousel as it circles around. Compare also with XIII.8.11, where the image of the smooth and muscled mountains on which the voices are bucking like horses comes directly from this image. The voices eliminated in the first passage are found in the second, and the carrousel's horses supply the rest.

XIII.8.23. The negative line which ended this passage, "they fall frenetically but you don't remember," is eliminated here. In the final version, memory is omnipotent ("incestuous memory," "disoriented memory," "labyrinths hanging on the shadow of my steps," VI.7.) and the desire to escape it is strong (see also note to the conclusion of XIII).

XIII.9.1–2. The poet tried out *tombées* ("fallen") after "lost," and the aurally similar *tombes qui voient* ("seeing tombs") after "harvest." The sound recurs also in line 10 and in the verb of line 14; furthermore, the verb appears three lines before this and was also to have concluded the preceding stanza before its eventual elimination. The role of these interior echoes, retained or discarded, is an essential one.

XIII.9.14–15. Another vertical expansion of complication of levels.

XIII.9.15-16. The crystal transparency which often seems to be the supreme value for the Dadaists and surrealists. See Breton's "Praise of the crystal," Tzara's essays on poetry and on art, and his frequent references to "glass corridors," "hours of windowpanes and of clearing," and so on.

XIII.9.21. The neutral and colorless verb "perched" is changed to the menacing ("fixed") which leads directly to the harsh series of "drives . . . hard . . . sterility . . . fixed."

XIII.10.3. The ordinary escalator steps, *les marches,* were changed later to these disquieting hands.

XIII.10. last three lines. Inversion is another form of reversal of the ordinary form of things; here the natural process corresponds perfectly to the Dada attitude. This technique is evident in the Dada films, such as those made by Hans Richter. See, for instance, the sequence in "8 x 8" where the pieces of paper reassemble themselves after being torn, or, in "Ghosts before Breakfast," the sequence of the fragments of coffee cups rejoining their parts.

XIII.2.17. A juxtaposition typical of Dada's more humorous imagery.

XIII.12. conclusion. See the earlier passage: "I know that I carry the tune in me and am not afraid/I carry death . . . " (part 3). The gravity is not lessened by the play on words (*ami, ennui, l'ami*) which is the verbal equivalent of the reversing of images. Tzara makes frequent use of this rearrangement in his prose poems, such as *The Antihead:* "Crystal with haggard eyes, with tousled hair, bitterness rusts our greatest pleasures. Crystal with haggard eyes, the bitterness of tousled hair rusts our pleasures, the insects. Crystal with haggard hair—bitterness rusts our pleasures. . . . Crystal of insect with haggard eyes, bitterness with disheveled hair rusts the bitterness with haggard eyes . . . " (XXXI of "Mr. Aa the Antiphilosopher," *The Antihead, Les Cahiers libres,* 1933, p. 59).

For Tzara, the concept of memory (see note to XIII.8.23) seems to be intimately connected with the notion of approximation, for which the "luminous forgetfulness" invoked in the last line is the only remedy. The Dadaists and surrealists declare war on memory as a restraint on liberty: thus the imaginative idea of burning down all the libraries. This literature is strongly oriented toward the present.

XIV.1.1. In the typescript, the line reads "the high white snows," but then the superfluous term "white" is discarded for one with moral overtones, "serious," which had been tried out elsewhere and discarded. Since the height of the snow itself determines the loftiness of the action, the whole line takes on a solemnity it did not have.

XIV.3.1. Originally, "to frighten me with its mask of horror." The line is turned away from the personal, but the idea of the horror is kept for the last line.

XIV.3.3. The original lament, "oh my god," which reminds us of some of the interjections in the *Twenty-Five Poems,* is altered from the personal to the more matter-of-fact statement.

XIV.3.4. One of many incomplete lines, deliberately left that way. In some cases, complete lines are transformed into incomplete ones, so that they will be incomplete witnesses to an approximate language.

XIV.3.6. The initial form of this image, "pressed like a fruit," is strengthened to "crushed" at the same time as the image of the foot is added.

XIV.3.8. The trivial and unlovely image of an *insecte glissant* is altered to the more appropriate image of the prey fleeing and unreachable.

XIV.3.10. Tzara used to spell this *athmosphère,* a fact interesting only for dating purposes. During the years 1925–30, his spelling grows gradually more consistent with ordinary French orthography.

XIV.4 and **5** in general. The reiteration of the word "consolation" over a number of stanzas is a subtle form of the lyrical repetitions related to it in sense: "morning morning/morning sealed with crystal and with larvae/morning of baked bread/morning of shutters in madness" (XV.9.). This entire passage has nobility of tone to suit the lines quoted before: "of a clear golden radiance—like the quickening widening beating of wings" ("Note on Poetry").

XIV.5.10. The word "consolation" which once appears on a notebook page alone, becomes the title of a poem (originally in *Permitted Fruit*) and is of considerable importance for the poet. It is perhaps the corresponding idea to that of approximation, its brighter double, its merciful echo. If the motif does not figure with that of fire in the concluding part of the poem, as the poet originally intended, it is still the necessary prelude to the final transfiguration and purification. After the haunting series of "almosts" and "slightly," where man is certain apparently only of his incomplete nature and insufficient capabilities, the final crescendo toward the end of the pilgrimage of language cancels out at last the pessimism of the beginning line: "sunday heavy cover . . . "

XIV.5.12. The hell was originally a rather frivolous *petit enfer.* As the poem grows and changes its character, the poet appears to change with it. The five years of writing and rewriting the epic were probably the most important ones for Tzara's personal and poetic development.

XIV.5.17. After "message," the first version read *manuel*, corresponding literally to the five fingers mentioned three lines above.

XIV.6.4. After trying out a series of three words related in sound (and in meaning, by a slight sadistic route), *fouets, souhaits, écoliers* ("whips," "wishes," "schoolboys"), the calm result surprises.

XIV.6.7. To the phrase "oh my god," once discarded (see above, note to XIV.3.3.), is added as an afterthought "my violin," perhaps to protect once more against the self-accusation of sentimentality and to preserve the unsettling character of the imagery.

XIV.7. The litany of a man whose humility ("a man is so few things") is immediately underlined at the start of the next stanza: "but what does man matter?"

XIV.7.1. The image of the cigarette was formerly much clearer: "a tree trunk place on the ashtray's edge/still smokes."

XIV.8.8–12. Reprise of the image of linen hanging like flames or licking tongues but with the addition of scarlet color and the further extension into the language-related images of palate, throat, beaks, and barkings.

XIV.8.14. The *aboie* suggested by the *becs* (beak=mouth=bark) was originally the vaguer and less colorful *s'agite* ("moves about"). All these images of the mouth and language led originally to a "mouth of nothingness" in the next stanza.

XIV.9.9–10. Related to the passage of the sun directly preceding, this is a response to the pathetic brief litany of man. The bright tone carries over to Part XV and to the quick arrivals of the carts, the silver coins on the counter of the rare morning, the images of fire, sparkling, crystal, sun, and light. But the superb one-line summary of all this optimism in the next part: "You are at the breakfast hour of your life" will be denied in the next lines by the unavoidable "artful net of age."

XIV.9.11. The form of the drops may have suggested the verb *perlent* ("pearling") and is also preserved in the image of the notes trilling. This image extends the language images just preceding (the tongue, the throat of the sky) to the realm of music; see, twelve lines below, "I sing."

XIV.10.5. This was to have been a very long line, as if it were the summit of the poet's determination.

272 Tristan Tzara ▶

XIV.10.7–end. For the importance of the theme of consolation, see the note to XIV.5.7. After the themes of burning, of birth, of fullness, and of morning sun ripening the offerings of men, the powerful recurrence of the word alone leads directly to the "unforesting" of the conscience (as the wolf is led out of the wood) and to the infinite which in some sense redeems the approximation. This is probably the most moving part of the poem, less grandiose than the conclusion, more fully developed than the beginning.

XV.1–4. in general. Particularly noticeable here are the images of nature and liquids, fullness and profusion: swelling udders, flowing metal and lava: acanthus, vine-plants, and honey; the inexhaustible bath, the unharnessed waves doubled by the accordion's folds. All these images lead to the "day waking in our breasts" at the conclusion of the second stanza, to the brightness of the "crystalline marriage" and the "marine sparkling," in the third stanza, to the positive setting of the "rare morning," "the breakfast hour" of life, the "prolific encampment of stars" (XV.4.10–11), and the head held high (XV.3.9), as well as to the images of innocence mingled with knowledge, such as the precocious milk spurting forth (XV.3.6) and the naked light deliberately clothed in fleece (XV.3.11–12).

XV.8.4-5. A remarkable combination of the ubiquitous dream imagery with the equally significant imagery of water and birth; in one sense, this can be considered the ur-image of the poem itself, as the heavy and prized sailboats laden with heat and light at the outset of Part XV yield finally the quiet and unobtrusive birth of the ship of poetic vision.

XV.9. in general. The repetitive litany characteristic of surrealist poetry is here a praise of transparency (crystal and windows and river), of beginning (larvae), and of simplicity (bread baking, shutters in the wind, squirrels, and the sweet smell of the iris). The clamor of the more brilliant and noisier parts of the poem is balanced by these moments of tranquillity and transparency, the quiet concerns of a poetry moving inward.

XVI.1.1. The contrast of the monstrous spectacle here with the calm beauty of the litany of morning just before it demonstrates violent alternation characteristic of Dada and surrealist thought. There is a similar stylistic alternation between the lines of epic proportion and the short lines, often the most moving in their sudden brevity (for example, XVI.3.11: "time mocks us").

XVI.2.2. The line was originally two, beginning with the heavy rhythm: "but now the wagon worn out with hopes with chances with turpitude carries me along."

XVI.2.3. This line also was originally two heavy ones, partly of the catalog type: "I know the lassitudes the aridities the shames the latitudes /and the good are as guilty and as full of merit as the bad."

XVI.2.13 and 19. The *dieux serrés* in line 13 ("the huddled gods") were originally the *dents serrées,* the "clenched teeth" in the later line.

XVI.2.25. See the deleted section of Part III.

XVI.4.5 and 6. Originally, there were far more concrete images "hands which hoe and steal," "hands which hoe and sow and pluck ..." "which give food to shoeless donkeys, ... " "which feed birds, dogs, cats." This twenty-one line passage focused on the image of hands is the human counterpart of the serious and confident hands of the shepherd and stands in the same relationship to them as does the approximate human language to the cosmic language perceived most clearly at the conclusion of the epic.

XVI.6.16. Example of the changing of the image to its opposite: these lines formerly read: "no subterfuges ... instead of "subterfuges."

XVI.7.5. The verbs were originally closer together: "swallows up and slowly devours," before being changed to the interior rhyme: *engloutit et asphyxie* ("swallows up and asphyxiates").

XVI.7.6. The vigor of the new rhythms and the electric flood so strong that it bursts the tympanum mocks the pathetic blossom of the unstable song in its surroundings of mediocrity (XVI.7.3.).

XVI.7–conclusion. Rarely do the changes seem a cause for regret; but here, the rare image of octopi fainting was formerly enhanced by their description as "implacable."

XVII.1.1–9. The constantly renewed freshness of vision enables man to view the cyclical spectacle of nature as a consolation, even while he realizes its imperfect and approximate character, parallel to his own imperfect and therefore recurring meditations.

XVII.2.11. The expression "what does it matter" preceded this line. Many such parenthetical expressions are inserted in pencil on the typed pages or in the notebooks after the original text and are finally eliminated or placed else-where. This expression is now found in XVII.10.13.

XVII.5. in general. See the description of variants in my introduction, pp. 18–19.

XVII.6.9. Here the concluding refrain of many sections was inserted, then removed: "and so many others and so many others."

XVII.6.19. See the elimination of the cushions described at the beginning of Part XI.

XVII.8.10. An earlier reference to the sentimental, "the painful throat of the well," was eliminated.

XVIII.3. in general. This passage furnishes the most profound and most poetic explanation of the effort, hope, and frequent failure implied in the language of an approximate man. It is a quiet prelude to the final waiting and the problematic center of the epic.

XVIII.3.1. In typescript: "between human appearances and intoxications." The rhythm was awkward and in the final version, the two trisyllabic nouns and their easy assonance contrast ironically with the depth of the difficulty.

XVIII.3.3. Formerly "of beings and things," a cliché then replaced by these references to language and, possibly, to the flowing of time.

XVIII.3.7. The line read *trop lourde carcasse* ("too heavy carcass"), before the final, less melodramatic form, related to the former by sound: *carcasse, cuirasse.*

XVIII.3.9. Formerly the more personal "in the depths of myself," before the poem was given its universal character.

XVIII.4.1 and **2.** Between the first two lines, a mediocre line was omitted: "and that's enough for men to live in good calm camaraderie." The whole section has been shortened; originally, five of the lines were longer. The parts now omitted added very little; for instance, line 2 ended with "dirty jugs of their bodies the catafalques"; line 3: "this peace whose mechanical progress wants to be called prayer"; line 6: "obscure with fisticuffs and spittings and revolts."

XVIII.4.8. In the first version, it was the poet's "adventures" which were enlivened by temptations, or, at another point, mediocre life itself: "temptresses adding spice to the dullness of life."

XVIII.5.8. The repetitive and circular motion of the windmills determines the echoes: originally *moulins-à-temps moulins-à-espoirs* ("time-mills hope-mills") where the sound of *vent* led to *temps*; finally, *tourments* is substituted, keeping the sound, but turning the sense toward the tragic.

XVIII.5.10. The image of the scythe was juxtaposed with the "agricultural instruments," but the final image of the tongues themselves serving as scythes contributes to the greater poetic strength of abstraction in addition to the suggestion of language, continued in the next line by the references to ear and to speech.

XVIII.5.13. The signal was first called apocalyptic, then biblical. The final poem retains all the possible grandeur of religious imagery while eliminating the more specific references to it.

XVIII.5.15. Originally, *pays et yeux* ("countries and eyes") then changed to *doigts* (the image of fingers probably suggested by the implied image of the Morse code), before the rhyming *voix* ("voices"). As we have seen, very often the final choice is one relating to speech or language; that it should be so frequently determined by verbal echo is appropriate.

XVIII.5.16. It was formerly the voice which was *en chair et en os* ("in flesh and blood") and the sound of the first word led to *chère* ("dear") in the next line, continuing the echo.

XVIII.5.16–18. Like the "materiality of construction of a simple image," the immaterial theme of language is here again linked to a material metaphor. See also the comparisons between the verbal structure of language and a tent made of infinite parallel forms which then somehow becomes a stream, between the word and nuggets of gold or honey, and so on.

XVIII.5.24–26. The circular images of the wheel and the propeller as they turn convey once more the infinite cycle of approximations and repetitions.

XVIII.6.9. A great alteration away from the literal collection of the letters "by the post office" to those age picks up.

XVIII.6.11. The subjective qualification "of the poet" appeared here but was eliminated with the other marks of the excessively personal.

XVIII.6.14. The impatiences formerly fell in the heat of fever itself, continuing the image of the thermometer, specifically, of the mercury of the entrails with which the poet wrote love letters (changed to the simpler "sap of the entrails," 1.8). But "ditch" suggests the imagery of death, a more chilling conclusion for the impatiences as they fall.

XVIII.6.15. Originally the end of the line read *des têtes grimacantes et grimées* ("grimacing and dirty heads"), another instance of a verbal echo.

XVIII.6.20. Note the constant allusions to game and gambling (see *Place Your Bets*). The evocation of chance contrasted with the sad mechanics of ordinary (nonchance) love described in line 22 was originally even harsher: "modern and hygienic comfort of love." Compare with Breton's conception of *L'Amour fou,* a marvelous product of chance. The manuscript in the Fonds Doucet stops at the end of this section.

XVIII.8.1. In proofs, the first line of this section goes with the preceding section.

XVIII.8.6. The unoriginal image of aid arriving "in its white dress," which appeared in typescript and in proofs, was changed to this opposite pole, in accord with the gambling metaphor which continues in line 8.

XIX.1.18. The word "pathetic" was eliminated here; Tzara continues his effort toward the unsentimental.

XIX.3.3. The word "unpleasing" as an adjective for the practice of the infinite was eliminated with the majority of allusions which could have been considered self-pitying.

XIX.3.4. "Structure" was originally "aspect"; together with the strengthening of the linguistic imagery and the toning-down of the sentimental or personal, there is increased emphasis on the structural, in the literal and figurative senses.

XIX.5. Corrections in the notebooks are almost unreadable. The repeated vow to fire and waiting begins at this point.

XIX.6 and **7.** Notice the repeated allusions to game—dominoes of stars, eucharistic games—played out against a cosmic background. The verbal congestion or ecstatic drunkenness in the sixth stanza is only the human approximation of those divine games. In the seventh stanza the reduction is even more severe.

XIX.8. Originally, this last section was divided into three but the massive accumulation is more impressive in the final text.

XIX.8.9-11. "Hearths of emotions" read originally "flames of words." The simpler and more beautiful word *flamme* is kept for the end, although the image of fire is retained. For once, the reference to language succumbs to a direct statement of emotion. After the approximations and the long pilgrimage of language, the gestures here lose all trace of the pathetic and all sense of limit. The poem is at once directed upward and toward the intensely personal by a slowly accumulating momentum: "a slow furnace . . . a slow fire . . . a fire . . . man . . . a man . . . your heart . . . I have pledged."

Unexpectedly, the final wait in the desert for the coming of the flame rejects the approximate. Tzara had initially placed part of the famous phrase beginning with "approximate man" before the line starting "harmony." He had also meant for the poem to end with the absorption of the individual into the general: "approximate man like me like you and like the others." But he eliminates this line and the stage is wholly occupied by the individual man of language as he passes from the journey of approximation with the others like him into this heroic solitude.

Notes to Other Writings

Notes to Other Writings

First Poems, originally written in Rumanian, are translated here from the French version, *Les Premiers poèmes,* by Claude Sernet (Paris: Seghers, 1965).

The Second Celestial Adventure of Mr. Antipyrine was written in its first stages on the back of an advertisement for a Dada ball in 1920. As Tzara is writing the play *Mr. Saturn* becomes *Mr. Aa* and *Tristan Tzara* becomes *Mr. Absorption.* The links between *Mr. Antipyrine* and *Mr. Antiphilosopher* are clear enough: philosophy gives you a headache, you take an aspirin (antipyrine), and so on. (Originally, this was a *Mr. Aa Manifesto.*)

Contrary to what is usually thought, this play was not written in one burst of enthusiasm. Many of the longer and more impassioned (more absurd, if one chooses) speeches were added later, after having been written separately. There are also passages added at the end of others; for instance, the speech of Mrs. Interruption, beginning "whistle swollen with loveless lemonade" was written apart from the rest; and the concluding speech of *The Disinterested Brain,* after "telephone there is no one left," was added later.

Twenty-Five Poems (1918)
"White Giant Leper of the Countryside"

Few changes on one manuscript, several on another.

1.10. According to the changes Tzara originally made, the "formation" was to be "colonies"; after that, a short passage was to be added: "the peninsula of his heart shrinks/confidence and swells swells black man's head." Other changes were to have been made: for instance in line 23, "kaolin" was to have been "alum"; in line 11, the sponges were to be compared with harvests (the echo *vendanges éponges* was deliberately created). It is often the case that between the manuscript and the proof, alterations are lost, or, as in the case of *Approximate Man,* changes made on the proofs were not carried out.

1.21. The phrase *Travelers' Tree* was inserted in the manuscript and then taken up later as the title of a major collection.

1.24. After another series of African or pseudo–African words which do not appear in the final poem, Tzara inserted: "dali bouli obok et tombo et tombo/here the reader begins to shout," with a hand drawn pointing to the final phrase. See his remarks in the letter to Doucet (introduction, note 4), on the subject of collage and of linguistic shock.

1.26. After trying this out on one line: "many rrrrrrr here the reader" (*beaucoup de rrrrrrrr ici le lecteur*) Tzara decided to have the "here" begin a new line. But the 1918 edition of *Twenty-Five Poems* had short lines and therefore it was impossible to tell what Tzara's intentions had been; in the 1946 manuscript indications were evidently not consulted. For the opposite error, with the same cause, see note to "The Liontamer Remembers."

"The Great Lament of My Obscurity Three."

There was another page to this poem, clearly marked with this title, continuing the imagery, and numbered in Tzara's writing as the sequel, but finally placed in the poem "me just touch me" (*moi touche-moi seulement*). The omitted section reads:

without knowing how nor why	sans savoir comment ni pourquoi
clustered short	serrés courtes
show the path	montrent le chemin
all at once	tout d'un coup
to rot in gold of great and	pourrir en or de pierre grande et
dense	
dense stone	grande
great	dense
dense	

and, on the page in capital letters, the exclamations: WEST! WEST!

"Drugstore-Conscience"

1.3. Originally, the image of leeches was the straightforward one of blood-letting associated with sickness: "the leech making itself a sickness"; the tree was added later.

1.11. Added in manuscript.

1.13. The wolf was merely resting on the bench (*le banc*) until Tzara inserted the single letter "1" to render the image more interesting. Thus many of the more startling images of Dada come about not through unusual vision but through minor alterations.

1.19. The possible origin of the title for the poem. As in many of these poems (see note for "Wise Dance March"), there is a decided contrast between two series of words: one intensely active, the other passive and restful. Here in the first series, one would have: "will be born," "fountains," "come in a spiral," "swell," "dig," "goes away," "pursued," "chases," "sharp," "fulgurating brightness electric," "pluck"; and in the other: "unmoving lord," "silence," "rests," "long," "heavily," and "stands immobile." The lily lamp can be considered as the link between the calm and the electric brightness. Tzara probably did not plan out these oppositions, but they are a frequent formal element of his work, probably indicative of two psychological tendencies (as borne out by his manuscripts and letters). At this period of his life, the active series is stronger; later, the visual predominates.

"Saint."

Dated 1917. The final phrase of the first line, originally *grandeur arborescente* is altered into *ascendance arborescente,* where the echoes *ance-ante* and the alliteration lend resonance to the ending.

1.6. "the sounds . . . coagulate" can be taken as a definition of Tzara's primary method, or as a description of the kernel from which the poem springs.

1.8. In the typed version before proofs, "concentration . . . couplings" was one line, a further "coagulation" or concentration.

"Wise Dance March"

1.1. To the separate words, "jesus flower shirt" (*jésus fleur chemise*), hyphens were added as afterthoughts to make the final unique noun. Originally, the line read: "the mirror breaks the lamp flees pushes is a great wheel smashing" (*la glace casse lampe fuit pousse est grande roue broyant [sic]*); the transformation of the *est* into *et* is typical, and the wheel, retained for the next line, is one of the circular images Tzara frequently uses.

1.2. Originally the line read: "for I am freezing," but the poet wishes at this point to turn everything away from the personal. See *Faites vos jeux,* in *Les Feuilles libres,* no. 32 (1923), p. 146. Tzara says he wrote to destroy the feeling which pushed him into doing so, that he had always dreamed of losing his personality and of becoming apersonal.

1.4. Originally the less startling image of bloodletting, "empty your veins"; the substitution of one word is a radical change here.

The poem again exhibits the balance between the two kinds of attitude, active and immobile. Here the contrast is between "breaks," "flees," "turn," "dance," "crush," "walk," "bite," "whistle" and "alone," "freeze," "put down," "empty," "know."

11.6 and **7.** Originally line 6 read: *siffle violon blanc* ("whistle white violin"), thus the expansion from whistle to bird, and the pun on "egg white"; in *The Antihead* Tzara puns on *blanc d'ange* (angel white) resembling the word "blancmange."

"Little Town in Siberia"

1.7. The pun is intended: in the manuscript we find *descend* ("descends") crossed out to become *décent* ("decent"). The opposing action is added afterwards, with the word "higher." Even when the initial writing of the poem did not include contrasting sets of actions, the poet occasionally added them later.

"The Liontamer Remembers"

11.4–6. Here, the very plain indications in the manuscript that the lines were meant to be choppy and short were overlooked. In the 1918 edition, one could not tell; perhaps the editors of the 1946 edition omitted to check the original where there were to have been five lines, not three. As it now stands, the phrase, "roll roll red," is swallowed up at the end of the preceding line, and loses the vividness intended.

1.6. The brightness of the color red sets the poem in motion, as in "Vanilla . . . " The force of the lines suffice to set them swerving. From the initial "look at me" to the final "see," the poem is set in the framework of visual activity.

"Springtime"

The title had a capital letter in the manuscript which it had lost by the 1946 edition.

11.10 and 11. In the manuscript, one line goes from "sow" to "the sky." In the 1946 printing where the verb "plant" comes at the beginning of a new line, the intended effect of the rapid accumulation of images and actions in one line is lost.

"Sun Night"

1.1. Originally, "descend its ice king," where the verb was probably suggested by the sinking of the sun at nightfall.

11.12 and 13. Originally, the line read *la sphère la planète* ("the sphere the planet"); then, perhaps to conform to interior rhyme, the phrase of *douleur et de fer* ("pain and iron") was substituted and *tempête* replaced *planète* again through suggestion of rhyme. In the manuscript, *la tempête* is on the same line as *la sphère*; again the 1946 printing chops it up.

Of Our Birds

"Circus"

This poem of 1917 and "The Showmen" of 1916 can be considered part of the same series as "The Liontamer Remembers" in the *Twenty-Five Poems*; the Dada accent on spectacle still finds its perfect metaphor in the circus ("Let's dance, Let's shout"). See also "Cosmic Realities Vanilla Tabacco Wakings" of 1914.

"Cosmic Realities Vanilla Tobacco Wakings"

X. After "consequently/lord lord/forgive me" the expression "of ice" was added in the typescript. Many of these poems are made more interesting by the addition of what might be considered irrelevant elements; the latter also have the effect of turning the direction away from the sentimental (see the introduction).

XV. The "TURNINGS" are lines which do indeed appear on the manuscript page as lines literally veering left and right.

"Arch"

11.9 and **10.** To arrive at the phrase "the most variegated," the words underwent the following transformation: 1. *le voile est rouge* ("the sail is red") with *bigarrée* added and crossed out; 2. *la nuit bigarrée* added at the end of the line; 3. *le voile bigarré;* and 4. the final result. The rearrangement of words is obviously of more significance than the object' depicted; Tzara's preoccupation is typically linguistic rather than visual. As an example of change by sound, *a mouvement intense* yields this *mouvement dense.* In the manuscript, a line describing a possible condition: "so we might seem ridiculous to him" is changed to the far stronger assertion: we are enthusiastic, therefore we appear ridiculous. The line was finally eliminated, perhaps because it was too personal.

"Boxing"

I.3. The simplest of the diverse visual and verbal techniques for attracting the reader's undivided attention to the language and the purpose of the poem, and to the self-conscious cruelty of the poet.

I.17–21. The interior rhymes in the original serve as a partial mockery of the poem: *LE SIFFLET . . . effet . . . reflet . . .* and are paralleled by *les yeux de fiel . . . oublié le ciel.* Elsewhere in the poem, Tzara uses half-rhymes: *craquent . . . hacrée . . . crale; tapis . . . merci; sonde . . . tombe . . . l'ombre. . . . l'ombre.*

II.1. One of the most important examples of the poet fleeing the sentimental and personal. See the letter to Doucet (introduction, note 4), and the passage in *Place Your Bets,* where Tzara speaks of trying to lose himself by writing. This line about the mechanical actions of the Pierrot was added, and in the addition, the term "sentimental" is crossed out (the addition originally read: *acharnement correct et sentimental* . . .).

II.13. "Transactions sensations": notice the similarity of sound in English as in French. Originally read: "kilometric transactions sensations."

II.14. The specification of when to applaud was added. Tzara places the spectacle firmly in the present.

II.23. A change for the more interesting, since originally the line read "surrounds the fields and the lake."

"SPEAKING OR INTELLIGIBLE WOOD SIGN OF EASTER ISLAND"

In the title, the sign on Easter Island was originally "writing"; notice the accent on language, written or spoken. Often Tzara draws heads on his manuscripts; here, however, he has drawn a sort of cubist landscape.

"The Showmen"

11.18–end. After "there is a machine" the rest was added later.

Cloud Handkerchief

The first production took place on May 17, 1924. According to Tzara, "The scene represents a closed boxlike space from which no actor can leave. All five surfaces are of the same color." To represent the places of action, post-cards are shown on a screen. The play, which was much admired by Louis Aragon for its *collage* form, is an elaborate investigation of the problems of theater and reality, poetry and madness, and the self, based on *Hamlet*. Lines from Shakespeare are interspersed with Tzara's own lines, in a combination at once lyric and self-mocking. The poet in the play wears a mask to hide from himself, he says in his own monologue, and another character comments: "No one understands this play."

Travelers' Tree
"The Lousy One"

A last stanza was added in proofs, of which lines 3 and 4 are particularly worth noting for the theme of the man and his approximation traveling as his double beside him on the journey toward completeness.

The typescript is full of changes, probably of initial aural inspiration; the successive modifications either rhyme or show assonance. In line 3, the qualifiers "frivolous or serious" (*frivoles ou graves*), exact opposites, become *frivoles ou rares,* slightly more imaginative as a choice, and finally *frivoles ou sidérales,* where the opposite feeling is retained but the second adjective expands into the cosmic. In line 10, the phrase, "root powerfully" in which the adverb intensified only the root's strength, becomes "root night" where the juxtaposition of the nouns, already strong semantically, also has a double direction for its strength: the root is *profound* like the depth of night, but it is also obscure or *hidden*. One of the most extraordinary examples of the rhyming modifications is found at the end of stanza 6: where the initial stages, the lines change from *ta vie est un paquet sorti d'un marécage/jeté aux fauves vents qui lêchent l'emballage* ("your life is a package taken from a swamp/thrown to the bestial winds licking the wrapping") to the trial phrase *l'a fait sortir d'une cage* ("brought it from a cage") before the final result: *lêchent leur naufrage* ("lick their shipwreck"). This example alone should suffice to prove that it is not a question of starting with the image of the shipwreck but with the sound *age*.

The images in lines 14–16 were originally the rhyming images of the *feuilles* in their rags and *nuage bas descendu en deuil* ("cloud descended low in mourning"). The substitution *d'automne* suggests in its letters *aumône*, and the phrase *grouille la vermine* ("vermin crawling") leads to the substitution *grouille la famine;* but the cluster of images remains much the same in sense, corresponding to Tzara's essential, albeit usually overlooked, principle of the "coagulation" of sounds.

Where the Wolves Drink

Tzara originally added "poèmes tzaristes" to the title in pencil. This is the time of Tzara's greatest self-consciousness as a writer, of his closest attention to his own style; the expression "Tzarist poem" is, of course, a pun but also partly serious.

V. "Traps in the Grass"

One of the poems for which there exists a list of words the poet wanted to use; it is clear that the poem's intended vocabulary dictates its images.

1.9. Originally, *la jeunesse a passé* [or then *a coupé*] *la route c'était le mauvais présage* ("youth has gone by on the road it was the bad sign"), where the explanation weighs heavily. In the final version, the simpler juxtaposition suffices.

1.10. Changed from the too personal: *sur chaque seuil que je voulais franchir* ("on each threshold which I wanted to cross") to the more general line as we have it now.

1.15. "unreadable": the sign and the reading continue to haunt the poet, as in his epic.

VI. "Lies of a Night"

1.1. The precious opening, *Il était une nuit* ("Once upon a night") is changed to the present phrasing, more interesting as it implies both the sweetness of lies and the echoes of mirrors in their falseness (see 1.7).

1.4. The sentimental idea of remorse is eliminated here in favor of the related image of "wakes."

1.6. The voracious beasts were once ferocious (*bêtes féroces*): notice the similarity in sound.

1.7. The image of the echo, like that of the double, is prevalent in the poetry of this period.

1.10. The "high spring" combining the concepts of nobility and genesis is akin to the later images of plenitude.

1.15. Compare, in *Noontimes Gained,* "I have been left out of everything."

Seeds and Bran

In pencil on the manuscript, the notation "experimental dream" is inserted, by which Tzara means the attempt to use the forces of the unconscious, as conducive to knowledge as are scientific experiments. Tzara agrees with the surrealists on the need to combine the impulses of day and night. In this manuscript the changes are of very little interest; from this time on, the initial impulse and the final version are on the same linguistic, poetic, and imaginative level. The word lists continue, and for some pages each word in the list can be traced. The average length of the lists is about 30 words.

Page 195, line 12. The initial form of this conclusion read: "the meanings of men" then, "of human beings," and finally, as happens also in *Approximate Man*, Tzara opts for the singular form, as the most specific and therefore the most universal. Compare: "the adventure of winter men" with "the adventure of winter man," where the plural is changed to the singular. The rest of the sentence, surrealist in imagery and in tone, was added. Many other such lyric passages are written apart from the rest to which they will be added later.

Tzara's most impressive writing is built upon formal repetition or on verbal echoes to which he attributed a great theoretical importance. The repeated expression: "It will be a question of" was added (p. 198, line 12 from bottom of page).

Noontimes Gained
Resumé of Night

X. conclusion. Here, a *luxueuse délectation* (luxurious delectation) was changed to a *luxueux enveloppement,* probably in order to remove from the expression the extreme of personal sensuality. The last line is greatly strengthened. First: *Telle est à-peu-près la nuit* ("such is night more or less"), it was given a more subjective quality: "Telle se présente à mon esprit la nuit" ("night appears like this to my mind"). But in the final version, lengthened at the end, the emphasis on the nightly presence of multiplicity, depth, and random possibility is far more successful. As we have seen, Tzara prefers to lengthen his lines at the end.

The Hand Passes
"Limits of Fire"

The title, exhibits the poet's fascination with fire and flame. At the time of *Approximate Man,* however, Tzara emphasized their association with the absolute, rather than their limitation.

"Waking"

The final sentence is partially a response to the coming of the flame in the desert at the end of *Approximate Man.* Here salt and the fire are allied with the mineral: "stony in my clothing of schist" as in Dada (the mountains of crystal) and ever since. But the accent now falls on life and on the heights of living, rather than on the desert and the trial by fire, as in T. S. Eliot's *Waste Land* and Tzara's epic of 1930. In the context of the above remarks, it is interesting to note that at the bottom of the page from *Noontimes Gained,* Tzara writes of marvels as if to balance his own lament: "dirty life . . . dirty life mixed with death."

Radiant Mutations
"Herald of Eyes"

Three changes are of interest for the particular sense of vigor they convey: the verb in "would like to get rid of them" is changed to the more violent and active: "snatch." When the words "what does your impatience matter" are added, the passage acquires a certainty of tone, and finally, in the place of a memory simply accumulating, the poet stresses the clear and positive action of standing erect.

"New Paragraph"

The changes toward force and positive action are just as frequent here. For example, the benevolent action of the rain becomes "your irritating action"; the neutral "bony resemblances" become "bony absurdities," which changes the direction of the image; then a "misunderstood mistake" is strengthened to the point of being an "exemplary error." Finally, two conditions about which one is ordinarily powerless to do anything are changed at last to one which properly causes indignation: "thanks to misery" becomes "thanks to poverty" before the final "thanks to fraud."

The references in the latter part of the poem to the idea of game and risk, *où se joue déjà,* and to the joy of battles were added in the manuscript; they give a strong sense of Tzara's personality imposing itself.

Noontimes Gained

"Bay Morning"

1.2. "the air of the fields" was originally "the air of time."

1.3. Originally *les fruits avaient aussi (souvent) le goût de leur sourire (appel)* ("the fruits had also [often] the taste of their smile [call]").

In the manuscript, the final stanza has the characteristic spontaneous quality of the lyric passages; it is untouched, whereas the rest of the poem undergoes many alterations.

1.17. Was originally *une vie qui suit ma vie à la distance de l'écho* ("at an echo's distance"), then *traînait en laisse* ("pulled on a leash"), and then "this leash of an echo." For the theme of the approximate man and that of the double walking beside the poet, compare this passage, added in pencil to the first stages of *Seeds and Bran:* "Man leads another on a leash or walks beside him."

Earth upon Earth

In this collection, Tzara's fascination with the power of language is evident. In *Berçeuse entre deux portes,* we see man as he is lost in language and in "Acceptance of Spring," the men who go on their way swallowed up in their own echo. Both descriptions could apply to Tzara and his poetic heroes.

"Acceptance of Spring"

Greatly changed, this poem is clearly one of those about which Tzara cared the most. The title itself is composed of two key words for his work. There are numerous references to light added in the manuscript: in 1.1 a boat of armor becomes a shining boat; the tongues of crystal, 1.11, are added, as are the words "of light" in 1.34 (originally "brief human enchantments"). And in the margin, Tzara works over another passage centered around the image of brilliance combined with that of journey.

As is true of all the poems of this period, numerous examples of moving toward the greater can be found. Probably one of the most impressive occurs in 1.8 which was first "offering themselves to the night," then became the more passive and undistinguished "offered to night," before the final state, where the acting subject is allied with the perceived greatness of the night. The natural prayer at the end was added last. In various versions, the poet tried out such discordant expressions as *son règne adorable* ("its adorable reign") and *se multiplie le coeur de son graine* ("the heart of its grain is the first multiplied"), the first unacceptable because of its coy overtones, the latter, because of the loophole it left for a sentimental reading.

Mine

The gradual lengthening of almost every one of the titles in this series of poems is indicative of Tzara's will to linguistic expansion. He changes "Vignes" to "Par les vignes," "Grenier" to "Le Grenier enchanté," "Gare" to "Gare par temps d'égarement," "Hôtel" to "Lumière d'hôtel," "Neige" to "Pleine neige," "Pont" to "Le Pont écartelé," "Lampes" to "Jeunes lampes," "Blessures" to "Blessures à rebours," and "Réveil" to "L'Eternel réveil."

"Through the Vines"

Another image of immobility allied with the certainty of a moment in its completeness (or, as Tzara, calls it often, its present plenitude) begins the second paragraph. Originally: "Immobile hours, plunged in palpitating unanimity, I knew plentitude," the sentence was changed to the present version in which the image of immersion is removed to stress instead, as in "I discovered," the active presence of the poet. The same combination of images recurs in *The Ox on the Tongue* (originally in *In Man's Memory*) where the deception of the human world and of human vocabulary is balanced against the un-self-conscious grandeur of natural silence. Here, however, the immobility is seen as imprisoning.

"The Horse"

Originally, the second sentence read "each step reinforced"; the change to *amplifiat* stresses not the repetition, but the expansion. All of Tzara's more important poems, starting with *Approximate Man,* are slanted in this direction.

There were three stages in the construction of the simple sentence "One day I saw solitude." First there was just the perception that one was alone (*je m'aperçus qu'on était seul*); then, the more intellectual realization (*me rendis compte de la solitude*), and finally, the far more effective (and more compact) verb of simple vision. Compare the ending of the Note on Art: *Comprendre, voir* ("Understand, see").

As an example of Tzara's frequent reversals from one verb to its opposite and of his tendency toward the majestic, compare the first version's "reducing" of his vision with the "enlarging" of the second. The object seen is the same, but the way of looking at it seems to depend, retrospectively, on the memory of the vision, or on its expression.

The poem is prefigured in a poem of October, 1941, "Départ" in *Entretemps: Ce cheval dressé l'or de sa tête sur la crête ivre des montagnes* ("This horse upright the gold of his head against the drunken crest of the mountains"). Compare it also with the first line of the poem from *The Hand Passes in Noon-times Gained: J'a vu le cheval immobile sur le sommet de la montagne* ("I saw the horse immobile on the summit of the mountain").

Tristan Tzara, with Hugo Ball and Richard Huelsenbeck, founded the literary and artistic movement Dada in Zurich in 1916. Later in Paris he joined Aragon, Breton, and Soupault in Dada and surrealist manifestations. Having become a communist, like many intellectuals of the time, he later participated in the Spanish Civil War and the French Resistance. He died in 1963.

Mary Ann Caws, Ph.D., attended the National Cathedral School, and went on to get her B.A. (cum laude) at Bryn Mawr in 1954, her M.A. at Yale University in 1956), and her doctorate from the University of Kansas in 1962; she holds an honorary Doctor of Humane Letters from Union College (1983). She is currently Distinguished Professor of English, French, and Comparative Literature at the Graduate School of The City University of New York, and on the faculty of the Women's Studies and Film Certificate Programs. Professor Caws was co-Director of the Henri Peyre French Institute from 1980 to 2002. She is an Officer of the Palmes Académiques, a translator, and the author of many books on art and literature.

The revised manuscript was edited by Joseph S. Phillips and Nancy Hanger.

Manufactured in the United States of America.

www.blackwidowpress.com

TITLES FROM BLACK WIDOW PRESS

TRANSLATION SERIES

A Life of Poems, Poems of a Life
by Anna de Noailles. Translated by Norman
R. Shapiro. Introduction by Catherine Perry.

Approximate Man and Other Writings
by Tristan Tzara. Translated and edited
by Mary Ann Caws.

Art Poétique by Guillevic. Translated by
Maureen Smith.

The Big Game by Benjamin Péret. Translated
with an introduction by Marilyn Kallet.

*Boris Vian Invents Boris Vian: A Boris Vian
Reader.* Edited and translated by Julia Older.

Capital of Pain by Paul Eluard. Translated
by Mary Ann Caws, Patricia Terry, and
Nancy Kline.

Chanson Dada: Selected Poems
by Tristan Tzara. Translated with an
introduction and essay by Lee Harwood.

Earthlight (Clair de Terre) by André Breton.
Translated by Bill Zavatsky and Zack
Rogrow. (New and revised edition.)

*Essential Poems and Writings of Joyce Mansour:
A Bilingual Anthology.* Translated with an
introduction by Serge Gavronsky.

Essential Poems and Prose of Jules Laforgue.
Translated and edited by Patricia Terry.

*Essential Poems and Writings of Robert Desnos:
A Bilingual Anthology.* Edited with an
introduction and essay by Mary Ann Caws.

EyeSeas (Les Ziaux) by Raymond Queneau.
Translated with an introduction by Daniela
Hurezanu and Stephen Kessler.

Fables in a Modern Key by Pierre Coran.
Translated by Norman R. Shapiro. Full-
color illustrations by Olga Pastuchiv.

Fables of Town & Country by Pierre Coran.
Translated by Norman R. Shapiro. Full-
color illustrations by Olga Pastuchiv.

*Forbidden Pleasures: New Selected Poems
1924–1949* by Luis Cernuda.
Translated by Stephen Kessler.

Furor and Mystery & Other Writings
by René Char. Edited and translated by
Mary Ann Caws and Nancy Kline.

*The Gentle Genius of Cécile Périn: Selected
Poems (1906–1956).* Edited and translated
by Norman R. Shapiro.

*Guarding the Air: Selected Poems of
Gunnar Harding.* Translated and edited
by Roger Greenwald.

I Have Invented Nothing: Selected Poems by
Jean-Pierre Rosnay. Translated by J. Kates.

The Inventor of Love & Other Writings
by Gherasim Luca. Translated by Julian &
Laura Semilian. Introduction by Andrei
Codrescu. Essay by Petre Răileanu.

Jules Supervielle: Selected Prose and Poetry.
Translated by Nancy Kline & Patricia Terry.

La Fontaine's Bawdy by Jean de La Fontaine.
Translated with an introduction by
Norman R. Shapiro.

Last Love Poems of Paul Eluard. Translated
with an introduction by Marilyn Kallet.

Love, Poetry (L'amour la poésie)
by Paul Eluard. Translated with an essay by
Stuart Kendall.

Pierre Reverdy: Poems, Early to Late. Trans-
lated by Mary Ann Caws and Patricia Terry.

Poems of André Breton: A Bilingual Anthology.
Translated with essays by Jean-Pierre
Cauvin and Mary Ann Caws.

Poems of A.O. Barnabooth by Valery Larbaud.
Translated by Ron Padgett & Bill Zavatsky.

Poems of Consummation by Vicente
Aleixandre. Translated by Stephen Kessler.

Préversities: A Jacques Prévert Sampler. Trans-
lated and edited by Norman R. Shapiro.

The Sea and Other Poems by Guillevic.
Translated by Patricia Terry. Introduction by
Monique Chefdor.

To Speak, to Tell You? Poems by Sabine
Sicaud. Translated by Norman R. Shapiro.
Introduction & notes by Odile Ayral-Clause.

MODERN POETRY SERIES

ABC of Translation by Willis Barnstone

An Alchemist with One Eye on Fire
by Clayton Eshleman

An American Unconscious by Mebane Robertson

Anticline by Clayton Eshleman

Archaic Design by Clayton Eshleman

Backscatter: New and Selected Poems
by John Olson

Barzakh (Poems 2000–2012) by Pierre Joris

The Caveat Onus by Dave Brinks

City Without People: The Katrina Poems
by Niyi Osundare

Eshleman/The Essential Poetry: 1960–2015

Concealments and Caprichos
by Jerome Rothenberg

Crusader-Woman by Ruxandra Cesereanu.
Translated by Adam J. Sorkin. Introduction
by Andrei Codrescu.

Curdled Skulls: Poems of Bernard Bador.
Bernard Bador with Clayton Eshleman.

Dada Budapest by John Olson

Disenchanted City (La ville désenchantée)
by Chantal Bizzini. Translated by
J. Bradford Anderson, Darren Jackson,
and Marilyn Kallet.

Endure: Poems by Bei Dao. Translated by
Clayton Eshleman and Lucas Klein.

Exile Is My Trade: A Habib Tengour Reader.
Translated by Pierre Joris.

Eye of Witness: A Jerome Rothenberg Reader.
Edited with commentaries by Heriberto
Yepez & Jerome Rothenberg.

Fire Exit by Robert Kelly

Forgiven Submarine by Ruxandra Cesereanu
and Andrei Codrescu

Fractal Song by Jerry W. Ward, Jr.

from stone this running by Heller Levinson

Garage Elegies by Stephen Kessler

Grindstone of Rapport: A Clayton Eshleman Reader

The Hexagon by Robert Kelly

How Our Bodies Learned by Marilyn Kallet

Larynx Galaxy by John Olson

LinguaQuake by Heller Levinson

The Love That Moves Me by Marilyn Kallet

Memory Wing by Bill Lavender

Packing Light: New and Selected Poems
by Marilyn Kallet

Penetralia by Clayton Eshleman

*The Present Tense of the World: Poems 2000–
2009* by Amina Saïd. Translated with an
introduction by Marilyn Hacker.

The Price of Experience by Clayton Eshleman

The Secret Brain: Selected Poems 1995–2012
by Dave Brinks

Signal from Draco: New and Selected Poems
by Mebane Robertson

Soraya (Sonnets) by Anis Shivani

Tenebraed by Heller Levinson

Wrack Lariat by Heller Levinson

LITERARY THEORY /
BIOGRAPHY SERIES

*Barbaric Vast & Wild: A Gathering of Outside
and Subterranean Poetry (Poems for the Millen-
nium,* vol. 5). Eds: Jerome Rothenberg and
John Bloomberg-Rissman

Clayton Eshleman: The Whole Art
by Stuart Kendall

*Revolution of the Mind: The Life of André
Breton* by Mark Polizzotti

WWW.BLACKWIDOWPRESS.COM